D1526426

Cambridge Studies in Cultural Systems

Rank and rivalry:
The politics of inequality in rural West Bengal

Cambridge Studies in Cultural Systems

Clifford Geertz, Editor

Rank and rivalry: The politics of inequality in rural West Bengal

MARVIN DAVIS
Department of Anthropology, Brandeis University

CAMBRIDGE UNIVERSITY PRESS

Cambridge
London   New York   New Rochelle
Melbourne   Sydney

Published by the Press Syndicate of the University of Cambridge
The Pitt Building, Trumpington Street, Cambridge CB2 1RP
32 East 57th Street, New York, NY 10022, USA
296 Beaconsfield Parade, Middle Park, Melbourne 3206, Australia

First published 1983

Printed in Great Britain at
the University Press, Cambridge

Library of Congress catalogue card number: 82-9747

British Library Cataloguing in Publication Data

Davis, Marvin
Rank and rivalry: the politics of inequality in
rural West Bengal. – (Cambridge studies in
cultural systems)
1. Castes – Bengal   2. Bengal – Political
participation
I. Title
305.5′122′095414   GN491.4

ISBN 0 521 24657 1 hard covers
ISBN 0 521 28880 0 paperback

Contents

Illustrations

Tables

Acknowledgments

The research and writing on which this study is based was supported by a grant from the Foreign Area Fellowship Foundation, a grant from the American Institute of Indian Studies, and a Sacher Faculty Grant from Brandeis University. I am genuinely grateful to each of these sponsors, as I am to the Danforth Foundation which sponsored my graduate education at the University of Chicago.

Among the individuals who have facilitated this study, each in his or her own way, and sometimes in ways unsuspected, I would also like to acknowledge and thank Victor Ayoub, McKim Marriott, Bernard S. Cohn, Ruta Pempe, P.K. Bhowmik, Biswanath Banerjee, Ralph W. Nicholas, Peter J. Bertocci, and Marguerite S. Robinson. A very special thanks is extended to all the villagers of Torkotala, and most deeply to M.G. Das. Thanks and much appreciation go also to SAB, BSD, MEC, EPS, T. and H.

Introduction

Stated initially, and somewhat over-simply, this study is a descriptive analysis of rank – relative highness and lowness – and those rivalries by which distinctions of rank and the behavior appropriate to ranked social units are variously maintained or altered, supported or challenged, in a village of West Bengal, India. The study aims partly to add to the general fund of ethnographic information about stratification and politics in rural India, and partly to advance the kind of analysis undertaken. With regard to this latter and more polemical aim, it is argued that a holistic anthropology is best concerned with both systems of action and meaning, and best examines social structural and cultural material in a manner that does not treat either as in some sense secondary, derived or epiphenomenal.

Hindu culture includes the premise of inequality. Hindu society is organized around ascriptive groupings of people into ranked families, lineages and castes. On this Indianists are generally agreed. It is also agreed that social position within a hierarchy of families, lineages or castes – to borrow from Weber – depends on considerations of status rather than of class or power. No similar agreement exists, however, on the specific criterion of rank, the basis of inequality, among Hindu status groups. The disagreements are particularly evident and have been debated most heatedly in discussions of caste, the primary unit of social organization in rural India. Attributional theorists like H.N.C. Stevenson (1954), for example, emphasize the physical nature of a caste and its placement along a continuum of purity and impurity, with the more pure castes held to rank above the less pure. Interactional theorists emphasize the exchange between castes of culturally valued foods and services, with the givers of food held to rank above the receivers, and the receivers of service held to rank above the givers. Here it is not the religious standard of purity and impurity, but behavioral dominance that seems to be at issue (Marriott 1959; 1968). Louis Dumont's (1970) purity-plus-power argument represents still a third perspective, in which the attributional element of purity is qualified by the interactional element of power, which it nevertheless

① purity

② exchange relations

③ purity plus power

1

'encompasses.' Each of these perspectives offers a different evaluation of physical nature and culturally coded behavior as the criterion of caste rank. Yet all are alike in treating physical nature and behavioral codes as distinct and separate features.

The relative merits of attributional, interactional and purity-plus-power perspectives are a matter of long-standing discussion.[1] Of all the criticism that can be justly leveled against each perspective, though, perhaps the most telling derives from a series or writings by Ronald Inden (1976) on marriage and rank among Brahmans and Kayasthas in middle-period Bengal, Inden and Ralph Nicholas (1977) on kinship in Bengali culture, and McKim Marriott and Inden (1974; 1977) on South Asian caste systems generally. Writing about Hindus at various times in history, and in various parts of South Asia, these authors suggest that physical nature and behavioural codes are not, as they have been treated, distinct and separate features. Unlike our own dualistic conception of the natural and the cultural (Schneider 1968), Hindus regard physical nature and behavioral codes as cognitively non-dualistic features. Each is immanent in the other; each is inseparable from the other; each is a reflection and realization of the other.

The evidence from Torkotala, a (pseudonymously named) village in West Bengal, also suggests that neither physical nature nor behavioral codes are the sole or even the primary criterion of caste rank in Hindu society. Instead, the rank of any caste depends mutually on its nature and code. But what kind of theory can account for the physical and the behavioral, the natural and the cultural, as a duplex criterion of caste rank? And given the great breadth of ideas like the natural and the cultural, are physical nature and behavioral codes the criterion of caste rank only? Or does the same duplex criterion apply to other social units as well? If so, what does this reveal about rank in Hindu society as a whole?

These are among the questions raised in the first half of this study, chapters 1 through 3, which offers a descriptive analysis of rank in the Bengali cosmos and society. To preview their contents briefly, chapter 1 examines the ecology and social composition of Torkotala and the surrounding kingdom, and provides an initial account of their adminis-tration and local history. This places the study in space and time, and introduces its human subjects. It also sets an immediate limitation to the scope of this study, for while Torkotala is seen to have a mixed population of caste Hindus and tribals, the land, people and social history of Torkotala are described almost entirely from the perspective of Hindus as they introduce themselves and their village in terms of the Bengali concept *des* or community. This is not to deny that many differences in perspective exist among caste Hindus and tribals, or to underestimate the importance of studying intra-cultural variability. But in the discussion of *des*, as throughout most of this study, the insider's perspective presented is, unless specially noted, that of caste Hindus. Unqualified reference to 'Bengalis,' as a result, may be read as referring to Bengali Hindus.

Chapter 2 begins a description of the Bengali cosmos and society in local, cultural terms. It also begins an expanded ethnography of rank that moves beyond the usual focus on caste as a unique institutional system of inequality to a recognition that Bengalis view the several worlds of the universe, the various life forms that inhabit those worlds, and all birth groups into which humans in society are divided, as organized into a series of ranked orders and ordered ranks; individuals, too, though the subject of individuals is not considered until chapter 3. Brief mention of a few generalizations drawn from this ethnography will provide an overview of the argument made.

Bengalis describe the several worlds of the universe as extending up and down along a north–south axis that transverses the entire cosmos and is topped by Brahma, the creator of the universe and all that is manifest within it, at its northernmost point. Each world of the universe is ranked according to its relative proximity to Brahma, with the higher, more northerly worlds ranking above the lower, more southerly worlds.

Inhabiting the several worlds of the universe are six kinds of life forms – gods, humans, demons, animals, plants and objects – which occupy a place and rank in the universe according to the extent to which their own defining features approximate those of Brahma.

The same premise of ranked inequalities which informs Bengali perceptions of the several worlds and various life forms of the universe also informs Bengali perceptions of the birth groups (*jati*) into which humans in society are divided, including categories of castes (*varna*), the interactional groups we call castes, and the more highly differentiated kinship units included within castes. It is in this sense that rank is an ordering principle of the Bengali cosmos and society as a whole.

The various *varna*, castes and kinship units into which humans in society are divided are all defined by their radical material substances (*gun*) or physical nature and the moral conduct or behavioral code (*dharma*) held appropriate to that nature, which are viewed by Bengalis as a single, if duplex, criterion of rank. Both *gun* and *dharma* are inherent in and directly imply the other. The rank of any birth group, as a result, can be demonstrated by its physical nature or its behavioral code. One is but the reflection and realization of the other. It is in this sense that attributional, interactional, and purity-plus-power theories of rank are unified by the recognition that nature and code, when understood in local, cultural terms, are not distinct and separate, but cognitively non-dualistic features.

The defining features, and thus the rank, of all human birth groups are not fixed and unchanging over time, but can be transformed for better or worse through the life activities of its members. It is in this sense that a unified theory of rank is also transformational, and that a transformational perspective reveals the internal dynamic by which the ordered ranks of Bengali society are continuously subject to flux. Included in chapter 2 is also a discussion of how the premise of ranked inequalities and the ideas which inform a transformational theory of rank are evidenced behaviorally in such acts as marriage, diet, food exchanges, and work.

The ethnography of rank begun in chapter 2 is extended still further in chapter 3 with a discussion of the individual (*lok*) in Bengali thought and action. Are individuals properly considered units of rank among Hindus? If so, are they defined and ranked by the same features of nature and code as are the more inclusive birth groups to which they belong? Can the defining features, and thus the rank, of individuals be transformed in much the same way and through similar acts as, say, those of castes? These are among the questions raised in chapter 3. In pursuing them the discussion completes the argument for a transformational theory of rank begun in chapter 2. It also aims to clarify the place and importance of individuals in a group-oriented India.

Louis Dumont (1970:1–20; for earlier statements see 1965a, 1965b, 1967) has argued that the individual as an elemental social unit, and the normative subject of thought and action, exists only in modern countries of the West, with their values of equality and liberty, and should not be considered a universal. In Hindu India, as in other traditional societies, Dumont holds, individual identities are submerged in the social groups to which they belong, while individual interests are subordinated to society as a whole, which bears primary value. Thus the individual only becomes an elemental unit in group-oriented India in the person of the world renouncer, the *sannyasin*, who, paradoxically, realizes his individuality in the effort to step outside society and merge with Brahma. Under all other circumstances it is the various birth groups to which an individual belongs – his family, lineage and especially his caste – which are the normative subject of institutions in Hindu society, and also the units of rank.

Modern individualism and traditional holism may well be opposed configurations. But any actual society, including that of Hindu India, can include both sides of this structural opposition, even when they are differently valued. To minimize or abbreviate the discussion of individuals because they are not the primary social unit in Hindu India, as Dumont does, is thus to leave unexamined the individuality of 'encompassed' persons. It is also to ignore the analytic problem posed by questioning the place and importance of individuals in a group-oriented society.

To explain more fully, it is the overriding importance of status groups like family, lineage and especially caste that marks Hindu society as group-oriented, while it is the preoccupation with ranking such groups that marks Hindu society as hierarchical. Membership in a ranked family, lineage, or caste is only one kind of positioning relevant to systems of social stratification though, and does not in itself situate individuals within the status groups to which they belong. Everyone within a corporate family or caste shares the same rank in relation to outsiders. But within the family or caste individual members still can be differentiated and are differently valued. To refer to the ranked position of an individual among others who share a common status, the sociologist Benoit–Smullyan (1944) used the term 'situs.' When added to the usual concern of Indianists with ranked status groups, an attention to situs may provide an analytic key to the opposition individualism–holism. Does the individual exist in holistic India?

As detailed in chapter 3, the evidence from Torkotala suggests that individual Bengalis retain a personal identity, have distinguishable self-interests, pursue their self-development, and can be ranked quite apart from any of the inclusive birth groups to which they belong. Individuals, in sum, have a situs different from their status as a caste member or any other status deriving from membership in a family or larger kinship grouping. Further, individuals are at times the normative subject of thought and action. Bengali Hindus regard the individual as a microcosm of the universe at large. The same processes of development that are general to the universe are replicated in the physical-cum-moral development of an individual. The same premise of ranked inequalities that orders the birth groups into which persons in Hindu society are divided applies as well to individuals. And, like the groups of which they are members, individuals undergo transformations of their defining physical nature and behavioral codes in accord with their own life activities. Included in chapter 3 is a discussion of these processes of individual development and transformation as evidenced in passage through a prescribed series of life-cycle rites and life stages.

The descriptive analysis of rank presented in the first half of this study proceeds at first through a cultural analysis of the sort identified with David Schneider (1968) and, among Indianists, with Ronald Inden and Ralph Nicholas (1977), but with differences. For Schneider, as for Inden and Nicholas, culture is defined as a system of symbols, a definition derived from works by Talcott Parsons, Clyde Kluckhohn and Alfred Kroeber (cf. Parsons and Shills 1961; Kroeber and Parsons 1958; Kroeber and Kluckhohn 1952). A symbol is defined, following Suzanne Langer (1960), as one thing that stands for another. If this view of culture were accepted literally, it would focus study on the vehicle or conveyer of meaning, the symbol, rather than on what is conveyed by symbols, and would thus misrepresent what is typically done in the name of cultural analysis. It would seem both more useful and more accurate, as a result, to define culture as a system of meaning. Or to elaborate, in this study culture refers to that complex assemblage of concepts and ideas, premises and understandings that constitute a system of meaning shared and transmitted by a group of people. Culture is conveyed through symbols, be they words or deeds.[2]

The component concepts and ideas that constitute a system of meaning may pertain to a single domain, such as religion or politics, or may pertain across domains. Portions of a system of meaning may also be more general or less general, in that some premises and understandings are shared by all within a society, while others are shared and transmitted by persons representing a segment of the whole society. Segmental meaning systems, and the relations between religion and politics as organizing cultural frames, are discussed in the second half of this study (chapters 4 and 5). Chapters 2 and 3 focus first on those concepts and ideas, premises and understandings of rank shared by all Bengali Hindus. The aim is to identify the basic units of the Bengali cosmos and society, how they are defined and differentiated locally, and how they are related one to the other in a peculiar construction – a Bengali construction – of reality. The effort, put differently, is to discover the system of meaning within which Bengalis perceive and interpret matters of rank, and to do so in cognitive terms that are used and understood by Bengalis in talking about their own cosmos and society.

At first glance an approach that seeks to describe a particular construction of reality in its own cognitive terms may appear tautological. It is not, as the analysis presented in chapters 1 through 3 should demonstrate. But an analogy made now may help clarify the strategy of cultural analysis that unfolds later. Physical scientists describe how the combinations and products of a limited number of atomic particles – neutrons, protons, electrons, etc. – result in all the various known elements, and how these elements – hydrogen, oxygen, carbon, etc. – may be differently combined to produce all the world's known objects, both organic and inorganic. In this way the material universe is seen as resulting from the combinations and products of a few basic units, and at each level of synthesis are the new and more complex units defined in terms of other, more simple units. In the same way does a cultural analysis seek to describe how the Bengali cosmos and society is constructed from the various combinations and products of a few basic cultural units, among them *des, jati*, and *lok*. This is to define a cosmos and society in its own terms, but after the pattern of physical scientists searching for the material (here conceptual) building blocks of the universe.

This said, it still may be asked if an effort to describe the Bengali cosmos and society in local, cognitive terms is not flawed on other grounds. Does a strict cultural analysis preclude the possibility of a comparative social science? Does such an analysis allow for the possibility of cross-cultural generalizations? It does, as the less ethnocentric ethnography towards which a cultural analysis strives allows for more accurate comparative statements and more truly universalistic definitions as well. A better emic, as Goodenough (1970: 98–130) has argued, allows for a better etic. Supporting evidence for this position is provided throughout the study, but of particular relevance in chapters 1 through 3 is the discussion of why certain universalistic definitions of clan and lineage do not apply exactly in Bengal, and why the Bengali family is not accurately defined either by the husband and wife as a minimal pair, or, following Goodenough, by the central importance of the mother. The whole of chapter 3, as already noted, bears on Dumont's argument that the individual is not a universal unit of comparison. Though not pursued in this study, a culturally informed ethnography of rank may also advance the comparison of caste, class and race as systems of social stratification, if only in clarifying how physical nature and behavioral codes are in some systems separate criteria of status and in others a single, if duplex, criterion.

Another and more biting criticism of the kind of cultural analysis identified with Schneider, and with Inden and Nicholas, is the observation that a system of meaning once uncovered, however internally consistent and elegant, is not readily verified. Also, a strict cultural analysis does not in itself consider actual patterns of behavior. These observations are not unrelated, for if the Bengali view of their cosmos and society as ordered by ranked inequalities was shown to inform ongoing social acts and situations, then this might well stand as a test for the cultural analysis through which the concern about rank and inequality was uncovered. It would also reveal something of the nexus between *systems of meaning* – the complex assemblage of ideas, concepts, and understandings that constitute culture – and *systems of action* – the network of personal and group relationships and related processual acts that constitute social structure. With this in mind, chapters 2 and 3 depart from a strict cultural analysis, considered incomplete in itself, to include also discussion of how the Bengali concern with rank at a cultural level is evident socially in patterns of marriage, diet, food exchange, work, and ritual observance, including those life-cycle rites that mark the physical-cum-moral development of individual Bengalis as they move through a series of life stages.

In departing from a strict cultural analysis, the ethnographic effort is to document the pervasive and fundamental importance of ranked inequalities to Bengalis, not only for how they conceptualize their cosmos and society abstractly, but also for how they conduct their day-to-day lives. The effort also is to argue by example for a particular view of the anthropological enquiry. Systems of meaning can be distinguished analytically from systems of action and studied separately, as Schneider has done for kinship in American culture and Inden and Nicholas have done for kinship in Bengali culture. Systems of action can also be studied in analytic isolation. But as the questions that mainly concern anthropologists are only partly about cultures as systems of meaning, and only partly about social systems as systems of action, such separate treatment may be of limited value. It may also be misleading, for social action of all sorts is in an important sense unintelligible apart from its cultural context, and to focus solely on the substantive content of meaning systems overlooks what is probably the essential functional role of culture: its role in directing and justifying action preferences. Social acts, in turn, have a role in affirming or denying a system of meaning. Systems of meaning and action, in sum, though analytically separable, are interdependent and do affect each other. As they are also experienced by actor and observer as a single, intertwined, inexorably related whole, a holistic anthropology is best concerned with both.

The research on which this study is based was planned as an exercise in political anthropology. Yet the report of that research begins with a rather extensive ethnography of rank. Why? Because it is the Bengali concern, even preoccupation, with ranked inequalities that defines the broad context of meaning in which political competitions in rural West Bengal are engendered, fought and won, or lost. Also, it is in part through political competitions that the ranked orders and ordered ranks of the Bengali cosmos and society are variously maintained or altered, supported or challenged. The second half of this study, chapters 4 and 5, examines this conjunction of rank and rivalry in detail. The aim is partly to advance what is known about politics in rural India, and partly to further the argument for a holistic anthropology by illustrating how our understanding of politics can be enhanced by complementing the usual concerns with political structure and process with an attention to political culture.

Students of politics in rural India are well aware that competitions are generated along two main lines of cleavage. The cleavage between castes and between castes and tribes defines the vertical axis of politics, and is reflected in competitions between ranked groups over the control of land, water, women, office, and other material resources, all of which have a bearing on the less tangible resource of status. The cleavage between big men defines the horizontal axis of politics, and is reflected in factional competitions between leaders, teamed with supporters from various castes and tribes, over the same kinds of material resources, plus recognition as the biggest of big men. Given that the material interests at stake in caste and factional competitions are much the same, discussions of politics in rural India have focused in the main on processual differences – say, in mobilizing support – between competitions structured around ascriptive, corporate teams like castes and voluntary, non-corporate teams like factions. Yet the local significance of caste and factional competitions – like the less often studied competitions between family members or between villagers and outsiders to a village – is in part independent of their structure and process and rests instead on the system of meaning in which they are embedded, something even the most astute observers of politics in rural India ignore or treat as 'a given' that does not require separate analysis (cf. Bailey 1960; Nicholas 1968; Robinson 1975).

I will illustrate this point, and thereby preview the material presented. Bengalis refer to politics as *sason* or rule, and then distinguish between two forms of rule: village politics (*gramer kaj*) and government politics (*sorkari kaj*). The distinctive contrast between these two forms of rule does not lie in the organization of political teams, the personnel who participate, or even the manner and means by which competition is waged, though there are differences in these regards. It lies instead in the broadly defined goal of political acts. That is, both village politics and government politics are identified behaviorally with rivalries over rank, and those rivalries are structured in much the same way; but in each form of rule are rivalries pursued with a different goal and in relation to a different normative framework. The many family, caste and factional competitions that instance village politics aim to protect and maintain the system of ranked inequalities described in chapters 2 and 3, a system considered divinely given, inherent in the nature of the universe, and thus beyond the agency of human change. This goal is defined in relation to the religious framework of Hinduism. It is expressed locally in equating politics with the administration of *dharma*. In the context of government politics, by contrast, rivalries aim to level, if not completely eliminate, the system of inequalities supported by considerations of *dharma*, and to substitute in its stead a polity, society and view of the cosmos ordered on the premise of equality. This goal is defined in relation to the Indian constitution and legal system, which also establish politics and religion as formally separate domains in a secular India. It is expressed locally in equating government politics with progress, a future better than the past.

Village politics and government politics are discussed in chapters 4 and 5 respectively. In each chapter the explanatory effort is to clarify why the many and varied competitions which occur in Torkotala are not an infrequent or unanticipated feature of life in rural West Bengal, by identifying the social processes which generate them. The effort also is to provide a cultural account of politics, detailing how village politics and government politics are both enactments of local morality. These related explanatory goals require complementing the now orthodox view of politics as a system of instrumental action – who gets what, when and how, in Harold Lasswell's paradigm – with an increased, more actor-oriented attention to politics as a system of meaning. What are the shared understandings of reality that inform political activity? What are the prizes, the goals, the valued ends towards which political activity is aimed? What are the qualities deemed to merit the political prize? Are these shared understandings, prizes and qualities peculiar to the domain of politics, or are they related to those which inform other social activity?

It is a commonplace that the ethnography generated during field work is colored by the questions used to elicit the information and the analytic perspective that both frames the questions and interprets the responses. In this light, to raise the above questions is to do more than fill an ethnographic gap. It is also to redirect the manner in which we approach the subject which is politics by adding to the usual questions about structure and process an attention to political culture that is lacking in accounts of politics in rural India, as in even the benchmark political studies of Evans-Pritchard, Gluckman, Fallers and Barth. This limitation of past political anthropology has not gone unnoticed (Winckler 1970: 334; Nicholas 1973: 64–7), and programmatic calls for a reorientation have not been entirely unheeded (e.g. Moore and Myerhoff 1975; Cohen 1976). But there is yet no consensus about how questions of structure, process and meaning can be integrated within a single framework.

In examining politics in a West Bengal village, this study adopts what Garfinkel (1967), following Mannheim (1952), has termed 'a documentary method of analysis,' or what can be identified in more familiar descriptive terms as the analysis of critical acts as social and cultural paradigms. The documentary method is similar to Gluckman's extended case method and van Velsen's (1967: 129–49) situational analysis in its detailed study of actual events within a broadly defined structural context. Yet it differs from both in the use to which case materials are put. For whereas case studies in the hands of British structuralists have been used mostly to detail patterns of choice and strategic action within the constraints of a given social system, the documentary method is intended to highlight politics as two-dimensional – as singular instrumental acts and as an embodiment or paradigmatic example of an underlying pattern of meaning that informs a number of different, ostensibly unrelated acts occurring at discontinuous points in time. Politics, in other words, is viewed instrumentally and symbolically.

Culture was defined earlier as a system of meaning. Political culture is that sub-set of concepts and ideas, premises and understandings that define the context of meaning in which political acts occur, are perceived and are interpreted. In attending to the symbolic nature of instrumental political acts, the documentary method aims to identify in what sense a particular competition embodies a pattern of meaning common to a variety of competitions, whatever their singularities and different material goals. In doing so, the documentary method takes into account that the meaning of a political act is socially authored and not intrinsic to the particulars of the act itself; that the meaning attributed to an act may be different for different participants and observers; and that an act may be attributed a different meaning at different points in time, even by the same person. In this regard the documentary method is similar to the analysis of action as an 'open' text suggested by Ricoeur (1971) and exemplified in Geertz's (1973) study of a Balinese cock fight. Where it differs from the symbolic analysis of action as text-analogues is in avoiding that form of reading a text which includes psychological interpretations of why people act as they do. Like the extended case method and the situational analysis of British structuralists, a documentary method restricts interpretation to the significance of overt behavior, be it in word or deed, and uses each of these two forms of behavior to help clarify the other.

The operation by which this is done, left vague by Mannheim and Garfinkel, is here formulated as two-fold. First, a pattern of meaning or 'theme' is identified which seemingly informs a number of unrelated acts occurring at discontinuous points in time. That theme may be formulated inductively after observing a number of political events, and in that sense originate from the action system. Or it may be formulated from the explicit statements of informants asked to interpret specific political events, and in that sense originate from the meaning system. In either case, a theme once uncovered is used to interpret additional events on Mead's (1932) observation that for actors in a given sociocultural system both the past and the future are informed by present understandings. This second operation of matching theme to additional events is here called 'fitting.' Through fitting, the applicability of a theme is tested and, when warranted, can be revised or even discarded. A theme that does fit may also be elaborated as more and more ostensibly unrelated events are seen to have a common underlying pattern of meaning. Fitting theme to events, it should be added, does not imply any determinancy or primacy between systems of meaning and action. It suggests only how the reflexivity between meaning and action can be documented as each is used to elaborate the other.

Mannheim (1952) described the documentary method as a common sense empiric by which actors interpret past, present, and future events by locating ostensibly singular acts within a common pattern of meaning. It is used in this study for much the same purpose, and to illustrate how politics can be studied two-dimensionally as a form of action that is both symbolic and instrumental. In the attempt by actors to maintain or alter a certain fit between systems of political meaning and action, can also be discerned the processes that generate competition. Thus chapter 4 details how the family, caste, and factional competitions which instance village politics, for all their differences, are alike in being occasioned by efforts to rectify or forestall a perceived lapse in moral conduct that threatens the ordered ranks of society. The three instances of government politics discussed in chapter 5 are differently occasioned by efforts to realize a greater measure of equality, be it political equality through a democratic system of rural self-government, social equality through legislation, or economic equality through a labor dispute.

The ethnography of politics presented in chapters 4 and 5 argues by example for a particular style of analysis that integrates questions of structure, process, and meaning. The specifics of that ethnography, in combination with the account of Torkotala history and administration begun in chapter 1, also argue for a reinterpretation of political competitions in rural India. To anticipate that ethnography now may help later in evaluating the individual documentary cases through which it is presented.

The Indian village has been described as a self-sufficient, well-integrated community in which all live in harmony and consensus. To judge from the historical experience of Torkotala, the Indian village never was independent of a superior political power, which at the very least claimed revenue rights to village lands, and never was free of competitions. Moreover, the occurrence of competitions at each level of social organization is not an unanticipated or aberrant feature of village life, either statistically or normatively. In discussing the politics of family life, for example, it will be seen that interpersonal rivalries over rank and behavioral dominance are a chronic feature of Hindu family life, and far from being disparaged as a lot of Machiavellian scrapping, these rivalries are perceived and legitimated locally as a moral means to insure the behavior appropriate to family members of different seniority and sex. The documentary cases presented also evidence that competition – or the lack of it – between particular dyads of the Hindu family is predictable, as is the time when those competitions will occur within the life cycle of individuals and the developmental cycle of the family.

The politics of caste is similarly an enactment of local morality, though it has been described otherwise. Leach (1960), Bailey (1963) and Beteille (1969) have each argued that castes are units of cooperation, not competition, and that when castes do compete they are acting in defiance of the principles of the caste system. A culturally informed study of politics in Torkotala differently suggests that both inter-caste and intra-caste competitions are consistent with a transformational perspective in which the defining features and rank of a caste are continually in flux, and thus continually open to challenge. They are also essential to maintaining the proper order of castes in a local hierarchy, for an apparently static order of ranked castes is not static at all, but constantly renewed and adjusted through competition. The occurrence of both forms of the politics of caste is predictable, and in inter-caste competitions there is even a patterned sequence to those changes in the generalized life style of a caste on which claims to higher rank are based. ✳

Beals and Siegel (1960a) have argued that factional competitions in Indian villages are the product of external pressures associated with situations of change, and in that sense are alien to village life. Again the evidence from Torkotala suggests differently. Every factional competition, whatever the material interests at stake, is also a test of those personal qualities of leadership by which big men are compared and ranked, with recognition as the biggest of big men, as *the* leader, being the cumulative result of many factional wins. This process of ranking factional leaders through their success in actual competitions lends to factional politics an open-ended, if episodic, quality as big men repeatedly test each other in a continuing rivalry over rank. It is a process, significantly, that is independent of external pressures on a village, and will perdure during periods of relative stasis or change so long as Hindus remain preoccupied with the individual as a unit of rank.

Competition can be divisive or integrative, and what is divisive in the short term can be integrative in the longer term. This is the case with village politics, for through the temporary disorder of family, caste, and factional competitions is upheld a lasting social order presumed to date from the very creation of the universe. Competition can also be innovative. Specific bones of contention often highlight strains in a social system, and the temporary disorder of politics can result in a new and better order. Indeed, the varied competitions that instance government politics are best seen in this light: as efforts to remedy the stressful inequalities of the present social order. Panchayati Raj, a system of rural self-government designed to extend into Indian villages many of the same features of a modern, democratic polity that already exist at higher administrative levels of the state; the Hindu Code, a body of civil legislation that removes judicial recognition of inequalities of caste and sex in certain matters of family law; and the Torkotala labor dispute, a competition over the wages and conditions of work for agricultural laborers – these are the three instances of government politics discussed in chapter 5. Each represents an effort to realize within Torkotala certain of the equalitarian ideals expressed in the Indian constitution and others encoded in the Indian legal system.

Exploring the conjunction of rank and rivalry in Torkotala politics highlights the utility of examining the relations between politics and other social domains. For as evidenced in chapters 4 and 5, the competitions that instance village politics and government politics are both informed by the same transformational perspective that informs Bengali patterns of marriage, diet, food exchanges, work and ritual performance. Like these other acts, political competitions are also a means by which the rank of an individual or group can be altered for better or worse. Anthropologists have long recognized the importance of life-cycle rites and other public ceremonies as a social means for marking a change of status of individuals and groups. The ethnography presented in this study suggests that political competitions are also usefully studied as rites that both mark and facilitate status passage.

Exploring the conjunction of rank and rivalry will also provide another indication of how a culturally informed analysis can contribute to a comparative social science, for contrary to universalistic definitions of politics as the ultimate arbiter of public goals and values (Easton 1965; Swartz, Turner and Tuden 1966), chapters 4 and 5, in combination, evidence that politics in rural India is sometimes subordinated to religion as the orienting normative framework, and sometimes defined as separate from and superordinate to considerations of religion. This observation bears on more than questions of definition because Louis Dumont (1971) has contrasted traditional and modern societies on the basis of whether religion or politics provides the over-arching normative frame, and has argued that politics has this orienting role only in individualistic societies of the West. The Torkotala material differently suggests that just as societies are neither entirely individualistic nor entirely group-oriented, actual societies, including Hindu India, may include more than one set of relations between politics and religion.

A traditionalist village politics and a progressive government politics co-exist in villages of rural West Bengal today, as they probably have since the British introduced their own equalitarian precepts and practices into the slowly modernizing colony of India. In Torkotala both forms of rule have support, for while Bengalis share a view of their society as presently ordered by ranked inequalities, they do not share the same evaluation of that order as necessary or just. Some Torkotala residents favor the protective bent of village politics. Others welcome the innovative changes associated with government politics. More commonly, Torkotala residents at different times advance and act in accord with both the themes of village politics and government politics. This will become evident in tracing the involvement of the same villagers through several documentary cases. Doing so will also 'personalize' the study in following named individuals as they variously react to the complex of changes that face Torkotala residents, as their village is increasingly integrated into the wider state and national levels of politics. Detailing the support given – or withheld – to Panchayati Raj, Hindu Code legislation, and the Torkotala labor dispute will also reveal the limitation of assuming that a progressive government politics will soon displace village politics, or that a traditionalist village politics will reject outright the innovations associated with government politics. As reported elsewhere in India, and will be argued for Torkotala, traditional and progressive forms are not always opposed or conflictual alternatives (Gusfield 1966; Rudolph and Rudolph 1967; Singer 1972). To past discussions of the structural amalgam which characterizes rural India as neither wholly traditional nor wholly modern, is added a processual complement in focusing on competition as a conduit of stasis or change.

The themes of village politics and government politics, when viewed substantively, represent culturally defined models of reality that are used to type actual competitions, thereby making them intelligible as instances of a more general pattern. They also serve to direct the interested participation of individuals in specific competitions, and to justify that participation. Torkotala residents, including the leading big men of the village, are not consistent in their support of a traditionalist village politics or a progressive government politics. But they are consistent in the language of claims used to justify their activity in each form of rule. Chapters 4 and 5 will document that a language of claims can be a forthright statement of actual reasons for pursuing a competition. Or a language of claims may mask actual motivation. In either case the importance of attending to the public statements that accompany political acts is that they are an expression of socially accepted reasons for acting in relation to culturally defined goals, of legitimate rationalizations for action whatever the actual motivation of actors. C. Wright Mills (1940) noted long ago that varieties of action each have their characteristic 'vocabulary of motives.' His observation is persued in the second half of this study to identify the language of claims characteristic of village politics and government politics, how each is used to condone competition differently, and what each implies for processes of change in rural West Bengal today. Change is not unique to either village politics or government politics. But as documented in chapter 5, each form of politics does have its own manner of rationalizing change in terms of a past or future Golden Age, and the language of claims that accompanies an effort at directed change can be critical to its success or failure. Chapter 5 closes the body of this study with a discussion of how the understandings of a traditionalist village politics were manipulated for the purposes of a progressive government politics in the instance of Panchayati Raj, and how a progressive language of claims was used with mixed results in the instance of Hindu Code legislation and during the Torkotala labor dispute.

The themes of village politics and government politics, the language of claims associated with each form of rule, and the many Bengali concepts and ideas presented throughout this study – all are created, shaped, and held in the minds of individuals. Yet culture transcends individual minds, is public, not private, and represents the system of meaning shared by members of a society. This shared system of meaning is also public in having behavioral expression in a variety of day-to-day social acts and situations, including patterns of marriage, diet, food exchanges, work, ritual performance, and even patterns of political competition. Indeed, it is through such day-to-day acts that a system of meaning and its component parts is variously maintained or altered, supported or challenged. Or so, in brief, is the combined argument of the separate halves of this study.

The field work on which this study is based was carried out from January 1971 through June 1972, and during the summer of 1977, in Torkotala and other villages of the former Narayanghar kingdom, which are now included in the larger Midnapore district of West Bengal State.

A comparable study of rank and rivalry could have been done almost anywhere in rural India. This study was carried out in rural West Bengal primarily because of the language training available in Bengali. It was done in Torkotala, rather than any other West Bengal village, in part because entry into Torkotala was both easy and uncomplicated. Entry was made easy by the introduction of a local social worker-cum-anthropologist who is known throughout the Narayanghar area for his relief and development work among tribal peoples. Entry was uncomplicated because the introduction permitted access to Torkotala as a village without obstructing access to any of the families, castes, factions and classes that divide villagers amongst themselves, which were the planned focus of study. My stated reason for wanting to live and work in Torkotala – to learn about those aspects of Bengali life not represented in English-language newspapers or books, and to convey this information to others who could not travel to India personally – also gained an extra measure of plausibility and acceptance from the activities of this social worker, for he sometimes played a similar role in clarifying the details of tribal life to caste Hindus.

The moderate size of Torkotala, its relatively compact physical plan, its location at a fair distance from any urban center and in the midst of a historic kingdom, its multicaste population, and its experience with Panchayati Raj – all were practical considerations which weighed on the feasibility of doing field work in a particular setting and the appropriateness of asking specific questions in that setting. Torkotala as an object village also promised to be an interesting research setting for, as villagers quickly made known, the history of Torkotala is closely tied to the fortunes of the local Pal Rajas and the history of the Narayanghar kingdom – a topic explored in chapter 1. Torkotala is also sufficiently representative as a sample village for one to see in it something about the whole of rural West Bengal and of rural India. This said, it was never intended that field work be done in a village that was representative in any statistical sense. To think that it could be is perhaps misleading, for in West Bengal, as throughout India, villages vary both in features such as population size that can be averaged numerically, and others such as having a dispersed, nucleated or hamleted physical plan, or having a single headman, a dominant caste or no clear village-level leadership that cannot be averaged but only counted as present or absent. Variations in structural form, in other words, cannot be represented in the case study of a single village.

'The locus of study,' as Geertz (1973: 22) has pointed out, 'is not the object of study. Anthropologists don't study villages (tribes, towns, neighborhoods . . .); they study *in* villages.' Their data is extremely specific and circumstantial, but the importance of that data, at least potentially, is not so much where it came from, as how far it can be taken by analysis and interpretation. From local truths to general visions . . . Or for the purposes of this study, from the ethnography collected almost exclusively in Torkotala, to generalizations that extend beyond Torkotala and neighboring villages. The transformational theory of rank and human development presented in chapters 2 and 3, for example, *may* well be part of the system of meaning common to Hindus throughout West Bengal, as throughout India. The processes identified as generating the family, caste, and factional competitions discussed in chapter 4, or the instances of government politics discussed in chapter 5, *may* be part of the system of action common throughout Hindu India. Some comparative evidence in support of these generalizations is marshalled at the close of the appropriate chapter or chapter section. But strictly speaking the ethnographic base for their full appraisal is lacking at present and must await comparable studies of stratification and politics elsewhere in rural India. For that reason this study is only suggestive, not certain, of general visions from local truths.

Field work was done exclusively in the local language, Bengali, and without the use of translators, a practice that is not uncommon among anthropologists and perhaps needs no defense as a field-work technique. What is generally a productive technique was particularly useful, even necessary, in this study to generate the linguistic data for a culturally informed analysis of rank and rivalry. Some of that linguistic data, most often in the form of Bengali terms and phrases, is presented when identifying those categories and ideas that are the conceptual building blocks of a Bengali construction of reality. The numerous Bengali terms identified may slow the reading of an English text, but if this be perceived by some as a practical difficulty better avoided, there are methodological reasons for including Bengali terms and phrases with an appropriate gloss as needed. They point the way to a comparative analysis for, as Indianists will note, many of the terms and phrases that are discussed are shared between Bengali and other languages of India. The concepts and ideas, premises and understandings that constitute culture are not always expressed through a single term, and key terms like *des* or *jati* or *lok* or

✳ \|\| *sason* may have a relative meaning that changes with context. There may also be a considerable gap between the organization of vocabulary and the organization of the underlying ideas it is used to express. For each of these reasons, language is not an immediate or perfect map to culture. Yet the terms and phrases used by Bengalis – what is said – to describe their reality and to elaborate why they act as they do within that reality is the raw data of a cultural analysis, and is best included as part of that analysis. If anything, it is a just criticism of this study that more and lengthier quotes from informants were not included as additional evidence for the cultural analysis presented. They could not be presented because while I was careful in the field to record key terms and phrases in Bengali, most conversations of any length were summarized and recorded in English. Hindsight suggests that for evidentiary purposes it would have been useful to run a tape-recorder, which I did not do at all, and to gather from informants more written texts, which I did only rarely.

Working without the aid of translators was a device to focus attention on the linguistic data needed for a cultural analysis while avoiding those problems attendant on filtering data through a third party. Working without the aid of formal field-work assistants was differently reasoned. Torkotala residents agreed to host one outsider – myself – in their village. To introduce another as a field assistant seemed an unwarranted test of hospitality, and one potentially counter-productive to this study of politics. Outsiders typically are viewed by Torkotala residents with wariness and suspicion. They are also associated with government-backed policies and programs designed to alter life within Torkotala – an association explored in the discussion of government politics. To employ a field-work assistant from outside Torkotala thus threatened to affect the very subject of this study, and to become part of it. To work with field-work assistants from within Torkotala had its own limitation. Namely, to be closely associated with any one individual or segment of the Torkotala population threatened to obstruct access to at least some families, castes, or factions of the village. During the whole of the research period, as a result, I maintained an independent residence and worked without formal assistants from within Torkotala. My practice also was not to rely on a select group of principal informants – so none can be identified here – but to circulate throughout the village daily, taking care over time to visit and speak with members of every household on most every topic of enquiry. If this practice was a slow and sometimes redundant data-gathering device, it was also invaluable for collecting cases of political competition from all segments of the Torkotala population. Over one hundred documentary cases of village politics and government politics were collected in all, some observed first hand, others reconstructed by informants from memories of the past, still others recovered from entries in a personal diary or log of village events. In another study, for another purpose, it will be interesting to use all of these cases to document statistically the what and how of politics in rural West Bengal: what is the full range of contentions that spark political competitions, what is the frequency with which each contention sparks competition, how are competitions of each type processed most frequently – as Robinson (1975) has done with material from a Sinhalese village. These are important questions, and though not ignored in this study, are also not answered as fully as possible given the relatively few documentary cases considered. This lack of numerical data is a limitation of any case study method. Yet on balance, it is the depth and detail of analysis facilitated by a case-study method which is here of greater advantage in documenting that there is a conjunction of rank and rivalry in rural West Bengal and why.

What people say, and what people do – these are the two kinds of evidence usually available to anthropologists working in the field. Both are integrated in a documentary analysis that is concerned equally with systems of meaning and action, with theme and event, rank and rivalry. In portions of this study textual sources are also used as evidence, not of actual behavior, but of culture, in words written rather than words spoken. In the chapters on rank, and in discussion of village politics, for example, reference is made to certain literature well known in Torkotala and throughout rural West Bengal, including the Srimad Bhagavata Mahapurana, Purusasukta, Bhagavad Gita, and Manu Dharmasastra. In discussion of government politics, reference is made to the Indian constitution, and to legislation contained in the Hindu Code. Both kinds of texts, religious and political, it will be seen, provide literal evidence of those concepts, ideas, and understandings that define the context of meaning in which Torkotala residents compete politically.

Whatever the evidence considered – words written, words spoken or deeds – the effort throughout this study is to describe and then explain patterns of rank and rivalry in rural West Bengal. That explanation proceeds at points through an analysis of the logic and meaning of those concepts and ideas, premises and understandings that constitute Bengali culture. And it proceeds at points through a causal – functional analysis of the network of personal and group relationships and those processual acts that constitute Bengali social structure. It is the integration of these two forms of analysis that marks this study as holistic. It is through a holistic anthropology that this study aims to advance our understanding of stratification and politics in rural India.

1. Des

On entering a village in West Bengal and being introduced to its residents, one of the first questions asked of a newcomer is, '*Apnar des kothay?*' By this question Bengalis understand, 'Where are you from?' 'Where is your *des*, your village, region, kingdom, country?' *Des* is a relative concept which carries all of these referents. And if the reply given is not at the level of specificity desired, the same question, perhaps in a different form, but probably not, will be asked again and again. To what end? To place a person spatially and socially, for the concept *des*, in addition to referring to a specific territory or geographic area, is also associated with three related concepts.

Desachar combines the roots for place (*des*) and customary behavior (*achar*) to denote that every geographic area has its characteristic way of life. *Deskal* incorporates the root for place and time (*kal*) to denote that every geographic area also has a history, unique and dissimilar from all other places. And *deskalpatro* combines the roots for place, time and man (*patro*) to denote the full singularity of a geographic area, which includes its social composition and its population. Individually and collectively these related concepts suggest why, when Bengalis enquire as to one's *des*, they are enquiring as well, albeit indirectly, into more than a named territory or division of physical space. Specifically, every *des* is known for its peculiar conjunction of land, people and local history.

Following the Bengali example, this chapter introduces a village of West Bengal with a discussion of what is understood locally when a person identifies his *des* as Torkotala. Torkotala is located approximately a hundred miles southwest of Calcutta in Midnapore district. Its physical setting within Midnapore, the social composition of its population, and the history and administration of the village are considered in turn. The discussion throughout also bears on a certain view of the Indian village that dates as early as 1830, when Charles Metcalfe wrote.

The village communities are little republics, having nearly everything they want within themselves, and almost independent of any foreign relations. They seem to last where nothing else lasts. Dynasty after dynasty tumbles down; revo-

lution succeeds revolution; Hindoo, Patan, Mogul, Mahratta, Sik, English
are all masters in turn; but the village communities remain the same.

(Cited in Kessinger 1974:25.)

This view of the Indian village as a timeless, self-sufficient, politically
independent entity is an idealization that does not fit contemporary rural
communities (Cohn 1968; Neale 1962; Srinivas and Shah 1960; Marriott
1955), and probably also did not fit villages of Metcalfe's time. Yet it is an
idealization that lingers on – especially about villages in past
time – because it is difficult to evaluate fully in the absence of historical
accounts of specific villages. Even the partial and selective history of
Torkotala recounted in this chapter can thus serve as more than a mere
introduction to a West Bengal village, for it will evidence how a durable
village like Torkotala may still be a village in flux. The physical bounds,
social composition and administration of Torkotala have not been
constant or unvarying through time, nor are changes in these and other
areas of Torkotala life unrelated to events originating both within and
outside the village. Torkotala exists now as in the past in relation to the
broader communities of which it is a part.

The land

Viewed from the air or on a map of physical relief, Midnapore district
appears as a sloping tableland. From its elevated margins to the north and
west where it meets the lower reaches of the Chota Nagpur Hills, the land
slopes gradually but continually to the south and east. Hilly terrain and
true forest regions give way to undulating ridges of scrub jungle, and they in
turn to a broad deltaic plain until the district lands flatten out completely
before merging with the Bay of Bengal.

Between the Chota Nagpur Hills and the Bay of Bengal, the gradual but
continual slope of this tableland remains unbroken. No topographical
features clearly divide the more elevated and less elevated portions of the
district. Yet Midnapore does consist of two geological subdivisions,
recognized and described locally as eastern and western Midnapore.
Marking this east by west division is an all-weather, motorable road, the
Orissan Trunk Road, which runs from Burdwan district to the north of
Midnapore, through the central portions of Midnapore district, and
southwards to Orissa. Midnapore Town, the seat of district administration,
Karagpur, a major railway junction in West Bengal, Narayanghar, Belda,
Contai and Dantan are among the major settlements which straddle the
trunk road. Torkotala village is located beside the same road some miles
south of Karagpur and north of Narayanghar Town.

East of the Orissan Trunk Road is an open, well-cultivated deltaic plain.

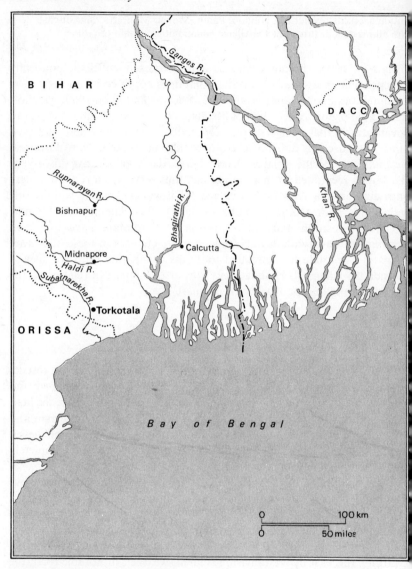

Fig. 1. West Bengal and Bangladesh

The soil is almost wholly alluvial. The land is both fertile and well watered, benefiting from periodic deposits of silt from the numerous waterways which lace this portion of the district. The Rupnarayan, which marks the northeastern boundary of Midnapore, the Kasai, which crosses the middle portions of the district before joining the Haldi, and the Subarnarekha, which waters the southwestern portions of the district, are the principal rivers. There are as well literally innumerable smaller waterways, tributaries and canals, which collect and carry rainfall for potential use as irrigation waters. Rainfall is as much as 60 inches a year. Though much of this rain is concentrated in a definite monsoon season from June to September, only the cold-weather months from November to January are dry. Warm-weather temperatures of 100° F or more are commonplace. The climate of eastern Midnapore is thus characteristically hot and humid. And when combined with fertile, alluvial soil, land and climate join to make this portion of the district ideal for rice agriculture. Rice is the principal crop of the area. Betel-leaf vines, date and coconut palms, sugar cane, papayas, mangos and guavas, plus a variety of garden vegetables, including tomatoes, squashes, peppers, egg plants, onions, cabbage and spinach, are also common crops in this portion of Midnapore.

West of the Orissan Trunk Road the flat deltaic plain is replaced by undulating ridges of scrub jungle. The soil is lateritic and far less fertile than alluvium. The climate is measurably colder and more arid. Monsoon rains are experienced, but the slope of the land and the resulting runoff make this potential boon an actual detriment because over time the continual action of water runoff has bleached the soil of needed nutrients. Unlike in the east, what is carried away by water runoff is not replenished by periodic deposits of silt. Rice can be grown in areas cleared of scrub jungle, especially in the depressions between ridges where moisture is retained longer and the soil is enriched by detritus washed down from the slopes. But betel-leaf vines, palms and those varieties of fruit trees and vegetables which require a considerable and continual source of water are not commonplace. Geologically, western Midnapore is a transition zone between the well-watered, fertile alluvial plain to the east, and a more elevated true forest region, the Chota Nagpur Hills, even further to the west.

Torkotala village straddles the Orissan Trunk Road and the east-by-west divisions of Midnapore district. All of the housing sites of the village lie immediately west of the trunk road, while agricultural lands owned by Torkotala villagers lie on both sides of it. Village lands thus share the geological features characteristic of both eastern and western Midnapore. To the immediate east and west of the Orissan Trunk Road, the soil is neither wholly alluvial nor wholly lateritic, but a bit of both. Torkotala village lands, as a result, are more fertile than the wholly lateritic soil further to the west and less fertile than the wholly alluvial soil further to the east. Chemical and natural fertilizers, rather than silt deposits, are relied on to retain this measure of fertility. The land is flat, and water runoff is not considered problematic. Yet coconut palms, papayas, guavas, mangos and other plants which thrive in warm, moist climates are absent. Scrub jungles are the most prominent growth on uncleared village lands. On cleared lands rice is the main agricultural crop.

The people

Just as the Orissan Trunk Road marks the geological division of Midnapore district, it also marks the primary social division of the district. East of the trunk road, the population is predominately of Bengali or Oriyan stock, and includes higher-caste Hindus. Brahmans, Baidyos and Kayasthas, plus those artisan castes known collectively as Navasakhya,[1] are the specific castes associated with eastern Midnapore. Also named in this regard are the Mahisyas, the single most populous caste in the district. Aside from the Brahmans, all of these castes are considered in Bengal as Sudras, but Sudras (*sat* Sudra) from whom a Bengali Brahman will accept drinking water. West of the trunk road, the population is predominately tribal. Lodha, Munda and Santal are the most populous of these tribal groups. Associated with them are those *asat* Sudra castes like Bagdi, Dom, Sunri, Dule and Hari, from whom a Bengali Brahman will not accept drinking water.

Both tribals and Hindus within and around Torkotala invest this social division of Midnapore with considerable importance. In 1971 settlements on both sides of the trunk road included persons of tribal and non-tribal stock as well as higher- and lower-caste Hindus. But the more elevated, less fertile scrub jungle and forest tracts of western Midnapore are considered to be the original *des*, the native lands, of those tribal populations whose traditional livelihood, in addition to agriculture, includes gathering fruits of the forest and hunting small game animals. The fertile, well-watered deltaic plains of eastern Midnapore, by contrast, are considered to be the original *des* of higher-caste Hindus of Bengali or Oriyan stock. Their traditional livelihood, in addition to caste-related artisan and trade activies, is settled rice agriculture, and has never included hunting and gathering forest produce. It is this association of eastern and western Midnapore with the people who live there, and the way of life and livelihood maintained by them, that invests the geographic east–west division of the district with social importance.

Befitting its location beside the Orissan Trunk Road, Torkotala village has a mixed population of caste Hindus and tribal peoples. Out of a total population of slightly more than 700 people in 1971, 46% of the villagers were caste Hindus. The remaining 54% of the villagers are Lodhas (27%) or Mundas (27%). Caste Hindus refer to both of these groups as *adhibasi lok*, denoting the people (*lok*) who were the first or original (*adhi*) inhabitants (*basi*) of the area. The same term is glossed here as 'tribals.'

Oral histories indicate that around 1898 Torkotala had a clustered settlement pattern with one outlying, loosely allied hamlet. Within the central cluster lived a mixed population of Sadgops and Brahmans as the principal landholders, and Bagdis as the main source of agricultural labor.

In addition there were one or two families each of certain Hindu artisan and service castes. Kumar, Kamar and Rajok (Dhopa) were among these castes. Napits came to Torkotala when needed from a neighboring village just east of the Orissan Trunk Road. One Hari family had a house at the edge of this clustered settlement.[2] Significantly, no tribal peoples lived in Torkotala at the time. The outlying hamlet was populated by Muslims.

The year 1898 is clearly known to Torkotala villagers because the date is imprinted on the steel girders of a railway bridge that spans a water conduit in the middle of nearby agricultural lands. It was after then that the bridge was built and tracks were laid for a branch line of the southeastern railway running from Karagpur, a railway junction to the north of Torkotala, through Narayanghar and southwards to Orissa. The railway line ran parallel to the Orissan Trunk Road along its western side, and on its course bisected the then residential heart of Torkotala. Many houses and housing sites, in addition to considerable agricultural lands, were lost to the laying of the railway tracks and the embankments on both sides of the tracks.

Brahman families in particular incurred the largest losses from the building of the new railway. Of the ten to twelve families then resident in Torkotala, all but three left the village soon afterwards. They were relatively recent migrants to Narayanghar from somewhere in Orissa and may have felt little attachment to Torkotala as their native village. In 1971 the descendants of only one of the three Brahman families which did try to resettle in Torkotala still remained in the village. Sadgop and Bagdi families also incurred losses of residential and agricultural lands with the building of the railway. Rather than leave Torkotala, though, they shifted their housing sites to the east side of the railway tracks where there remained areas of uncleared scrub jungle. Hence the settlement pattern of Torkotala took on a new form. Families which were undisturbed by the laying of the railway tracks remained at their present housing sites and came to constitute a hamlet west of the railway tracks, referred to simply as West Hamlet. East of the railway tracks a newer and much larger East Hamlet was founded. Agricultural lands of the village continued to lie on both sides of the railway and on both sides of the trunk road.

The outlying Muslim hamlet was located just to the south and west of the clustered Hindu population, less than five minutes walking distance along circuitous mud banks which divide one plot of paddy land from another in this part of Midnapore. The hamlet is described as having numbered several hundred people. Its residents earned their livelihood not as landholders or agricultural laborers, but as buyers and sellers of cattle. Present-day residents of Torkotala, none of whom are Muslim, say they do not know why the Muslims left Torkotala. It appears that Torkotala Hindus never lamented their leaving and may even have provided some incentive, perhaps because they were Muslims and perhaps because they traded in cattle, a particularly invidious occupation to Hindus. The Muslim hamlet was not in the direct path of the new railway line, and it is unlikely that they, like the Brahmans, left the village on account of losses incurred when the railway was built. It is acknowledged by Hindus that until the late 1950s descendants of these Muslim inhabitants of Torkotala returned to the site of their abandoned hamlet each year to visit the burial place of a saintly ancestor. In the late 1950s a Hindu, not of Torkotala, but of the Narayanghar area, removed the stones which marked the burial place and used them to build a bench of sorts under a great banyan tree on his own property. After that the Muslims no longer returned to Torkotala yearly, and the same individual who removed the stones later arranged to acquire legal title to the land on which the Muslim hamlet stood. Today this land is no longer considered part of Torkotala.

As the discussion thus far indicates, the actual lands and people included in Torkotala, as well as the settlement pattern of the village, have not been constant and unvarying through time. Then how is the village qua village defined? In a manner that recognizes and can reflect flux over time, Torkotala is defined by its residents as the *des*, the physical-cum-social community over which the authority of the traditional headman actually applies. It is described and mapped according to the following divisions.

In 1971 Torkotala village was divided into eight hamlets, or *para*. Each of these hamlets has defined physical boundaries and is recognized as a named territorial unit by all Torkotala Hindus and tribals. As with all referents of *des*, these physical divisions of the village are recognized as social divisions as well. All Hindus live in one of two hamlets: one west of the railway tracks that has its nucleus among the families that did not relocate after the building of the railway, and one east of the railway tracks that has its nucleus among families that did relocate at that time. All Lodhas live together in one of four Lodha hamlets, which lie south of the Hindu hamlets. All Mundas live together in one of two Munda hamlets, which lie north of the Hindu hamlets. No Lodhas live among Mundas. No Mundas live among Lodhas. Both Lodhas and Mundas live apart from caste Hindus. Thus the primary physical divisions of Torkotala, the hamlets, parallel and reflect the primary social divisions of the village.

Genealogical materials indicate that both the Lodhas and Mundas are new to Torkotala since the early 1930s. They came first as part of the wave of migrant laborers from western Midnapore on which Hindu cultivators of Torkotala and villagers further east relied to help harvest the principal rice crop of the year in late November and early December. They stayed when Sadgop landholders of Torkotala offered to employ them as agricultural laborers on a seasonal or yearly basis. Persons of the Bagdi caste, until then the principal agricultural laborers of the village, were at this time beginning to acquire and cultivate their own lands and thus did

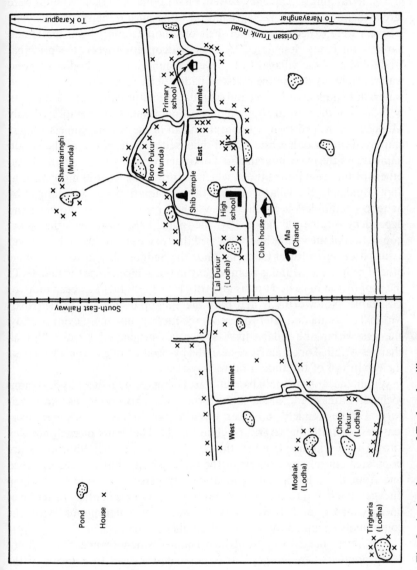

Fig. 2. A sketch map of Torkotala village

27

not need or want to work the land of others. To do so, in the context of life in Torkotala as in other Indian villages, implies a definite inferiority in rank and wide-ranging dependency as well. First Lodhas and then Mundas were hired, therefore, to do the agricultural tasks once done by Bagdis. The laborers were expected to build their own houses apart from the Hindu hamlets on lands designated by their Sadgop employers, the principal landholders of the village. In this way, around outlying bodies of pond water, originally dug in the midst of paddy fields as a source of irrigation water, did hamlets of Lodha and Munda agricultural laborers develop on both sides of the central Hindu hamlets. Some landholders employed only Mundas and helped them settle to the north of the Hindu hamlets. Others employed only Lodhas and helped them settle to the south of the Hindu hamlets. As the early migrants to Torkotala became settled, relatives and others of the tribe joined them, which in turn attracted still more Lodhas and Mundas to the village. At first this immigration was encouraged by Sadgop landholders because the newcomers provided an economical and dependent source of labor. By the mid-1950s, however, the tribal population of the village had surpassed that of caste Hindus and there was a surfeit of agricultural laborers. Thus the Sadgops began to discourage other Lodhas and Mundas from settling in the village. Since the mid-1950s the proportion of caste Hindus and tribals in Torkotala has been more or less stable. Noteworthy is that both the Sadgop decision to settle tribals within Torkotala and later to discourage further settlement evidence how changes within the village have sometimes originated locally. Not all changes within Torkotala have been the by-product of external events like the expansion of the Indian railway system.

Within the largest Hindu hamlet, East Hamlet, are further physical-cum-social divisions of the village in the form of neighborhoods, also known as *para*. Unlike hamlets, no clear physical boundaries or topographical features separate the several neighborhoods. The limits of each are well known to Torkotala Hindus, though. Three of the neighborhoods are populated entirely by persons of the Sadgop caste, but are distinguished one from the other as being inhabited by persons of different Sadgop lineages. Each of these neighborhoods represents a residential clustering of lineage mates, and their physical limits are coterminous with the compounds occupied by individual families of the lineage.

The fourth neighborhood of East Hamlet is defined negatively as not being populated by Sadgops. It is populated instead by persons of the Tontoby, Bagal, Kayastha and Brahman castes; also some Bagra-Khatriyas, who were formerly known as Bagdis.[3] What members of each of these castes share in common is that they cleared and settled the scrub jungle which remained in East Hamlet after the three Sadgop neighborhoods already existed. This fourth neighborhood is referred to

Table 1. *The population of Torkotala village, 1971*

Hamlets	Compounds	Households	Males	Females	Total	% of total population
Hindu						
East	30	42	107	112	219	
West	14	23	60	64	124	
Subtotal	44	65	167	176	343	46.4
Munda						
Boropukur	12	15	47	33	80	
Shamtaringhi	17	19	60	55	115	
Subtotal	29	34	107	88	195	26.4
Lodha						
Lalpukur	7	11	14	28	42	
Tirgheria	9	11	34	43	77	
Moshak	6	7 } incomplete census data[a]				
Chotopukur	9	10				
Subtotal	31	39			c.200	c.27.1
Totals	104	138			c.738	

[a] The census data are incomplete because of slow but continual population turnover in these hamlets.

descriptively as 'the neighborhood closest to the trunk road.' Each of the Sadgop neighborhoods, by contrast, is named and referred to by the surname of the lineage mates which reside in it.

The second Hindu hamlet, West Hamlet, is not internally divided into neighborhoods. Though neither quite as large in area or population as East Hamlet, it is not size *per se* which accounts for this difference. Rather, Torkotala residents generalize from the instance of East Hamlet to argue that West Hamlet does not have neighborhood divisions because none of its residents castes is represented by a residential clustering of lineage mates. An observer could add that in other villages, both to the east and west of the Orissan Trunk Road, neighborhood divisions exist even in the absence of such residential clusterings of lineage mates. In a large hamlet of mixed Hindu castes, for example, neighborhoods may separate one caste from another, a clustering of Brahmans from a clustering of Tambulis, or one category of castes from another, say *sat* Sudras from *asat* Sudras. The Lodha and Munda Hamlets of Torkotala, like West Hamlet, are also without neighborhood divisions of any kind.

Scattered throughout the hamlets and neighborhoods of Torkotala are 104 compounds and 138 households, both known in Bengali as *ghar* or *bari*. The houses are built of mud, dried hard by the sun, and have either thatch, baked mud tiles or corrugated tin roofing. The house of a major landholder may have several rooms, including separate areas for cooking, sleeping, and the storage of rice and valuables, in addition to a veranda where visitors are usually entertained. The very largest houses built within the last ten years may be two stories tall. In addition to the main residential building, a compound usually will include sheltered quarters for cows, goats and chickens, and an open area or yard, one part of which is used for stacking and storing dried paddy straws after the rice has been threshed. Another part of the yard may be used for a small vegetable garden. Torkotala village has no electricity; kerosene lanterns or oil lamps are used for illumination at night. Bathing is done outside the house in a pond of standing water. A compound may include its own small pond. Within the Hindu hamlets it is more common for neighboring compounds, especially when related by ties of kinship, to share usage rights in one large pond. Drinking water is taken from open wells or hand-pumped tube wells.

Among Hindus and tribals of Torkotala each compound is typically inhabited by patrilineally related kinsmen who live together as a family. If the family consists of several pairs of spouses and children who recognize the leadership and authority of a single male head, then the number of separate households within the compound is not distinguished. If several pairs of spouses and their children live as separate families, then the number of separate households is recognized, and each will have its own male head. Thus within the village as a whole there are more households than compounds. But in all cases, *ghar* and *bari* refer both to the physical setting and the social unit which occupies it – the compound and its members, the house and its household.

Hamlets, neighborhoods, compounds and houses are the important physical divisions by which Torkotala residents describe and map their village. Significantly, each of these physical divisions is recognized locally as a social division of the village as well. Hamlets are populated by caste Hindus, Lodhas or Mundas, but not by a mixture of these peoples. Neighborhoods are identified in Torkotala with the residential clustering of lineage mates. Compounds and houses are identified with the families who occupy them. The whole of Torkotala village is identified with its founders and first settlers, the Sadgops, but includes as well all who accept the leadership of the traditional village headman, a Sadgop by caste.

Local history and administration

Torkotala was founded by Sadgops with the support of the Pal Raja of Narayanghar, himself a Sadgop by caste, who retained revenue rights to village lands which were cleared and settled. Hence the history of the village is intimately tied to the fortunes of the Pal Raja and the history of the Narayanghar kingdom. The following account, told by a male of the royal lineage, indicates how the line of Pal Rajas first began, and suggests how the Narayanghar area, once infamous as the home of tribal peoples and lower-caste Hindus, became the site of a Sadgop kingdom.

In the time before Gondobah Pal became the first Pal Raja, the *des* now called Narayanghar was known as Narayanpur (the place of the god Narayan). It was the *des* of tribal peoples and very low-caste Hindus.

Gondobah Pal was a Sadgop from Burdwan. He came to Narayanpur from Burdwan on the trunk road, which even then [in the thirteenth century] was a pilgrimage route for persons on their way to the Jagannatha temple in Puri. Gondobah Pal spent only one night in Narayanpur. But during that night the goddesses Brahmani, Rudrani and Indrani appeared to him in a dream, and said that they were lying uncared for at the side of a nearby pond. Gondobah Pal was told to build a temple for the three goddesses and to see that they were properly worshipped. During the dream, the goddesses also revealed the name of a medicinal plant which grew near the pond and told of its wonderful curative powers for all kinds of ailments.

When Gondobah Pal awoke the next morning, he went to the pond where he had seen the three goddesses in his dream and, to his surprise, found them lying there, uncared for, in the form of three stones. The dream had shown itself to be true. Gondobah Pal hid the stone goddesses in the waters of the pond, vowing to build them a proper temple on returning from his pilgrimage to Puri.

Later the same day, Gondobah Pal continued southwards along the trunk road on his pilgrimage to Puri. Days of travel passed before he finally arrived. It was during his stay in Puri that Gondobah Pal learned that the wife of the local Raja was pregnant. Not only was the Rani pregnant, she had been in labor for days without being able to deliver the child. Her pain was immense. None of the Raja's physicians were able to relieve the pain or induce delivery of the child. The Raja, in his distress, thus looked to others in the kingdom for help and decided to have a public statement issued to the effect that any person who could relieve the Rani of her pain and deliver his child would be made a Raja over a group of villages now under his control.

On learning of this statement, Gondobah Pal immediately realized that the medicinal plant revealed to him in his dream by the three goddesses would relieve the Rani of her distress. He searched for the plant (the name of which is now forgotten), and having found it, cut off a twig. With the twig in hand, Gondobah Pal then presented himself to the Raja, explained his purpose in coming, and soon afterwards was given a chance to minister to the Rani. With the simple act of putting the twig next to the Rani's (left) ear the child was delivered quickly, without further pain. Both the mother and child, a son, lived in perfect health.

The grateful Raja asked Gondobah Pal the secret of his medicine. Gondobah Pal answered by telling of his dream at Narayanpur. He also told of the events of the following day and how he had vowed to build a temple and arrange for the regular worship of the three stone goddesses now lying uncared for in the water of the pond. As it happened, the villages of Narayanpur were under the rule of this very Raja, who immediately granted them to Gondobah Pal as the basis for a new kingdom, separate but still loyal to his own. This was in AD 1264.

Gondobah Pal was made Raja of Narayanpur with a simple ceremony. The Raja placed a mark of sandlewood paste on his forehead and titled him Gondobah Pal, Srichandon Raja. [*Chandon* means sandlewood paste. *Sri* is an honorific form of address. Srichandon Raja means the sandlewood paste Raja.]

In due time Gondobah Pal, as Raja, returned from Puri to his home in Burdwan and then from Burdwan to his new kingdom in Narayanpur. With him came many other Sadgops from Burdwan. Across from the pond where the three stone goddesses had lain a great temple was built and dedicated to Brahmani [a manifestation of Durga]. Not far from the temple a great *rajbari* [or Raja's house] was also built. It was then that Narayanpur became known as Narayanghar, the *ghar* or fort of the god Narayan. The great *rajbari*, surrounded by high walls and a large, broad moat, was like a fortress. Narayanghar is a far more glorious name than Narayanpur.

This account, which is far more detailed but in its outline identical to the accounts told by Torkotala villagers and by other persons of the Narayanghar kingdom, is important for several reasons. In its entirety it provides the charter for the presence and prominence of Sadgops in Narayanghar. Namely, Gondobah Pal, a Sadgop by caste, was made a Raja by reason of the very special medical assistance given to the wife of a Raja of Orissa at Puri. He was made Raja of Narayanghar, rather than any other place, because it was there, during a break on his pilgrimage to the Jagannatha temple in Puri, that the three goddesses revealed themselves to him in a dream, and that he learned from them about the wonderful curative powers of the plant which he later used to assist the Rani. In its specifics the account dates the presence of Sadgops in Narayanghar from about AD 1264. It was then that Gondobah Pal, along with many other Sadgops from Burdwan, raised a great temple to Brahmani, built a residence, and began to clear and settle the lands of the new kingdom. From that time onwards Sadgops have been the dominant caste in Narayanghar. Within Midnapore district as a whole, it is the more populous and wealthy Mahisya caste which enjoys this position. In its specifics the account also indicates how this special enclave of Sadgops was established. Simply, Gondabah Pal encouraged fellow Sadgops to migrate from Burdwan to Narayanghar to settle the uncleared lands of his new kingdom. Torkotala was among the many villages of the kingdom which were founded by these Sadgop settlers.

Judging from genealogical evidence, it is likely that Torkotala was not settled until the eighteenth century, but no exact dating is possible. The Pal Rajas did not keep a record of when villages in their kingdom were founded, and Torkotala Sadgops do not possess genealogies from which the first settlers of the village can be deduced with certainty. The genealogies which can be reconstructed include from two to eight generations. In one instance 21 generations were noted, but the genealogy is considered by other Sadgops of the village, including lineage mates of its possessor, to be a falsified document. (It was falsified to support claims being contested in court to certain lands as ancestral property – which it did successfully!)

From the founding of the village to the present, the *Mukhya* or headman of Torkotala has always been a Sadgop by caste. It is because of their position as founders and headmen of the village, and because they remain the largest landholders in the village, that Torkotala in 1971, with a minority population of Hindus, is identified locally as a Hindu village, and more specifically as a Sadgop village. Historically the Sadgops of Torkotala, through the village headman, have also benefited from a special administrative alliance with the Pal Rajas of Narayanghar. That is, the headman represented the local land-revenue interests of the Raja in Torkotala, seeing to the cultivation of village lands and assisting revenue officials in their collections, when they came to the village. In return the headman could call as needed for the support of the Pal Raja to bolster his personal administration of village affairs or to back the Sadgops as a caste in matters of inter-caste rivalry.

The *Mukhya* was the sole headman in Torkotala until the first decade of this century. Then events occurred which culminated in Torkotala, unlike other villages in the area, being led by two headmen: a *Mukhya* and *Raj Mukhya*. The relationship between these two village headmen is explained locally with this analogy. Just as a Hindu king is aided in the day-to-day administration of his kingdom by ministers as active seconds, so the *Raj Mukhya* is aided in his day-to-day administration of village affairs by the *Mukhya* as his active second. The *Raj Mukhya* is the ruling or principal headman of the village. As befits a principal headman, he does not himself actively work; rather he supervises the work of others, in this instance that of the *Mukhya*. But if the *Raj Mukhya* is the principal headman of Torkotala, how did he accede to this position so late in village history?

The pertinent events occurred between 1900 and 1910. Biswanath Maiti, a Sadgop, was the wealthiest and most influential villager of his generation. He married his daughter to Tijendra Pal, a poor but well-born member of a cadet branch of the royal lineage. It is customary, both normatively and statistically, in Bengali society for a bride to leave her natal home after marriage and return with her husband to his home or the home of his father, which is usually located in a different village. Residence is usually virilocal, and marriages between families of the same village are statistically rare. This customary pattern was not upheld in the marriage of Biswanath Maiti's daughter, though. Rather, Tijendra Pal took up residence in Torkotala in the house of his wife's father. This involved a definite loss of prestige for Tijendra, who placed himself in a position of dependency, and a definite gain in prestige for Biswanath, who evidenced his considerable wealth in being able to support his daughter's husband under his own roof. The arrangement also had very practical benefits for both parties. Biswanath Maiti had no sons of his own. Thus it was expected that Tijendra would assume management control of the Maiti lands after Biswanath's death. Inheritance rights to the land would later pass, upon his birth, to Biswanath's grandson. Tijendra did assume the management of Maiti lands after Biswanath's death, as expected. Then unexpectedly, Tijendra Pal manipulated his newly gained control over these lands, in combination with his status as a member of the royal lineage, to have himself designated *Raj Mukhya*. Tijendra simply declared his intention to become *Raj Mukhya*, a previously non-existent position, and stated that he had the personal support of the Pal Raja. As no one in the village, including the *Mukhya*, could successfully oppose Tijendra when backed by the Pal Raja, Torkotala came to have a second headman. When Tijendra died in 1941, he was succeeded as *Raj Mukhya* by his eldest son, Anil, who continues to live in Torkotala. It is expected that Anil will be succeeded by one of his sons, and he by one of his sons, so that the position of *Raj Mukhya* passes as an hereditary right to males of the Pal lineage.

The *Mukhya* and (more recently) the *Raj Mukhya* are assisted in their administration of the village by another official whose position dates from the very founding of Torkotala. The work of the *atghariya*, or village crier, involves circulating through the village to inform heads of households of an impending village meeting. It may include as well carrying messages or bearing items outside the village. The crier is appointed by the village *Mukhya* and works under his direction. Their relationship is likened to that between the Raja and his ministers and the *Raj Mukhya* and *Mukhya*. Namely, the crier is the *Mukhya's* active, laboring second. Like the two village headmen, he receives no salary or lands for his work; only the regard of fellow villagers and the honorary prestation of areca nut and betel leaf on the occasion of births and marriages and certain worships in the village. The position of crier has always been held in Torkotala by persons of the Bagra-Khatriya caste. The Bagra-Khatriyas, then known as Bagdis, are the agricultural laborers who settled Torkotala at the same time as their landholding employers, the Sadgops. Their 'right' to the second and more laborious of the traditional village offices is based on a claim to being 'the second founders' of Torkotala.

Since the mid-1860s, when British legislation created the *thana* as the local unit of police administration in Midnapore, the list of Torkotala officials has also included a *chokidar* or village watchman. Before then police functions were executed by henchmen who served in the employ of the local Raja in exchange for rent-free lands. Like the henchmen of earlier times, it is for the watchman to protect against village crimes and to report their occurrence to local officials, in this case police officers stationed in Narayanghar. The watchman also has the additional responsibility of collecting and reporting fortnightly the statistics of births and deaths in the village. For his work the watchman of the British Raj received a salary, and in some instances also received village lands to cultivate rent free. In 1971 the Torkotala watchman received only a salary. Part of that salary is paid by the West Bengal state government through the local police office, and part is paid from taxes collected from villagers for police work done on their behalf. The watchman thus remains, as he was during British rule, accountable to two parties. He is a villager in the service of fellow villagers; and he is a member of the regular constabulary, a government employee. In Torkotala during the last 40 years the position of watchman has been held by one Bagra-Khatriya, two Lodhas, and, presently, by a person born to the Sadgop caste but later outcasted for consorting with Lodha females. While the position is valued for the cash income it brings, the work of policing the village in the service of other villagers is considered demeaning.

Raj Mukhya, Mukhya, atghariya and *chokidar* are the four named positions of village-level leadership in Torkotala. Two of these positions, *Mukhya* and *atghariya*, date from the founding of Torkotala and thus may be considered traditional offices of village administration. Succession to both is maintained as a hereditary right of males of the incumbent lineages. The positions of *Raj Mukhya* and *chokidar*, by contrast, date much more recently in time, though Tijendra Pal and then his descendants have tried to obfuscate this fact and claim the position of *Raj Mukhya* as a traditional village office. One other official common in rural Midnapore and throughout West Bengal is the *tulsidar* or land-revenue collector. As the collector of revenues and especially as the recorder of local land holdings, the *tulsidar* had an influential role in Torkotala affairs in the past. Within this century, though, he has been superseded in importance, first by the British-appointed tax collector and more recently by revenue officials of the West Bengal state government.

Whereas the *tulsidar* was in the employ of the Pal Rajas, the tax collector was a salaried official of the British, appointed by the district magistrate of Midnapore, with responsibility for collecting both land revenues and the *chokidari* tax from the several villages under his jurisdiction. Torkotala villagers can no longer recall the first such tax collectors in their locale. The last, a Sadgop of the village, Radhanath Mahabarto, is well remembered. Like Biswanath Maiti before him, Radhanath Mahabarto was the wealthiest and most influential man of the village until his death in 1947. The rivalry between Radhanath and Biswanath's son-in-law, Tijendra Pal, was a pervasive and recurrent feature of political life in Torkotala during their lifetimes. It is continued by descendants of their respective lines, so that today the Sadgop caste is divided by three major political cleavages, each corresponding in large part to one of the three Sadgop neighborhoods in East Hamlet. The rivalry between these divisions of the Sadgop caste will re-enter the discussion in chapters 4 and 5. For present purposes it serves merely to identify the factional groupings among Sadgops, which also

represent the major factional divisions within Torkotala as a whole. The
Maiti–Pal lineage is led by the present *Raj Mukhya*, Anil Pal, the son of
Tijendra Pal. The Mahabarto lineage is led by the present head of the
statutory village council (to be discussed shortly), Atul Mahabarto,
Radhanath Mahabarto's younger brother's son. And the third lineage, the
Bhunai, is led by the present *Mukhya*, Haripado Bhunai.[4]

It is clear that the administration of Torkotala affairs has never been left
solely to the village headmen. The Sadgops as a caste have always exercised
leadership in the village, so much so that a meeting of Sadgop heads of
households is often described not as a caste council, but as a village council.
In addition, certain wealthy men have always been leading figures in village
affairs. Biswanath Maiti, Tijendra Pal and Radhanath Mahabarto are but
three such persons introduced thus far. The very saintly or the very worldly
wise have also been influential. In the late 1940s and early 1950s, for
example, village affairs were swayed by an itinerant Jogi of the Nath sect,
who lived periodically in Torkotala in the compound of the village
Brahman. During his irregular but frequent periods of stay in the village,
the heads of most households sought his advice on the widest range of
concerns. Significantly, Torkotala villagers also hold that village-level
administration is not the sole responsibility of named officials, a single
caste, or exceptionally able or gifted individuals. It is the shared
responsibility of the headmen of the Lodha and Munda hamlets, caste
leaders at the level of caste organization, lineage elders at the level of
lineage organization, heads of households at the level of family organization, and individual adherence to moral conduct at the personal level.
The discussion will return to what is meant by proper administration for
the village as a whole and for each level of social organization in chapter 4.
Here it is sufficient to acknowledge the orienting premise expressed by
Torkotala villagers: if individuals and groups at every level of social
organization properly adhere to the moral conduct enjoined for them, then
the affairs of the village as a whole would be in order.

This picture of overlapping administrative levels, from the individual to
the family, through lineage and caste, to village-level officials and,
ultimately, outside of the village to learned Brahmans or Jogis or the Raja
himself, represents a model of how Torkotala villagers conceptualize the
traditional lines of authority and responsibility for village-level
administration before or in the absence of any centralized state authority.
The actual administration of Torkotala in 1971 evidences how traditional
lines of authority within the village and kingdom have been altered or
circumscribed by a number of historical events originating outside the
village. Foremost among them is the declining fortunes of the Pal Rajas of
Narayanghar.

The declining fortunes of the Pal Rajas

From circa AD 1264, when Gondobah Pal became the first Pal Raja of Narayanghar, until 1844 when Prithviballabh Pal became the 26th in an unbroken succession of Pal Rajas, the royal lineage was able to retain direct rule over its kingdom. This was accomplished, however, only by recognizing a series of superior rulers. The Pal Rajas, for example, recognized their dependence on the goodwill of the more powerful Rajas of Orissa, and took care to acknowledge this dependence without at the same time relinquishing active rule over their kingdom. In part this consisted of 'gifting' a portion of the revenue collected from lands of the kingdom in implicit exchange for an umbrella of protection; and in part of patterning religious celebrations of the Narayanghar kingdom after those of the Orissan Rajas. After Durga Puja, the quintessential Bengali religious celebration for royal households, for instance, the second major religious celebration of the Narayanghar kingdom consciously and purposely parallels that maintained by the Raja of Puri. Specifically, the Jagannatha temple in Puri is famed as the temple of Jagannatha (Krishna), Lord of the Universe, Subadra, his sister, and Balarama, his brother. The image of Jagannatha worshipped at the temple, legend tells, was to be hewn from the trunk of a tree by the famous carpenter Visvakarma. It was left incomplete, with only indistinct human form, however, when Visvakarma was interrupted in his work by Indra-mena, the then king of Utkal (Orissa). Indra-mena was vexed at this untoward occurrence, but nevertheless worshipped the roughly hewn tree-trunk as his god. The image of Jagannatha worshipped in Puri today remains a roughly hewn, brightly colored piece of wood which bears little resemblance to the human form in which Krishna is usually represented. The images of Brahmani, Rudrani and Indrani that are worshipped by the Pal Rajas of Narayanghar have the same appearance: brightly colored wooden images of indistinct human form. It is also no coincidence that the major religious celebration of the Jagannatha temple in Puri, the *rathjatra*, is replicated on a smaller scale at the Brahmani temple in Narayanghar. In both instances *rathjatra* or 'the car festival' consists of parading images of the gods through the public streets on huge wooden cars or chariots, elaborately bedecked with rich cloth and scented materials, in a great procession of the gods and devotees. During the rest of the year, the gods are confined to the temple.

The supremacy of the Hindu kings of Orissa did not go unchallenged. It was only during the seventeenth century, though, that the next superior rulers of the Narayanghar kingdom, the Moghals, were able to dominate thoroughly and to consolidate their administration of the general area now known as Midnapore district. As part of Midnapore, the Pal kingdom of

Narayanghar was administered as a province of Orissa, to which a governor was sent from the imperial Moghul court in Delhi. It was his charge to police the area and to see to the collection of land revenues, the mainstay of the imperial treasury. The Pal Rajas assisted the governor in this work by seeing that the land revenues were collected by their agents and officials, all Hindus, and then honoring the Moghul governor with a portion of the total revenues collected. The Moghuls, for their part, did not actively intervene with the internal administration of the Pal kingdom, but left the Pal Rajas in direct control. This pattern was not altered substantially until the late ninteenth century during the lifetime of Prithviballabh Pal when the British supplanted the Moghuls and established themselves as the supreme rulers of Midnapore and Narayanghar, as well as the greater province of Bengal and Orissa.

As mentioned earlier, Prithviballabh Pal was the 26th in an unbroken succession of Pal Rajas. He reigned from 1844 until his death in 1933. The following account, told by a male of the royal lineage, recounts why the active rule of the Pal Rajas over the Narayanghar kingdom ended when it did.

As an old man, Prithviballabh Pal was seemingly without interest in the affairs of the kingdom. He built a second *rajbari* some miles distant and to the west of his ancestral home. There he lived apart from his wife, the Rani, who maintained the original *rajbari*. Either the Raja spent his days sitting idle, or else he entertained lavishly with no regard for the rupees being spent. At no time did he administer over the collection of land revenues of the kingdom and this, in combination with his lavish entertainments, gradually left the Raja impoverished.

If you ask why Prithviballabh Pal turned away from his work as Raja, I think it was because he had no sons of his own. The first eighteen generations of Pal Rajas each had one and only one son who lived to rule the kingdom and to father a successor. The nineteenth Pal Raja had three sons. The eldest became Raja after his father's death. The younger two sons were each given revenue (*zamindari*) lands for their personal expenses. From then until the time of Prithviballabh Pal whenever there was more than one son the eldest became Raja. Prithviballabh Pal was the first of his line, after 26 generations, not to have any sons. This, I think, is why he lost interest in the affairs of the kingdom. He could see the end of the royal lineage.

Prithviballabh Pal turned his interest elsewhere. Before death he wanted to complete a pilgrimage to Calcutta to bathe in the sacred Ganges (there known as the Hooghly). To this end he took a loan of three lakhs from a merchant family in Calcutta, the Laha family.

Prithviballabh Pal made his pilgrimage to Calcutta accompanied by a great number of friends and servants. Afterwards he was not able to repay the loan which financed the pilgrimage. The Laha family then took recourse in the British courts. And eventually Prithviballabh Pal was ordered by the courts to give up rights to collect the revenues to almost the whole of the Narayanghar kingdom in default of the loan. This did not leave the Raja landless. There were still considerable lands held in the name of the Rani which had not been forfeited by court order. And there was also a great deal of land held in the names of gods which remained under the administrative control of the Raja. But with the loss of rights to collect the revenue on farm lands in much of the kingdom Prithviballabh Pal was no longer the largest or even the second largest landholder in Narayanghar. The Laha family was now the largest landholder. And a branch of the royal lineage, with whom Prithviballabh Pal had some enmity, was the second largest.

When Prithviballabh Pal lost the legal right to collect revenues on much of the farm lands of the Narayanghar kingdom, he also lost *de facto* control over the cultivators and tenants of those lands, the persons who paid the revenues. These persons continued, perhaps, to view Prithviballabh Pal with the high regard due to their Raja. And the Raja continued to preside over ceremonial and religious functions of the kingdom, including Durga Puja and *rathjatra*. But in all matters regarding land and disputes over land, persons of the kingdom were now accountable to the Laha family who, in turn, were accountable to the British.

Torkotala was one of the villages which came under direct control of the Laha family. Present residents of Torkotala were not alive during the lifetime of Prithviballabh Pal. Nevertheless, Sadgops and other caste Hindus express a very definite opinion of this period as a turning point in the administration of their village and the kingdom as a whole. Villagers state that it was only towards the end of Prithviballabh Pal's reign, when he had withdrawn his active concern for administering the affairs of the kingdom, and especially after the loan from the Laha family was defaulted, that their fathers began to take land and other disputes to the British courts for settlement. Until then all disputes that could not be settled within the village could be settled by appeal to the Pal Raja.

This subjective view of the past is plausible but cannot be confirmed by documentary evidence. Yet as a statement of belief and as an indication of how Torkotala villagers perceive changes in the administration of village affairs, it is of considerable importance. It suggests that the traditional pattern of administration altered when the administrative alliance between the traditional village headman and the Pal Rajas altered. When the *Mukhya* no longer represented the interests of the Pal Rajas as the principal landholders of the village, he could no longer rely on support from them for his leadership of village-level affairs. Influence as a village leader thus came to depend more than ever before on one's personal capacity for leadership and on one's personal resources, especially wealth, which could be mobilized to attract and retain a political following. It is in this context that large landholders who could mobilize the artisan and service castes in their employ, plus their tenants and agricultural laborers, began to rival the *Mukhya* as the effective head of Torkotala village. The position of *Mukhya* still retained some of the customary high regard given to traditional offices in Bengali society, but as it was no longer buttressed by support from the Pal Rajas, the actual *Mukhya* became but one of a number of individual landholders in the village who competed for influence over village affairs on the basis of personal resources.

As to the affairs of the kingdom, Prithviballabh Pal adopted a son, Satiscandra, shortly before his death. Satiscandra Pal was able to regain revenue rights to some of the lands lost during his father's reign by repaying portions of the debt to the Laha family. He acquired other lands by clearing unsettled areas of the kingdom of scrub jungle. The royal lineage never recovered active rule over the Narayanghar kingdom, though, and while the title of Raja was never formally given away or taken away, Prithviballabh Pal is considered the last Pal Raja of Narayanghar. Satiscandra Pal lived out his days as a large landholder and *zamindar*. His sons, the 28th generation of the line dating from Gondobah Pal, continue to occupy the royal residence, to maintain the Brahmani temple, and to preside over those religious worships most closely associated with the Pal Rajas. Durga Puja and *rathjatra* continue to be performed yearly. Over the years, though, the political influence of the Pal lineage in Narayanghar has gradually but continually been reduced. Perhaps most immediately this is the result of *zamindari* abolition laws of the mid-1950s which sought to eliminate absentee landlords as well as intermediaries between the government and cultivators in tax collection, and then later legislation in the 1960s which placed successively lower ceilings on the amount of land any family could cultivate as a personal holding. Each new land ceiling reduced not only the potential income that could be earned by cultivating agricultural lands but also the number of tenants and laborers who would be dependent on a single landholder. This meant, from the vantage point of landholders, a definite loss of political influence because in rural India economic dependency implies wide-ranging political dependency as well.

For whatever reasons Torkotala villagers may have turned for support or assistance to the Pal Rajas in the past, in 1971 they turned to the West Bengal government as represented by its officers in Midnapore district. Midnapore Town, the administrative seat of the district, is located north of Torkotala on the Orissan Trunk Road. The villagers rarely go to Midnapore Town except when involved in court cases. The registration of land titles and other property transactions can be done in a local office in Narayanghar. The local land revenue office is also located in Narayanghar, as is the local police office. State and national elections have always been held in the village primary school. And other contacts with the district administration are rarely taken directly to Midnapore. More often they are mediated through the office of the Block Development Officer (BDO).

The development block in which Torkotala is located has its offices in Belda, a town south of the village along the Orissan Trunk Road. It is headed by the BDO and managed with a staff of extension officers who have expertise in fields such as agriculture, animal husbandry, social education, public works and the running of economic cooperatives. Also included on the BDO staff is a multipurpose village-level worker whose job it is periodically to visit villages in the block to enquire as to what government assistance might be needed. It is through the village-level worker, the several extension officers and the BDO that Torkotala residents usually contact the administrative apparatus of Midnapore district, whether petitioning for funds or merely seeking advice. It is the BDO, for example, who sees that improved varieties of seeds, fertilizer and chemical insecticides are demonstrated and made available in the block. And it is the BDO who allocates government funds for the sinking of new wells, the building of new schools or the funding of other local public works.

It was also the BDO and his staff of extension officers who, in 1962, introduced into Torkotala and other villages of the block the system of rural self-government know locally as Panchayati Raj. The history and operation of this system of self-government in Torkotala will be considered in detail in chapter 5. For now it is sufficient to point out that the introduction of Panchayati Raj added several new elements to the administration of Torkotala village affairs. Outside the village, for example, the head of the area *panchayat* or council now rivals the BDO as the most important official to whom villagers look for advice and assistance in those village affairs, including competitions, which cannot be settled locally. The support of either the area council head or the BDO, both of whom have government funds to allocate, is also considered necessary to the successful execution of development projects within Torkotala. Their influence in village affairs extends beyond their control of government funds, though, for Torkotala villagers view both men as representing the full weight and power of the state government. Just as the *Mukhya* once relied on support and assistance from the Pal Rajas, so today any individual with aspirations to village leadership must have the support and assistance of government officials outside the village. The BDO and the area council head are the government officials who are most important in this regard.

Within Torkotala the introduction of Panchayati Raj has meant the establishment of a *gram panchayat* or village council, legalized by statutory law, where historically there had never been a formal village council; and the election of two new village officials, an *Adhyaksa* or village council head, and the second in charge, the *Upo-adhyaksa*. Two Sadgops, Anil Pal, the *Raj Mukhya*, and Atul Mahabarto, contested the election for village council head. Atul won, and has held the position in the absence of a second election since 1962. The second in charge is the lone Bagra-Khatriya on the statutory council. In this the leadership of the new council, a Sadgop headman and a Bagra-Khatriya second, does not differ from the traditional leadership of the village. The operation of the village council does represent a departure from the past. For example, Atul Mahabarto, even in the absence of a second council election, is well aware of the potential power of the electoral process and – against the day of a possible second election – has openly sought to buttress his position of village leadership in a way that the *Raj Mukhya* and *Mukhya* never found necessary; namely, by winning the support and following, and the potential vote, not only of other Sadgops and landholders of the village, but of the more numerous Lodhas and Mundas. Much of the work of the village council, as a result, has focused on spreading adult education in the village, establishing an economic cooperative and sinking new tube wells in the outlying hamlets occupied by Lodhas and Mundas. More than the other two village headmen, Atul Mahabarto has also made a concerted effort to understand the statutory laws of West Bengal and to cultivate personal contacts with the officers who administer those laws and the programs of the state government within Midnapore district. It is not surprising, therefore, that Torkotala villagers, when reflecting on the work of the *Adhyaksa*, summarize the recent changes in village administration represented by the introduction of statutory councils with this short formula: the *Raj Mukhya* and *Mukhya* do the work of the village (*gramer kaj*), or village politics. They see to births, marriages and deaths, to worships and to the settlement of all disputes between these events. The *Adhyaksa* does the work of the government (*sorkari kaj*), or government politics; he sees to progress and change. Village politics and government politics are the subjects of chapters 4 and 5 respectively.

Summary and discussion

Just as newcomers to a West Bengal village introduce themselves, this chapter has introduced a village of West Bengal with a discussion of those features which characterize Torkotala as a unique *des*, namely, its land, people and local history. In doing so the village has also been discussed in relation to the several broader *des* of which it is a part, especially the former Narayanghar kingdom and the present-day Midnapore district.

Geologically Torkotala village and the Narayanghar kingdom represent a transition zone between the deltaic regions of eastern Midnapore and the less fertile, lateritic regions of western Midnapore. Socially the village and kingdom represent a transition zone of another sort, an ethnic frontier between predominately higher-caste Hindus of Bengali or Oriyan stock to the east and tribal peoples and lower-caste Hindus to the west. As the history of Torkotala instances, this social division of Midnapore has become increasingly blurred in recent decades. Though not discussed above, Torkotala villagers are also aware that the geological divisions of the district, while subject to immeasurably slower processes of change, are also in flux. The major river systems of Midnapore, as in West Bengal as a whole, have gradually but continuously followed the slope of the land and evidenced an eastward movement of their stream beds (Nicholas 1962). Symbolizing the geologic flux for Torkotala villagers is a moribund stream located three miles west of the village which in some time past carried silt as part of the active deltaic system now confined to eastern Midnapore. The Orissan Trunk Road, which runs north and south through the length of the district, conveniently marks the geological and social divisions of Midnapore.

Historically the Narayanghar kingdom represents a third transition zone, a march area for armies and pilgrims between Orissa to the south and regions of Bengal to the north and east of Midnapore. It is because of its strategic location beside the Orissan Trunk Road that the Narayanghar kingdom, a relatively small and infertile area, has received so much attention from a series of superior rulers. Torkotala adults are aware of this aspect of local history. Torkotala children learn of it through the biographies of all 26 Pal Rajas, which are taught in the local primary school and used pedagogically as temporal markers of major changes in village life.

The history of Torkotala recounted in this chapter, as partial and selective as it is, points to the error in that view of the Indian village as a timeless, self-sufficient, village republic, as a community that is static and closed. Specifically, for Charles Metcalfe or others to characterize a durable village as timeless and unchanging is to confuse the village as a type of community with the historical experience of an actual community. Some of the changes experienced within Torkotala stem from events originating within the village: the Sadgop decision to settle tribal Lodhas and Mundas, for example. Other changes stem from events originating outside Torkotala, especially as they reflect the fortunes of the Pal Rajas and, since Independence, the activities of the West Bengal state government. The Sadgop founding of Torkotala, the changing settlement pattern of the village, the presence of a British-paid village watchman and tax collector, the development work of the BDO, the existence of Panchayati Raj – these and other instances of life within Torkotala being affected by external events also evidence that Torkotala never was an independent political entity, a so-called village republic. In fact and in local perception Torkotala exists, now as in the past, in relation to the several broader *des* of which it is a part.

Interwoven with the discussion of the land, people and history of Torkotala is also an initial description of how the village has been administered through time. The union of these seemingly separate topics is not arbitrary, for Torkotala villagers perceive within the spatial organization of Bengali society the structure by which their village is administered. Every physical division of space is also regarded as a social division, so that land and people are never disassociated. Further, these physical-cum-social divisions are seen as localized administrative units with recognized heads or leaders who are responsible for the proper management and supervision of its affairs. This is as true for a household as it is for a hamlet, village, kingdom, district or state.

Within Torkotala, the *Mukhya* and crier occupy the traditional positions of village-level leadership. They are now assisted in this work by a watchman and two additional headmen, a *Raj Mukhya* and *Adhyaksa*. The work of each of these officials is further complemented by the headmen of the Lodha and Munda hamlets, caste leaders at the level of caste organization, lineage elders at the level of lineage organization, heads of households and personal adherence to moral conduct by individuals. Though not themselves villagers, historically the Pal Rajas, and more recently the BDO and the head of the area council, have also played important roles in the management of village affairs. Exactly what is understood locally by proper administration, and how individuals and groups at each level of social organization contribute to it, will be considered in greater detail in chapters 4 and 5. But first it will be useful to examine further the sociocultural context in which Torkotala villagers act politically, and make evaluations of proper administration. This is one aim of chapters 2 and 3, which in examining how the Bengali cosmos and society are ordered also develops a transformational theory of rank.

2. Jati

The spatial organization of Bengali society is premised on an association between land and people. According to this premise all of West Bengal and India, indeed all of the world, can be described and mapped as an overlapping series of larger and smaller *des*. All *des* are of the same genus, only increasingly localized species of the genus. Each is differentiated from the others by its unique conjunction of land and the people who inhabit the land, their history, and the customary way of life maintained by them. When viewed together, the multiple referents of *des*, village, region, kingdom, country, etc., form a continuous spatial ordering of society.

The social organization of Bengali society is premised on an analogous association between *jati* and their proper place in cosmological and social space.

A *jati* may designate a sex, a family, a descent grouping, a caste or a category of castes. It may also designate a nationality or even a life form, say Man. There is no contradiction in this, and the multiple referents of *jati* are not inconsistencies of language use. Like *des, jati* is a relative concept whose appropriate referent varies with context, and whose range of referents reflects the segmentary nature of Hindu social organization. But whatever the specific referent, the term *jati* is applied to persons who share by circumstances of birth a common physical nature and a common set of natural and moral activities thought appropriate to it. The term is perhaps best glossed as 'birth group.'

It will be remembered that one of the first questions asked of a newcomer on entering a West Bengal village is, 'Where is your *des*?' Introductions are never complete, though, until another and more delicate question is asked: '*Apnar jati ki?*': 'What is your *jati*?' If the reply given is not at the level of specificity desired, this question also will be asked again and again. To what end? To place a person socially and to know how he fits, according to his birth groups, into the ranked orders and ordered ranks of society.

Following the Bengali example, this chapter continues the introduction of Torkotala village with a discussion of those *jati* which are recognized locally. It also begins an ethnography of rank which goes beyond the usual

45

focus on caste as a unique institutional system of inequality. The opening sections of this chapter consider those properties of rank general to each life form in the Bengali cosmos and to all the birth groups into which humans in Bengali society are divided. It is argued that the entire Bengali cosmos and society is ordered by the premise of ranked inequalities, and that all life forms and human birth groups are ranked by the same criterion. As noted in the Introduction, the evidence from Torkotala also suggests that attributional, interactional and purity-plus-power theories of rank, as they developed through studies of how castes are ordered high and low, are each misleading in treating physical purity and patterns of behavior as distinct and separate features. In Torkotala, as throughout West Bengal – and perhaps among Hindus throughout India – the rank of a caste, like that of all other *jati*, depends mutually on its radical physical nature and behavioral code, which are viewed locally as a single, if duplex, criterion of rank. One is but the reflection and realization of the other. And a change in one entails a necessary and corresponding change in the other. The closing section of this chapter builds on this refinement in ethnography to develop a transformational theory of rank in which the defining features, and thus the rank, of a caste, and those more highly differentiated birth groups included within a caste, are seen to alter for better or worse according to the life activities of their members. Patterns of marriage, diet, food exchanges and occupation are each examined to illustrate this transformational process.

Both the premise of ranked inequalities, and the standard of nature and code as a duplex criterion of rank, are readily stated by Torkotala Hindus, though not all are equally knowledgeable of the details these bald statements adumbrate. There is a social distribution of knowledge. But the ethnography of rank presented below is not the esoteric knowledge of specialists, of males or females, of the high-caste or the well-educated. Aside from one Brahman family, Torkotala Hindus are of Sudra or Untouchable castes, and even those adult men and women who do not read can describe, at least in part, the several worlds and life forms of the Bengali universe from accounts heard in conversation with others or during public readings of respected texts like the Srimad Bhagavata Mahapurana, Bhagavad Gita and Manu Dharmasastra, which are a regular feature of village life. The ranking of categories of castes, castes and kinship groups is also not esoteric knowledge, nor a matter of sterile logic. A cosmos and society ordered by ranked inequalities represents for Torkotala Hindus a shared construction of reality which is considered authoritative and against which individual villagers form their own understanding, however partial or deviant, of what is really real. The discussion below provides a synoptic account of this commonsense understanding of the Bengali cosmos and society, a picture of the whole formed from conversations with literally every Hindu family in Torkotala. That the discussion emphasizes what is shared over intra-cultural variability is not to deny the many differences in perspective that do indeed exist among Bengalis, or even to under-estimate the importance of studying such variation. But for purposes of this study, what is critical is the shared system of meaning which defines the common cultural context in which Torkotala villagers act politically. That shared system of meaning includes a cosmology of ranked orders, to which the discussion now turns.

A cosmology of ranked orders

The Bengali universe is divided into three major worlds. *Lok* is the generic term for all of the worlds of the universe; it is also the specific term applied to the celestial and terrestrial spheres and to the air or atmosphere in between. *Tola* designates the subterranean world of the universe. *Narok* designates the infernal world. Each of these three major worlds is visualized as extending up and down along a north–south axis which transverses the entire universe. Brahma, the creator of the universe and all that is manifest within it, stands at the northernmost point of this axis. The southernmost point is marked as the last place to which the creative energies of Brahma, through the rays of the sun, penetrate.

Each of the three major worlds is differently valued according to its more or less northerly location in the universe, and thus its relative proximity to Brahma. *Lok* ranks above the subterranean world of *Tola*, and *Tola* above *Narok*, which is located below and to the south of it. Within each of these major worlds are seven subdivisions or minor worlds, all of which are similarly ranked according to their position along the north–south axis which transverses the universe. Inhabiting the several worlds of the universe are six kinds of beings or life forms. Man (*manusa*) is the modal form against which all others are compared. Deities (*debata*) are viewed as a life form superior to humans. Various demonic beings (*apodebata*) – giants, titans, spirits and ghosts, for example – represent man in his crude or debased form. The remaining three kinds of beings are animals (*jangam*) or 'moving beings,' plants (*gachpala*) or 'stationary beings,' and objects (*basto*) or those beings mined or taken from the earth, like metals, minerals, stone and water. Animals, plants and objects are considered successively lower forms of life than humans, but they share with humans and gods and demons a common origin in Brahma. It is because of their common origin that all life forms in this cosmology are viewed as sharing the essential nature of Brahma, as being animate and divine, but to a greater or lesser degree.

From Brahma first emanated *purusa*, the male, cultural principle of the universe, in which is embodied hard, structuring, but relatively inert matter. Then *prakriti*, the female, natural principle of the universe, in which is embodied soft, energetic, but relatively unstructured or undifferentiated matter. From the joining of male and female principles was created the phenomenal world and all that is manifest within it.

Even more specifically, all creation depends on the continued union and reunion of *purusa* and *prakriti* over time, and the resulting mixtures and products of the three modes in which primordial matter is constituted – namely, *sattvagun, rajagun,* and *tamagun.*

These three *gun* are the substance or matter by virtue of which all that is manifest in the universe is physically determined – the 'stuff' of which the universe is made. Together they are the constituent elements of all matter; not the attributes of matter, but the three modes in which matter itself is constituted. In Brahma the three *gun* exist in a state of active but stable equilibrium, a state in which their potential effect as matter is never realized. Thus is Brahma described as a pure principle without material properties. When not in a state of active equilibrium, though, it is the interplay and intermingling of these *gun*, as informed by the differentiating principle of *purusa*, that determines the physical nature of all that is manifest in the universe.

Sattvagun is the material mode which illumines and reveals the phenomenal world for what it truly is – namely, manifestations of the one supreme principle, Brahma. *Sattvagun* resides in the mind, is white in color, generates goodness and joy, and inspires all noble virtues and actions. It is present in greater or lesser degree in all life forms, but is most prominent among deities.

Tamagun is the material mode which veils and suppresses the true reality of the universe and leads humans, in ignorance, to be uncommonly attached to sensual and material desires. *Tamagun* resides in the body, is black in color, and engenders stupidity, laziness and fear, and all sorts of base behaviors. It is present in all life forms, but is especially prominent among plants and objects. The chasm between *sattvagun* and *tamagun*, between true knowledge and veiled ignorance, is bridged by *rajagun*, the material mode which activates the other two *gun*. Residing in life itself, *rajagun* is red in color, and produces egoism, selfishness, jealousy and ambition. It is present in all life forms, but is especially prominent among demonic beings and animals.

All life forms in the universe share the same *gun* with Brahma. Yet each has a distinct physical nature, and all are distinguished from Brahma, because these common *gun* are present in the various life forms in different proportions and in different sets of relations to one another. Figure 3 indicates how these differences are perceived by Torkotala Hindus. It also indicates how each life form in the universe is ranked according to the

Life forms (in rank order)	The disposition of *gun*			Relation of *gun* to each other: relatively active or suppressed
	sattva	*rajah*	*tamas*	
Brahma	×	×	×	active
				suppressed
Deities	×			active
		×	×	suppressed
Humans	×	×		active
			×	suppressed
Demons		×		active
	×		×	suppressed
Animals		×	×	active
	×			suppressed
Plants			×	active
	×	×		suppressed
Objects				active
	×	×	×	suppressed

Fig. 3. The physical nature of life forms in the universe

extent to which the disposition of its own *gun* approximates that of Brahma, the apical being in the Bengali cosmos.[1]

Sattvagun, rajagun and *tamagun* are ranked in descending order; thus so are the life forms characterized by the dominance of each. A rank ordering of life forms is not the only consequence of the manner in which the three *gun* are present and related to each other, though. For just as Bengali perceptions of physical space are premised on the association of land and people, so are Bengali perceptions of cosmological space premised on an association of every world with an appropriate life form or forms. Demonic beings, to illustrate, occupy the subterranean world of *Narok*. Within the world of *Lok*, deities occupy the celestial sphere; humans, animals and plants occupy different regions of the terrestrial sphere. Between the terrestrial and celestial spheres, in the world of atmosphere, live the souls of human ancestors and other beings, including animals, prior to their rebirth in new physical bodies.

There is another consequence of the manner in which the three *gun* are

present and related to each other. Bengalis hold that matter is never inert
never fully inanimate; it is always and inexorably related to activity. As ;
result, the universe as a whole, each of its worlds, and the life forms tha
inhabit those worlds are all associated with a range of activity held to reflec
and realize their physical nature. These activities are considered natural i
the sense that they are inherent in and inseparable from a given physica
nature. And they are considered moral in the sense that they reflect anc
realize the regularity and order proper to that physical nature. *Dharma* (o
rta) is the term usually applied to the regularity of cosmic processes: th
rising and setting of the sun, the cycle of the seasons, and the movement o
the stars. The natural and moral activities held proper and right to eacl
life form, including humans, are also termed *dharma*.

To summarize the discussion thus far, the entire Bengali cosmos i
ordered by the premise of ranked inequality; and all life forms within th
cosmos are defined and ranked by the same radical material substance
(*gun*) and the behavioral codes or *dharma* appropriate to those *gun*. As wil
be discussed, a cosmology premised on ranked inequalities defines in par
the cultural context within which Torkotala villagers marry, choose thei
diets, exchange food, work and even compete politically. Before examin
ing this fit between meaning and action, though, a cosmology of ranke
orders will be shown to have its reflection in a society of ordered ranks

A society of ordered ranks

Bengalis view all persons as belonging to a number of birth groups whicl
are defined and ranked according to their internal physical nature and th
outward behavior held appropriate to that nature. For example, the genu
Man (*manusajati*) is initially segmented into persons who are Hindus anc
persons who are *mleccha*. Hindus are persons who have the Hindu
behavioral code from birth. *Mleccha* is a sanskritic term used to describ
non-Hindus, persons not born of Hindus and who do not share th
behavior incumbent on Hindus. In some contexts the term is also used tc
stress the lowly or less than civilized manner of non-Hindus.

In 1971 there were no *mleccha* resident in Torkotala aside from myself
Both the tribal Lodhas and Mundas are distinguished from caste Hindus o
the village, but this difference is considered one of degree and not of kind
That is, both Lodhas and Mundas are perceived as sharing some but not al
of the beliefs, practices and institutions of Hinduism. Though not full
Hindu, neither are they *mleccha*. The Lodhas and Mundas of Torkotala ar
all integrated into the social, economic and political life of the village. Botl
groups worship Hindu deities on occasion. Yet they also maintain ar
ethnic identity apart from Hindus, have their own headmen and priests

and maintain ritual practices that are distinct from their Hindu neighbors. Muslims, by contrast, are referred to as *mleccha*. The outlying Muslim hamlet that was once part of the village has since been abandoned and there are presently no Muslims resident in Torkotala.

'Jati' as categories of castes ('varna')

Hindus are next segmented into *varna*. The Manu Dharmasastra describes the four *varna* of the Indian Great Tradition as Brahman or priest; Kshatriya or warrior-chief; Vaisya or merchant; and Sudra or menial. In an earlier hymn, the Purusasukta, the same *varna* are described as arising respectively from different portions of Purusa, the Primeval Man. Appropriate to its point of origin, each *varna* has a defining physical nature and behavioral code, and also a rank. Thus the Brahman *varna* – born from the mouth of Purusa – has as its code the teaching of the Vedas, performing sacrifices and worships, and accepting gifts from the three lower ranked *varna*. Its special sphere of activity is to exercise godly power (*brahman*). The Kshatriya *varna* – born from the two arms of Purusa – has as its code the ruling functions of protecting and providing. Its special sphere of activity is to exercise royal power (*ksatra*). The Vaisya *varna* – born from the thighs of Purusa – has as its code the production of wealth through agriculture, animal husbandry or trade. Its special sphere of activity is to exercise productive power (*vis*). The Sudra *varna* – befitting its lowly birth

The varna (in rank order)	The disposition of *gun*			Relation of *gun* to each other: relatively active or suppressed
	sattva	*rajah*	*tamas*	
Brahman	×			active
		×	×	suppressed
Kshatriya	×	×		active
			×	suppressed
Vaisya		×	×	active
	×			suppressed
Sudra			×	active
	×	×		suppressed

Fig. 4.   The physical nature of the four *varna*

The *varna*	Spheres of activity			
(in rank order)	*brahman*	*ksatra*	*vis*	*seva*
Brahman	×	×	×	×
Kshatriya		×	×	×
Vaisya			×	×
Sudra				×

Fig. 5.   *Varna dharma*

from the feet of Purusa – ranks lowest of the four *varna*. Its code and special sphere of activity is service (*seva*) for the three higher *varna*. Only the Sudra *varna* is not enjoined to learn the Vedas and thus is not included among the 'twiceborn', those who have a ritual rebirth on initiation to the learning of Vedic teachings. The Sudra, Vaisya and Kshtriya *varna* are all enjoined to give gifts to Brahmans.

The rank of each *varna* depends mutually on its physical nature and behavioral code, which are a single, duplex criterion. The rank order of the four *varna* can thus be represented analytically in either of two ways. On the one hand *varna* rank corresponds to the portion of the divine body of Purusa from which a *varna* was born, as represented in figure 4, for each portion of Purusa's body is characterized by *sattvagun, rajagun* and *tamagun* in different proportions and in different sets of relations to each other. On the other hand the rank order of the four *varna* corresponds to the behavioral code appropriate to each, as represented in figure 5. The Brahman *varna*, according to this line of reasoning, ranks highest because the well-being of society, which depends on the faithful propitiation of the deities, requires their exercise of godly power. In addition, Brahmans also have the capacity to exercise the distinctive powers of the three other *varna*. Ranked just below the Brahman *varna* is the Kshatriya *varna*, whose members cannot make offerings to the deities directly, but who are charged with ruling over the affairs of people on earth by exercising royal power. Kshatriyas also have the capacity for productive work and service. The capacity of the Vaisya *varna*, by contrast, is limited to productive work and service. Occupying the lowest rank of all is the Sudra *varna*, whose contribution to the social division of labor is limited to menial labor and service only. Other than in times of distress, each *varna* is enjoined to act within its own special sphere of activity.

As represented in the Purusasukta and other texts, the four *varna* are exhaustive units which apply to Hindus throughout India. As understood from their own life experiences, Torkotala Hindus, like Hindus elsewhere in Bengal, hold that only the Brahman and Sudra *varnas* are indigenous to contemporary Bengali society. Why this discrepancy with the scriptural texts exists is inexplicable to them; Bengali society is simply viewed as exceptional in this regard.[2] Torkotala residents also recognize an additional category of Hindus, the so-called 'Untouchables' (*asprisya*), which includes those Hindus who are not mentioned as being born from the divine body of Purusa. Like Sudras, the *dharma* of an Untouchable is service; however, Untouchables are distinguished from and ranked lower than Sudras by their association with the most demeaning and invidious of service tasks. The disposition of *gun* among Untouchables is marked by a dominance of *tamas* even greater than among Sudras.

The four-fold scriptural division of Hindus does not meet the criteria suggested by Nadel (1953:174–9) for the recognition of a system of social stratification. The *varna* are ranked, and are organically related through a functional division of labor. They are also exclusive units, since no one can belong to more than one *varna*. But it is questionable if the *varna* are exhaustive units because Untouchables are not mentioned in scriptural texts as a fifth *varna*, and Kshatriyas and Vaisyas are not thought indigenous to contemporary Bengal. Also, the four *varna* are not interactive groups in the sociological sense. They are categories which class together many castes on the basis of shared rank and certain common features attributed to their point of origin on Purusa. In doing so the *varna* categories provide a conceptual framework for integrating the many localized castes of different *des* into an all-India ideological scheme.

Further integrating the Indian Great and Little Traditions are less inclusive categories similar to the literate, four-fold division of Hindus, but lacking any scriptural basis and having a reduced territorial span. These regional and sub-regional *varnas*, as Richard Fox (1969) terms them, can only with difficulty be fitted into the all-India scheme; yet they function similarly in being indigenous ideological schemes which merge localized castes on the basis of certain attributional features and rank. Perhaps the best known regional *varna* scheme is the tripartite division of Brahman, non-Brahman and Adi-Dravida in much of South India (Gough 1952; Beteille 1965). The dual division of Bengalis into Brahman and Sudra *varnas* is another regional *varna* scheme. Following the folk geography of Bengal, the variety of Brahman castes are further distinguished as Rarhi Brahmans from western Bengal, Dokkhin Rarhi Brahmans from the area just south of Rarh, Varendro Brahmans from northern Bengal, Bangaj Brahmans from eastern Bengal, and Utkal Brahmans from the area of Bengal closest to Orissa (Utkal). The single Brahman family now resident in Torkotala, and the majority of Brahmans present in the Narayanghar kingdom, are Utkal Brahmans. Bengali Sudras are broadly categorized as *sat* Sudras from whom a Brahman will accept drinking water and *asat* Sudras from whom a Brahman will not accept water. *Sat* Sudras are associated with eastern Midnapore, *asat* Sudras with western Midnapore. Befitting its location along the trunk road which marks the east–west division of Midnapore district, Torkotala has a mixed population of Sudra castes.

'Jati' as caste or tribe

Unlike the sub-regional, regional or society-wide *varna* schemes, a set of localized, interactive castes do meet Nadel's criteria for a system of social stratification. Castes are true sociological groups, and they are exclusive, exhaustive units. Castes are ranked, and the multiple castes in an interactive community form an organic system of complementary, interdependent units. They are differentiated according to their respective *jibika*. *Jibika*, like *dharma*, is an outward expression of inward nature, but of a more limited sort. *Jibika* denotes 'living, existing, the practice of livelihood.' It is epitomized and symbolized by the characteristic occupation or work of a caste, but includes as well the generalized life style attendant on pursuing that occupation – patterns of dress, diet, food exchanges, service exchanges, and ceremonial practices, for example – and the way in which pursing that life style brings a caste, as a corporate unit, into interaction with other castes. The fuller implications of *jibika* as a generalized life style are evident when castes are considered as interacting social groups.

Castes as social groups are ranked, corporate bodies which are generally defined by descent, marriage and occupation. As such they constitute an ethnic group, a unitary society that is integrated biologically, culturally, socially and politically, while also maintaining interactions with other similarly constituted ethnic groups. Castes are ideally endogamous marriage units and thus represent a genetic or biological pool unto themselves. It is in this sense that all members of a caste are held to share, actually or potentially, the same physical nature and, more specifically, the same blood, the physiological source and central symbol of a common physical nature. Ideally members of a caste also share the same occupation and, thereby, the same economic circumstances of life. And they share a common pattern of ritual and ceremonial practices as well. It is likely, too, that individuals spend more time socially with others of their own caste than with persons of any other caste. Within a village they may live in the same hamlet and thus interact with each other as neighbors. Members of a caste, even when not resident in the same village, may meet periodically to regulate and enforce caste practices, or to protect the interests of one of their members in a rivalry. A caste council may exist for just that purpose. As an interacting social unit members of a caste represent both in their own eyes and in the eyes of others a miniature society within the larger society constituted by all castes of the immediate community and wider locale.

There are twelve castes and two tribes resident in Torkotala village. As mentioned earlier, the Lodhas and Mundas are seen as distinct from the twelve Hindu castes of the village in sharing some but not all of the beliefs, practices and institutions of Hindus. The Boisnabs of the village also occupy a special place in relation to other caste Hindus as followers of a religious sect. It is well recognized by all within the village, including the Boisnabs, though, that the ancestors of present-day Boisnabs were at one time ordinary caste Hindus. This ancestry is reflected in the use of double caste names such as Mahisya Boisnab or Bagra-Khatriya Boisnab. A brief description of each of the castes and tribes resident in Torkotala, and their respective *jibika*, follows.

Lodha

The Lodhas trace the ancestry of their tribe to a people, the Shabar, mentioned in the epic Mahabarta. The Shabars were extremely proficient in forest living, and had remarkable skills in hunting and gathering forest produce. They were, as a result, a highly regarded birth group and, so it is said, were on a par with Brahmans, with whom they exchanged daughters in marriage. The standing of the Shabars gradually fell, though, as society changed from a pattern of forest living to a pattern of settled agriculture, for which the Shabars were not well suited. Thus the new name, Lodha, which is held to reflect the reduced status of these once highly regarded people.

In this century the Lodhas have experienced both territorial and economic displacement as the forests of western Midnapore, their original *des*, have been gradually cleared by caste Hindus who practice settled rice agriculture. Lodhas are still found scattered throughout western Midnapore, but the population and economy of their *des* is no longer as they once knew it, and increasingly the Lodhas have come to live amongst caste Hindus in settled villages and to practice agriculture, either as cultivators, laborers, or both. The Lodhas first settled in Torkotala some four decades ago, when they were employed as agricultural laborers by the landholding Sadgops of the village. Both men and women worked in the fields then. In 1971 few still did. In part this reflects a reduced need for agricultural laborers as the size of individual holdings has been reduced by a series of land reform acts passed by the West Bengal state government in the 1950s and 1960s. It also reflects a general dissatisfaction with the Lodhas on the part of Hindu landholders of the village. From their perspective the Lodhas never took well to agriculture, and are not industrious workers. The Mundas, as a result, are presently the principal source of agricultural labor in Torkotala village. In 1971 most of the Lodhas of Torkotala had no regular employment. Lodha women relied on begging for their principal income. Lodha men worked irregularly as day laborers on government construction teams which periodically repair sections of the Orissan Trunk Road or as gang laborers on the Southeastern Railway. More often the Lodha men are seen idle, or else hunting field animals, with bow and arrow in hand, or fishing with a variety of nets and traps. Rice is their preferred diet staple when available. But without personal landholdings or steady employment, hunting and fishing, plus periodic handouts of food by government sources, have become for the Lodhas the main means of sustenance. The Lodha diet, more out of necessity than preference, thus includes small field animals and a variety of fish, including shrimps and mollusks which Mundas and caste Hindus of the village consider inferior foods. Largely because of their impoverished condition, the Lodhas are held suspect for the recurrent thefts of rice from paddy fields and storehouses which are a regular feature of life in Torkotala. Indeed, non-Lodhas of the village often describe thievery and dacoity as the characteristic occupation of the Lodhas, noting that until 1952, when the practice was revoked by the Criminal Tribes Act, the Lodhas were listed in all government records as a Criminal Tribe. Since 1957 the Lodhas have been listed as a Scheduled Tribe.

Table 2.   *The population of Torkotala village by caste and tribe, 1971*

Caste or tribe	Compounds	Households	Persons		Total	% of total population
			Males	Females		
Lodha	31	39	incomplete census data[a]		c.200	27.1
Munda	29	34	107	88	195	26.4
Sadgop	27	21	66	75	141	19.1
Bagra-Khatriya	9	21	40	57	97	13.1
Bagra-Khatriya Boisnab	4	5	10	8	18	2.4
Bagal	3	5	13	13	26	3.5
Jogi	3	4	12	7	19	2.6
Kayastha	2	2	5	5	10	1.4
Tantoby	2	2	5	2	7	0.9
Brahman	1	1	7	4	11	1.5
Rajok	1	1	4	2	6	0.8
Mahisya Boisnab	1	1	2	2	4	0.5
Hari	1	1	2	1	3	0.4
Mahisya	0	1	1	0	1	0.1
Totals	114	138			c.738	99.8

[a] The census data are incomplete because of slow but continual population turnover in these hamlets.

The Lodhas have gradually withdrawn their participation from village affairs in the last fifteen years. Increasingly they have gone outside the village for employment. Within the village they no longer participate in public meetings. They did not choose in 1962, for example, to nominate one of their number for membership in the village *panchayat*. The Lodhas do participate in the village celebration of Kali Puja; one of their number participates in the animal sacrifice to Kali. And Lodhas do attend the Shib Puja, though they are not permitted to participate as devotees. All other worships are held apart from caste Hindus and Mundas of the village. The Lodhas have their own priests and headmen. They are served by the same Napit who provides barber services for caste Hindus of Torkotala.

Munda

Like the Lodhas, the Mundas differ from caste Hindus in being organized into totemic clans. Also like the Lodhas, the first Mundas came to Torkotala from western Midnapore about four decades ago as agricultural laborers. But quite unlike the Lodhas, the Mundas are well integrated into the social, economic and political life of Torkotala village. Though all the Mundas were landless when first coming to Torkotala, by 1971 many had managed to buy land of their own, or had arranged to sharecrop lands owned by others. As a sign of this relative prosperity, comparatively few Munda women are seen working the fields alongside their husbands. The Munda diet is essentially similar to that of caste Hindus, meaning rice is the staple, and mutton and chicken (but no other meat) is eaten when available. The Mundas are also more restrictive than the Lodhas regarding which varieties of fish they will eat, and it is never alleged that they, like Lodhas, will eat birds. Unlike others of the village, though, the Mundas do hold a special place in their diet for rice beer. The Mundas have their own headmen and tribal council. Yet they also participate in village councils and are well represented by three persons on the village *panchayat*. At least one person from each of the two Munda hamlets is usually invited to *ad hoc* village meetings. Regarding communal worships, the Mundas attend Kali Puja and participate in the Gajan as part of Shib Puja. Other worships are done separtely by their own priest. The Mundas also have a Napit and Rajok from amongst their own birth group.

Sadgop

A good deal was written about the Sadgop caste in the previous chapter. The Sadgops of Torkotala are essentially an agriculturalist caste which migrated to Midnapore district from areas of Bengal to the north after Gondobah Pal was made Raja of Narayanghar. Since that time the Sadgops have become the most populous caste in the Narayanghar kingdom, and its largest landholders as well. In combination with the prerogatives and influence of a Sadgop Raja, their large numbers and extensive landholdings have given the Sadgops a dominant position in the kingdom at large and in specific villages of the kingdom, including Torkotala. As already mentioned, all of the headmen of Torkotala are Sadgops by caste. Sadgops also head the worship committees, school committees, the committees to run the village club house, and are invariably at the head of other, shorter-lived village projects as well.

The Sadgops are generally recognized as a purified section of the Goala caste, who are associated, like Krishna from whom they trace descent, with tending cattle and providing milk and milk products. They attained their higher position by adopting agriculture as their caste-related occupation. Today all of the Sadgop males of Torkotala work as agriculturalists. Most are landholding cultivators who employ others to do the actual physical labor of rice agriculture. A few Sadgop families have fallen on harder times and must supplement their income from meager landholdings with work as agricultural laborers. Even in hard times, though, Sadgops of Torkotala typically do not labor for other castes;[3] they are employed instead by fellow Sadgops of the village. In such instances Sadgop men can be seen plowing the fields with their own hands, an activity which is devalued, first, because it involves physical labor, and second, because it may involve injury to those life forms which live in the soil. Sadgops who can afford to hire others to plow will not plow themselves, even though they may do other agricultural tasks. Sadgop women are never seen working in the fields, even in the most impoverished families. In addition to their agricultural activities Sadgop families also keep cows for milk and raise chickens and goats for sale. Most other castes in the village, including the lone Brahman family, do the same. The village Brahman also follows the Sadgop lead in including mutton and chicken in his diet. Only the Boisnabs of the village are vegetarians.

Bagra-Khatriya and Bagra-Khatriya Boisnab

Both of these castes have essentially the same history, and with certain differences due to Boisnab practices, the same generalized life style. This is true because Bagra-Khatriya (B-K) Boisnabs, as their double name suggests, were originally B-K by caste.

The B-K were known in Torkotala until the late 1950s as Bagdi. The Bagdis are *asat* Sudras from whom a Bengali Brahman will not accept drinking water. They seem to consist of a mixed lot of people who came from the area of northwestern Midnapore which is known as Bagri. But it is uncertain whether this name was given to the land because of its association with the people, or to the people because of their association with the land (Midnapore District Handbook 1961, 1:59). Originally the Bagdis may have been fishermen. They have also been described as an aboriginal group of woodcutters and litter carriers (Bhattacharya 1968:444).

Table 3. *The occupational pattern of castes and tribes in Torkotala village, 1971*

Caste or tribe	Traditional or caste-related occupation	Present-day occupation/s
Lodha	Hunting and gathering forest produce	Day labor Agricultural labor
Munda	A combination of hunting and gathering and settled agriculture	Agriculture Agricultural labor
Sadgop	Agriculture	Agriculture
Bagra-Khatriya	Fishermen? Wood cutters? Litter carriers?	Agriculture Agricultural labor
Bagra-Khatriya Boisnab		Agriculture
Bagal	Cattle tenders	Agricultural labor Agriculture
Jogi	Religious mendicants *kirtan* singers	Religious mendicants *kirtan* singers Repairing unbrellas Agriculture
Kayastha	Agriculture	Agriculture Carpentry
Tantoby	Weaving	Agriculture Agricultural labor Carpentry
Brahman	Religious perceptor and priest	Priest Agriculture
Rajok	Washerman	Washerman Agriculture Agricultural labor
Mahisya Boisnab	Agriculture	Teaching Agriculture
Hari	Removing carcasses; beating leather drums; assisting at births	Removing carcasses; beating leather drums; assisting at births
Mahisya	Agriculture	Weaving Agriculture

The B-K are the 'second founders' of Torkotala, the laborers who helped clear the lands and settle the village alongside their Sadgop employers. During this present generation, the B-K were able to acquire lands of their own for the first time, and thus stopped working in the employ of others. In 1971 only a few B-K families still worked as agricultural laborers. The remainder own their own lands, and after the Sadgops represent the second largest landholding group in the village. One person of this caste also works as a skilled carpenter. B-K males will generally plow their own lands. B-K Boisnab males, by contrast, will not, for fear of inadvertently harming the life forms which live in the soil. The Boisnabs also differ in keeping a strict vegetarian diet. The B-K do not, eating meat and eggs according to their cost and availability. Ideally Boisnabs marry amongst themselves. However, when a suitable Boisnab partner is not available it is acknowledged that a B-K partner will be accepted in marriage. This occurs rarely, but it does occur, and thus the distinction between the B-K and B-K Boisnab castes is somewhat blurred. Still, both birth groups regard themselves and are recognized by others as distinct castes.

Bagal

The Bagals are traditionally associated with work as cattle herders. In 1971, though, the Bagals of Torkotala village worked as agricultural laborers, cultivating smaller plots of their own on the side. Based on their traditional association with cattle, the Bagals have recently advanced a claim to be Goalas by caste. It is unlikely that this claim will be recognized by other Hindus of the village, though, at least not in the immediate future, for Sadgops are aware that their own caste is regarded as a purified section of Goala. For the Bagals to establish their claim as Goalas would be indirectly to link the Sadgop and Bagal castes to each other, a link which the Sadgops adamantly deny.

Jogi

The Jogis are a birth group who identify themselves as belonging to the Nath sect. Little is known about the origin and development of the Nath sect. What is known suggests that members of the sect trace descent from a number of Buddhist ascetics, followers of Gorakhnath, who combined Buddhist thought and yogic saivism to emphasize the cultivation of the body as a means for spiritual attainment (Dutt 1969, 2:124–5). The Jogis of Torkotala village are not aware of and do not observe whatever these sectarian practices are. Neither are they aware of those differences in belief or practice that would separate themselves from caste Hindus. When asked about such matters, they invariably lament the departure of the itinerant Jogi, an exemplary member of the sect, who was mentioned earlier as having lived in Torkotala periodically in the late 1950s and early 1960s. In 1971 members of the Jogi caste earned their living singing religious songs, *kirtan*, which they learned from the itinerant Jogi, in favor of alms. They also do repair work of sorts, especially sewing umbrella cloths. Like all other castes in Torkotala, the Jogis combine their other work with work as agriculturalists. The Jogis are aware that they should not plow the land themselves, for the same reason that a Brahman or a Boisnab does not plow. Actually they do plow, for the Jogi families of Torkotala are too poor to hire someone else to do this work for them. Still, the Jogis view themselves as religious men on a par with Brahmans and Boisnabs. Others in the village do not view the Jogis with similar high regard, though.

Kayastha

In Bengal, where the Kshatriya *varna* is thought absent, the Kayasthas are included among Sudra castes, but considered the very highest of the Sudra castes. Like Brahmans, the Kayasthas of Bengal can be grouped by locations, so that one hears of the Kayasthas of western Bengal, northern Bengal, eastern Bengal, and the like. Crosscutting this categorization by locale is another that distinguishes between Kayasthas who work as scribes and writers, and those who do agricultural work. This latter group is held in lower esteem and they are referred to as *langol* Kayasthas, the Kayasthas who use the plow (*langol*). The two Kayastha families resident in Torkotala are both *langol* Kayasthas who work as agriculturalists and do their own plowing. The head of the one of these families is also an accomplished carpenter. Both families are relatively poor, and both are newcomers to Torkotala within the last twenty years. Neither participates actively in village affairs.

Tantoby

The Tantobys are traditionally associated with work as weavers. Neither of the two Tantoby households in Torkotala presently earns any income from weaving, though, or even knows how to weave. One of the households is headed by a woman who works as a day laborer in Sadgop households and also cultivates a small plot of land. The other household is headed by a male who earns his income from a combination of agricultural labor and day labor as a carpenter's assistant. Members of his household can also be seen, on occasion, selling mustard seed oil in the Narayanghar market. Neither of the Tantoby households takes an active part in village affairs.

Brahman

There is only one Brahman family residing in Torkotala village. Phani Babu, its male head, is an Utkal Brahman, literally a Brahman from that part of Midnapore district which forms the border between Orissa (Utkal) and Bengal. Phani Babu divides his time between cultivating his landholdings with the help of hired labor and serving as a priest (*purohit*). He is responsible for the daily worship of Sitala, the village goddess, and the god Shib. Every Thursday he also worships Lokkhi in most of the Sadgop households of the village. Like other Brahmans of the Narayanghar kingdom, Phani Babu eats mutton and chicken when available. He does not himself plow the fields or do any manual labor related to the agricultural process.

Rajok

The male head of the single Rajok family resident in Torkotala divides his time between cultivating a small plot of land, doing agricultural labor for

B-K households, and performing his tasks as a washerman. That he does not spend more time working as a washerman is largely because villagers prefer to save the expense, however slight, and wash their own clothes on all but ritual occasions like birth or marriage and when clothes are soiled by menstrual blood. Because the Rajok caste washes impurities from clothes, it is considered unclean and does not receive the services of a Brahman priest. In Torkotala Rajoks do receive the services of the village Napit, though. The male head of the lone Rajok family in Torkotala is a member of the village *panchayat*.

Mahisya and Mahisya Boisnab

The relationship between these two castes is analogous to that between the Bagra-Khatriya and B-K Boisnab castes. As their double caste name suggests, Mahisya Boisnabs were once simply Mahisyas, who later became Boisnabs. Certain differences in belief and practice are evident between these two castes. From the standpoint of other birth groups in the village, only a few are considered significant. Like the Brahman caste, Boisnabs never plow the soil. Also they do not eat non-vegetarian food or participate in the animal sacrifices which are a central part of Kali Puja and Durga Puja. In this they differ from local Brahmans and other caste Hindus. Both the Mahisya and Mahisya Boisnab are regarded as *sat* Sudras from whom a Brahman will take water. Mahisyas are also served by Brahmans as priests, while Mahisya Boisnabs are served by their own priests.

The Mahisyas are generally regarded as a purified offshoot of the Kaibartta caste, though individuals may not admit to this. In Midnapore district as a whole, the Mahisyas are the dominant agricultural caste, both in numbers and in size of landholdings. They are not similarly well represented in the Sadgop kingdom of Narayanghar, though. Indeed, the lone Mahisya Boisnab family and the lone Mahisya, who lives in Torkotala without his family, are both migrants to the village within the last twelve years from areas to the southeast of Narayanghar. Kengal, the Mahisya, earned his living as a weaver and sharecropper, but during most of 1971 was detained in jail on suspicion of theft. MGD, the head of the lone Mahisya Boisnab family of the village, combines agriculture with a number of other avocations. He is a teacher in the village primary school, the only one of three teachers who is himself a Torkotala villager, and is also head of the village economic cooperative.

Hari

The single Hari family resident in Torkotala, reflecting its status as Untouchables, lives separated from other families of the village at the outer edge of East Hamlet closest to the railway tracks. The male head of the Hari household has responsibility for removing animal carcasses from the village when necessary, for cleaning what ash and bone may remain at funeral pyres after cremations, and for beating leather drums at the larger village worships, including Kali Puja and Shib Puja. The female head of household is called upon by Hindus to assist at times of birth, which duty includes cutting the umbilical cord of the newborn. It is because of these caste-related tasks that the Haris are attributed the status of Untouchable. It is also alleged that Haris eat cow meat. The Hari of Torkotala are not served by Brahmans, or by Napits or Rajoks.

These 14 birth groups exhaust the number of castes and tribes resident in Torkotala village. Still others are known to Torkotala villagers through the weekly market held just south of Narayanghar Town every Thursday. Persons from throughout the kingdom visit this market weekly to buy, sell or trade those goods and supplies which they do not produce themselves. Torkotala villagers are thus aware of castes and tribes that are present throughout the Narayanghar kingdom, and not just those resident in their own village. From persons who have migrated to the village from outside the kingdom, they are also aware of birth groups and customs outside Narayanghar, and take interest in learning more.

Of the multiple castes represented in the Narayanghar kingdom, only four visit Torkotala regularly. Napits come to do their work as barbers, to act as go-betweens in arranging marriages, and to assist Brahmans in preparing the materials used in worship. Two Kamar brothers and their families lived in Torkotala until recently and did their caste-related work as iron smiths. The eldest brother died in 1966 and the younger brother left soon afterwards. Since then Kamars from another village, one mile to the north, visit Torkotala when called and especially during the busy agricultural periods, to repair farm tools and sharpen cutting edges. Two permanent work areas, consisting of a sheltered earthen fire pit and portable bellows, are maintained in the village for their work. Kumars or potters have not lived in Torkotala during this century. There is a large settlement of Kumar families just half a mile south of the village, though, and it is from them that Torkotala residents acquire whatever earthen pots may be needed. The Narayanghar market is an alternative source for such earthenware. Malakars are the fourth and last caste which visits Torkotala regularly. They supply the garlands used to adorn the gods at times of worship. Other requirements of worship, including the sweets which are offered to the gods, are usually bought at the Narayanghar market. The same is true of metal containers and utensils used for cooking and serving food. In West Bengal as a whole carpentry work is usually associated with the Sutrodhar caste. In the Naryanghar kingdom this work does not seem to be restricted to persons of the Sutrodhar caste, and is practiced by

Table 4.   *The rank order of castes and tribes in Torkotala village, 1971*

Rank	Birth group
1	Brahman
2	Sadgop
3	Kayastha, Mahisya Boisnab
4	Bagra-Khatriya Boisnab
5	Bagra-Khatriya, Malakar, Napit, Kamar
6	Jogi, Bagal, Kumar, Tantoby
7	Rajok
8	Lodha
9	Munda
10	Hari

Note: based on opinion data presented in the appendix.

anyone who has the skills. Torkotala has two accomplished carpenters, a Bagra-Khatriya and a Kayastha by caste. They are assisted by a male of Tantoby caste.

In their own descriptions of the castes and tribes resident in Torkotala and of others who visit the village regularly, or are known from dealings at the Narayanghar market, Torkotala villagers usually comment on their relative rank with respect to each other. Such evaluative statements of rank are couched in the most abstract terms, so that a birth group will be described as high or low (*ucchu* or *nichu*), big or small (*boro* or *choto*), good or not good (*bhalo* or *bhalo na*). When asked to explain why this is so, and what is meant by these expressive but vague terms, Torkotala villagers will then elaborate on some aspect of the *jibika* of the caste or tribe in question to support their judgement. The same aspect of *jibika* is not consistently cited in this regard. What does remain consistent, though, is the assumption that all castes and tribes, like all *varnas*, all life forms and all worlds of the universe, can be placed in a series of ordered ranks, as in table 4.[4]

'Jati' as clan, line and family

Individual Bengalis can rank the four *varna* and the castes of their local, interactive community in an inclusive ordering of like units. Thus does the cultural premise of ranked inequalities have its actual sociological reflection in villages like Torkotala. With regard to the still more highly differentiated groups into which *varna* and castes are segmented, the correspondence between cultural premise and sociological reality is more complicated. That is, while individuals can rank a limited number of these birth groups, the sociological conditions for ranking all *gotro*, all *kul*, all *bongso*, or all *poribar* (to be defined below), even in a single village, do not exist.

A *gotro* is usually glossed in the anthropological literature as a clan. It resembles a clan in that members are said to share descent and a common natural substance, semen, inherited from the *gotro* founder. Through shared semen, *gotro* members also share a common behavioral code enjoining exogamous marriage. But unlike a clan, a *gotro* is not considered a kin group in any specific sense, and Torkotala villagers, like Bengalis elsewhere, do not consider it possible or even reasonable to trace ties of descent between persons of many different castes and *varna* who claim the same *gotro* affiliation. Also, unlike usual conceptions of a clan, a *gotro* never acts as a corporate unit. Further, membership in a *gotro* is affected by marriage, as unmarried women in Bengali society belong to the *gotro* of their fathers, while married women change affiliation and belong to the *gotro* of their husbands.

Gotro are commonly compared and ranked according to the founding Vedic sage (*rsi*) from whom their defining nature and code is inherited. This said, Torkotala villagers admit that a rank order of all sages, and thus a rank order of all *gotro*, is not readily established. There is general agreement that the first sage, as the exemplary representative of the kind, stands above all others, the second above the third, the third above the fourth, and so forth in sequential order. But there is no similar agreement on the order in which sages appeared in the universe. Thus when asked to rank the *gotro* of their village, Torkotala residents often proceeded as if an inclusive ordering could be readily established – only to explain later, somewhat apologetically, that perhaps there really was no need to do so. It is with regard to the exchange of women in marriage that *gotro* affiliation has its central importance in Bengali society; and in arranging a marriage, the primary consideration is not whether *gotro* stand high or low, but whether they are different or the same.

A *kul* includes all of the male descendants of a common ancestral male, referred to as seed-male (*bij-purus*), together with their wives and un-married daughters. Whereas the seed-male of a *gotro* is a god-like being who inhabits one of the heavens, the seed-male of a *kul* is an actual human being who lived in some ancient time past, the exact number of generations ago now being long forgotten. A *kul* is known by the surname (*paddhabi*) of its seed-male. Pal, Bhunai and Mahabarto, to illustrate, are the surnames by which the principal Sadgop *kul* of Torkotala are known. Individual members of a *kul* are then further distinguished by a personal name, Anil Pal, Atul Mahabarto or Haripado Bhunai, for example.

Just as a *gotro* appears to resemble the anthropological clan, a *kul* appears to resemble the anthropological lineage in being a unilineal descent group of considerable, but more limited, genealogical depth. This seeming resemblance is tempered by an important difference, though. As in the more inclusive *gotro*, the female membership of a *kul* is not fixed or unchanging through time; it is altered by marriage. Unmarried women belong to the *kul* of their fathers, while married women belong to the *kul* of their husbands. A *kul* therefore emphasizes lineality, but is not a descent group as such. Moreover, whereas the physical nature and behavioral code of an unmarried woman is initially defined by descent (i.e. by the semen of her father), upon marriage these defining features become mixed and altered as the married woman lives in contact with her husband and persons of his *kul*.[5] The changing membership and features of women are reflected in the distinction between daughters of the *kul* (*kuler kanya*), who will eventually marry and leave the group to bear children for others, and wives of the *kul* (*kuler bou*), who will bear children for the line. It is on the in-marrying wife that the continuance of the line depends.

It is through the patterned giving and receiving of women in marriage that a *kul* demonstrates and determines its relative rank among similar groups. Where there is a reciprocal exchange of daughters in marriage, whether in the same generation or in different generations, two *kul* are held to have equal rank. If daughters are given in marriage in one direction only, it is the receiving *kul* that is held to rank higher. Though able to state this principle of rank, Torkotala residents are unable to make an inclusive ordering of all *kul* within the village because persons of different castes rarely intermarry and are generally unaware of the various *kul* within castes other than their own. The anthropologist could construct an inclusive ordering by combining the rank order of castes with the rank order of *kul* within each caste.

The practice of ranking *kul* according to the patterned exchange of daughters solidified in an extreme form in Bengali society in the system of marriage known as *kulinism*, which dates from the reign of King Adisura in the eleventh century AD, and flourished until the nineteenth century. King Adisura wanted to perform a rather elaborate but uncommon sacrifice, so Brahmans of the kingdom were assembled and told to make the necessary preparations for the rite. But as the specific rite was unknown to them, the Brahmans requested King Adisura to send messengers to a place in northern India, Kolanca, where lived five Brahmans famed for their thorough knowledge of Vedic teachings and practices. King Adisura did this. In due time the five Brahmans, accompanied by their families and five Sudra servants, and their families, came to the kingdom of Bengal. Because of their greater knowledge of the Vedas, King Adisura judged these five Brahmans and their Sudra servants to be of higher standing (*kaulinya*) than the indigenous Brahmans and Sudras of the kingdom. They and their descendants became known as *kulina* (Inden 1976:53–60).

The specific qualities which distinguished *kulinas* from the indigenous Brahmans and Sudras of Bengal, in addition to a greater knowledge of the Vedas, are variously described in different texts, but all are characterized by the active presence of *sattvagun*. According to one text cited by Ronald Inden, these *sattvik* qualities include being endowed with good conduct, humility and knowledge, performing famous acts and pilgrimages, showing devotion for sacrifices and marriages with *kulinas*, being absorbed in one's caste-related occupation, being generous, and being constantly purified through austerities (Inden 1976:61). Included in this listing of *sattvik* qualities, significantly, is the exchange of daughters in marriage with other *kulina*.

Torkotala villagers, of course, have no direct knowledge of this historical period. Nor can they list the specific *sattvik* qualities which distinguish some birth groups as being *kulina*. It is also unlikely that their ancestors ever participated in *kulin* marriages. As an elaborate system of restrictive marriages, *kulinism* only existed among certain Brahman castes and among Kayasthas, the highest of Sudra castes in Bengali society, and was never a prominent feature of life among those lower ranking castes, including Sadgops, which predominate in the Narayanghar kingdom. Nevertheless, the logic of exchanges which marks *kulinism* as a highly restrictive marriage system is the same logic by which Bengali Hindus currently compare and rank *kul*.

A *bongso* is a localized segment of the larger *kul* which recognizes the common seed-male, but also emphasizes its descent from a more immediate ancestor of the line. Like a *kul*, a *bongso* includes in-marrying wives and excludes out-marrying daughters. New *bongso* can arise at varying generational depth. But at whatever depth they do arise, *bongso* differ from *kul* in being a known, interactive body of patrilineally related kinsmen. Members of a *bongso* may reside in a single village and may even constitute a separate hamlet or neighborhood within that village. The Pal, Bhunai and Mahabarto neighborhoods in East Hamlet are all examples. But whether localized in a single village or dispersed among several villages, the *bongso* is the principal interactive body of kinsmen beyond the family. It is the senior males of the *bongso* rather than persons of the more impersonal, widely scattered *kul* who actually see to marriage negotiations. It is to persons of their own *bongso* that Torkotala villagers turn most often in times of emergency, for help in the fields, or for support in times of competition. *Bongso*-mates may also cooperate by holding rights to ancestral lands in common. Or they may hold other kinds of property and rights in common. The office of *Mukhya*, for example, is held in common by the Bhunai *bongso*, even though the actual *Mukhya* is from a single Bhunai household. Similarly, the office of *Raj Mukhya* is held in common by the Pal *bongso*. Perhaps most importantly, *bongso*-mates also hold certain ritual obligations in common. It is they who cooperate to offer worship to ancestors of the line, and it is they who cooperate on the occasion of a birth or death, the addition or removal of a person to or from the descent line.

As within the more inclusive *kul*, Torkotala villagers can rank the *bongso* of their own caste according to the patterned exchange of giving and receiving daughters in marriage, or by the refusal to exchange daughters in marriage. They are generally unaware of the marriage patterns among *bongso* of other castes and thus cannot construct an inclusive ordering of these units. The anthropologist could do so by combining the rank order of castes with the rank order of *bongso* within each caste.

The family (*poribar*) is the smallest natural and moral unit into which persons in Bengali society are grouped. It is defined locally in terms of its male head, the husband/father, and consists of his wife, his unmarried daughters, and his sons, whether married or not. As long as a daughter remains unmarried she belongs to the family of her father, as well as to his *bongso, kul* and *gotro*. After marriage she changes affiliation and belongs to the family, etc. of her husband and his father. A son, by contrast, belongs to the family of his father both before and after marriage; indeed, for as long as his father remains alive. Only upon the death of the father does the family consisting of himself, his wife and his children cease to exist.

A central difference between the family and larger kinship groupings, therefore, is that a family contains only living persons and only exists for a limited duration; it desists on the death of the husband/father. A *bongso* or *kul* persists for as long as living males of the birth group continue to bear sons who remember their common dead ancestors and honor them through worship and offerings.

During his lifetime the husband/father is the symbol of family unity and is referred to as *malik* (head) or *korta* (the doer). In principle he exercises rule over all family members and over all affairs of the family, both internally with regard to the interaction of family members, and externally with regard to representing the family in affairs of the line and caste, and in public village affairs as well. Members of the family, as a fully corporate body, are held, in turn, to participate in the actions of its head and to share the fruits or results of those actions. This ethic of shared responsibility and gain applies normatively to all activities of the family head. It applies most centrally, and herein lies the behavioral code particular to the family, to living together in a shared house, benefiting from common property and wealth, bearing the same rank, and eating from the same source of food (Inden and Nicholas 1977:17–18). Members of a family also share that kind of love which enjoins the male head to support, protect and nourish the members of his family. In their physical nature, too, members of a family are defined by sharing, and all members of the family are said to share the physical nature of the husband/father.

In principle all families of Torkotala can be ranked in an inclusive ordering of like units according to the rank of their respective male heads. Yet like the ranking of *kul* and *bongso* of castes other than their own, Torkotala residents cannot in fact and see little reason to rank families apart from considerations of marriage, and marriage is usually with families of one's own caste.

A unified transformational theory of rank

Bengalis regard physical nature and behavioral codes as cognitively non-dualistic features and as a duplex criterion of rank. Thus the rank order of life forms and the various birth groups into which people are divided will be the same whether approached from an attributional or from a behavioral perspective, as indicated for *varna* in figures 4 and 5. This suggests why attributional, interactional, and purity-plus-power theories of rank, each with their different evaluation of physical nature and behavioral codes as the criterion of caste rank, can be reconciled in a unified theory: nature and code are each but a reflection and realization of the other. But why should a unified theory of rank be transformational?

Consider again the Bengali view of creation, this time in more detail. Bengalis regard everything in the world as an emanation from Brahma through the union of *purusa* and *prakriti* (the male and female principles of the cosmos). Thus creation is not the origination of something new, but a transformation (*poriborton*) of that which already existed in latent form into that which is manifest and apprehensible as part of the diverse, phenomenal world. The diversity of life forms in the phenomenal world all have the same creative source. All life forms are also alike in being constituted of the same primordial substance, *prakriti* – or, more specifically, the three *gun* of which *prakriti* is constituted. They differ only in the way these constituent *gun* are variously combined and mixed by the differentiating principle of *purusa* in union with *prakriti*.

The original union of *purusa* and *prakriti* is continually and eternally replicated over time, so that all life forms are perpetually undergoing change and transformation as the internal disposition of their *gun*, and the *dharma* appropriate to those *gun* is altered. Through activities in accord with *dharma* and through mixing one's own physical nature with that of *sattvik* substances, for example, the defining features of a birth group are transformed positively and its rank elevated; for, in these ways, individuals of the group and the birth group as a whole become more cognizant of Brahma and lead a more uplifting spiritual life. Through activities in disaccord with *dharma* and through mixing one's own physical nature with that of *tamasik* substances, the defining features of a birth group are transformed negatively and its rank lowered; for, in these ways, individuals of the group and the birth group as a whole act in greater ignorance of Brahma and lead a more debasing, animal-like life. Activities that increase the *rajasik* qualities of a birth group only confirm the essential nature of humans, for it is the condition of humans living in the temporal world of earth to act out of strong passions and sentiments.

It is this concern to regulate the activities of a birth group and the material substances which are contacted and mixed with its own physical nature that has been interpreted by attributional and purity-plus-power theorists of rank as a preoccupation with purity and impurity. To Stevenson (1954) or Dumont (1970:46–61), for example, impurity is marked by involvement with life processes (such as birth and death) and life substances (including the effluvia of the human body: hair, sweat, blood, semen, feces, urine and rheum of the eyes, for example). Purity is marked by the lack of involvement with such processes and substances. Rank is then said to be determined by the relative degrees of purity and impurity. The greater the purity, the higher the rank. The lesser the purity, the lower the rank.

From the perspective of a transformational theory, by contrast, the concepts of purity and impurity do not refer to specific material qualities gained or lost according to involvement with life processes and life substances as such. Rather, the concepts of purity and impurity refer to a summary evaluation and statement of the *gun* and *dharma* that characterize an activity or substance or birth group as a whole. And these evaluations, to be understood as measures of perfection, are relative and subject to change. Only Brahma, who is totally beyond the effects of all *gun*, is entirely and eternally perfect. For all others, perfection is gained or lost according to how activities and contact with material substances are manipulated to combine and mix one's own defining features with others that have a greater or lesser dominance of *sattvagun*. According to its own defining features, what is imperfect to one birth group will be perfect to another. But the rank of each depends on the same features – nature and code – and the same strategy: to increase the dominance of *sattvagun* over *rajagun* and *tamagun*.

The defining features of human birth groups are not fixed and unchanging through time; nor are they strictly determinative in the same sense that one's genetic make-up is held determinative in Western scientific thought. Bengalis distinguish between two inextricable orders: the natural or given order (*prakriti*) and the man-made, or manipulated or cultural order (*sanskriti*). All that exists in the former is said to simply occur (*hay*) as the natural and moral result of cosmic processes. All that exists in the latter does not simply occur, but is made (*kara*) by specific manipulative acts on the part of men and women.

Conception and parturition happen in the given order, so the features of *gun* and *dharma* by which a birth group is initially defined are said to simply occur as a natural and moral result of cosmic processes, which include the process of human reproduction. Apart from this natural-process component of birth, however, many of the pre-natal rites associated with birth, and most life activities afterwards, are enacted in the man-made order; and through manipulative acts birth groups can transform their constituent *gun* and *dharma.* Marriage, diet, food exchanges and occupation are the specific acts considered below to illustrate this transformational process and the fit between systems of meaning and action. *Varna*, and especially castes, are the specific birth groups referred to. But the same transformations, *mutatis mutandis*, apply as well to other acts and to other birth groups.

With regard to marriage as a manipulative act, consider the following text, excerpted from an essay entitled 'An enquiry into the factor of compatibility of men and women for the production of eugenic offspring,' written in Bengali by a Torkotala village schoolmaster.

Only through the compatible union of man and woman can a healthy, happy and unbreakable married life be achieved and can desirable offspring be procreated. Only by the observance of a few natural laws can this compatible union of man and woman be achieved.

Accepting the theory that biologically every man and woman is a member of the same species, that of *Homo sapiens*, and so any man and woman could possibly mate with each other, still this is unacceptable and untenable scientifically because it cannot simply be denied that one man is born differently with different qualities from another man due to special genetical make-up, heredity and inherent tendencies... *mug, masu*, and *arhar*, to illustrate, are all pulses. But we cannot say there is no difference between them in quality or taste. Judged in this light how can it be asserted that all human beings are of equal quality, all indistinguishable save the division of man and woman; this is beyond one's understanding.

In keeping with their natural differences human society was divided into four, ranked groups – Brahman, Kshatriya, Vaisya, and Sudra.

... many foreign thinkers after realizing the scientific truth which worked behind this division have admitted its value. To maintain the qualities of each *varna* there was the system of intra-*varna* marriages called *samanulom bibaha*. And to gradually raise persons of lower qualities to higher qualities there was the system of inter-*varna* marriages. These marriages between persons of different *varna* were of two types. In the system called *anulom bibaha* a man of higher *varna* could marry a woman of lower *varna*. *Protilom bibaha* is the opposite; a man of lower *varna* could marry a woman of higher *varna*.

Of the three forms of marriage listed in the text, *samanulom bibaha* – a marriage (*bibaha*) between persons of the same or equal value, at par (*samanulom*) – is the preferred form and also the statistical norm in rural West Bengal. Between 1930 and 1970, for example, 124 out of 127 Torkotala marriages (98%) were between persons of the same caste. The

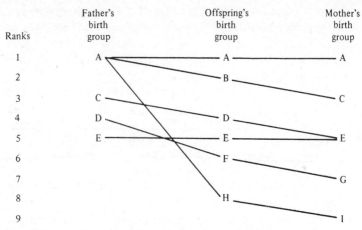

Fig. 6. The rank of offspring in *samanulom* and *anulom* marriages

offspring born of such isogamous marriages share the same features and rank as their parents, as graphed in figure 6.

When a male is of higher *varna* or caste than the female, this is referred to as *anulom bibaha* – a marriage which is regular or proper, one that is favorable, propitious (*anulom*). Such marriages are not preferred, but neither are they proscribed. Three of the 127 recorded marriages (2%) in Torkotala were of this pattern. *Anulom* marriages result in offspring whose physical nature and behavioral code, and thus their rank, lie somewhere in between – but not necessarily midway between – that of their parents. The union of closely matched birth groups A and C will produce a birth group B, midway in features and rank. But the union of more dissimilar birth groups A and I will result in a birth group, say F or G or H, whose features and rank most closely resemble that of I, as shown in figure 6. This is because of the heavy dose of *tamagun* associated with the lower caste.

This said, two qualifications are recognized by Torkotala villagers. First, while inter-*varna* marriages are held to generate a distinctive third group – a particularized caste – castes may be sufficiently similar to each other that marriage in the *anulom* pattern does not always produce offspring who belong to a third birth group. When a male and female of the next lower caste marry, the offspring born of such a union are held to belong to the higher ranking caste of their father. For this reason, when *anulom* marriages do occur, it is preferred that they occur between a male and female of very similar castes; such marriages most nearly approximate the preferred *samanulom* pattern. Second, while *anulom* marriages are sanctioned, that sanction has limits. A Sudra female, even though of lower *varna*, is never an appropriate marriage partner for a twice-born male, their defining nature and code being too different to allow for a propitious union and mixture in marriage.

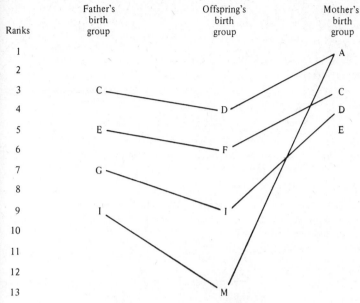

Ranks	Father's birth group	Offspring's birth group	Mother's birth group

Fig. 7. The rank of offspring in *protilom* marriages

When a female marries a male of lower ranking *varna* or caste, this is referred to as *protilom bibaha*. *Protilom* refers to that which is against the grain of society, it being deemed improper that a female would marry and intermix her features with a male of lower ranking birth group. *Protilom* marriages are thus negatively sanctioned in Bengali society, and while such hypogamous unions do occur, they occur but rarely. None were recorded in Torkotala village. The rank of offspring born in *protilom* marriages is always below that of their father, as graphed in figure 7.

The logic by which the several kinds of marriage are judged can be summarized as follows. Of the several kinds of union in marriage, unions between persons of the same *varna* and caste are best; those in which the female is of higher *varna* or caste than the male are worst; the rest, in which a male is of higher *varna* or caste than the female are middling, and with them it is better when the male and female are of birth groups more similar than dissimilar to each other.

Marriage is a critical act for the defining features and rank of a birth group because it is through marriage, and subsequent sexual intercourse, that blood is transmitted to offspring who continue the birth group. Blood is viewed by Bengalis as the physiological source of life, and transmitted within it are the *gun* and *dharma* which differentiate one caste from another. To protect one's blood from adverse mixtures, therefore, is to protect the defining features and rank of the birth group as well, and in a very literal, material sense. The same concern, to protect one's blood from adverse mixtures, also informs patterns of food consumption and the exchange of food between castes.

Like all other substances, blood has its physical source, namely, food. By an intricate series of transformations food which is eaten is changed into digested food (*rasa*), and digested food into blood (*rakta*). Blood is then transformed into flesh (*mangsa*), flesh into fat (*meda*) and fat into marrow (*majja*). From marrow is produced semen (*sukra*) and uterine blood (*artthava*), the direct physical source of life. Conception occurs and the process of human reproduction begins when semen from the male and uterine blood from the female unite in the female womb. In a rather indirect way, but in a way that is no less final for its indirection, then, Bengalis are what they eat.[6] For this reason the foods that are ingested and transformed to combine and mix with one's blood are of particular importance to Torkotala residents.

Different foods have different effects on the body through the blood. Believing that a non-vegetarian diet of meat, eggs, and fish, certain grains, some vegetables, including onions, peppers, garlic and squash, even some fruits, such as mangos and plantains, and a variety of other foods, are all characterized by *rajagun*, Bengalis describe these as hot foods (*garom khabar*) which excite the body and temperament. Foods normally included in a *rajasik* diet can become *tamasik* if they are stale, spoiled, smelly or sour. There are some foods, including alcohol and beef, that are always *tamasik*. Such hot foods give rise to empassioned, excited activity, to anger, greed, cruelty and lying – all low-valued *rajasik* and *tamasik* traits. Vegetarian foods, whose eating involves no injury to the providing source, are generally characterized by *sattvagun* and are described as cold foods (*thanda khabar*). Milk and milk products, including clarified butter, are prime examples. Cold foods give rise to self-control, forbearance, discrimination, truthfulness and contentment, all valued *sattvik* traits.[7]

The best possible diet for humans is one that consists solely of milk and milk products or, failing that, a diet which mixes milk and milk products with fruits and nuts, for this diet involves no injury to life forms. Clarified butter (*ghi*) from cow's milk is another food whose consumption causes no harm to life forms. A diet of such foods is also valued because it approximates the diet of Brahma, who is not dependent on food at all. Brahma is said to subsist by 'taking air.' This, of course, is impossible for humans, but it suggests why persons who are devoutly intent on achieving liberation and escaping the cycle of rebirths in this life-time train their bodies to have minimal dependence on foods of any sort. In doing so they approximate, in manner of diet, the nature of Brahma.

In addition to the kind of food consumed, the social source of food consumed also has its effect on the defining features and rank of a caste, for foods become mixed with the features of those persons who contact them during preparation, cooking and serving, and thus transmit natural and moral qualities whenever exchanged. Bengalis hold that castes of higher rank are characterized by a greater measure of *sattvik* qualities, while castes of lower rank have a greater measure of *rajasik* and *tamasik* qualities. Thus the general rule governing food exchanges seeks to minimize adverse mixtures by emphasizing the transfer of food between equals, or failing that, from high to low, from greater levels of *sattvagun* to lesser levels. This said, a qualification must be added because on inspection it is clear that Torkotala villagers do accept some kinds of food from lower-ranking castes and tribes. That is, as all foods do not convey natural and moral qualities to the same degree, some foods have a wider exchange value than others and are freely given and received among a wider number of birth groups.

The exchange value of specific foods depends not on whether they be of the vegetarian or non-vegetarian variety, but on the manner in which they are processed for consumption. Villagers distinguish, for example, between raw food (*sidha* or *kacha mal*) stuffs, drinking water (*jal*), foods prepared other than in boiled water (*jal khabar*), foods prepared in boiled water (*bhat khabar*), and foods prepared with clarified butter (*ghi khabar*). In addition, distinctions are made between foods which remain after the gods have eaten (*prasad*), and foods which remain after humans have eaten (*etho* or *jhuta*). Each of these kinds of food has a different exchange value.

Prasad refers to food which, having been presented by worshippers to the gods as an offering, is then left by the gods to be eaten by humans. As gods are *sattvik* in comparison with the humans who worship them, all worshippers will accept *prasad*. *Prasad* usually consists of fruits native to the area, confections made of milk or milk products, and confections that mix milk and sugar; rice preparations made with milk and sugar and clarified butter are also a common offering. However the specific offerings differ among deities – and thus the nature of *prasad* – can vary considerably; they may even include the flesh of animals, as in Kali Puja and Durga Puja. But whatever its specific content, *prasad* is freely accepted by all worshippers, irrespective of caste.

Etho or *jhuta* (food leftovers of humans) has a very severely restricted exchange value because to ingest it involves a more significant transfer and mixing of *gun* than to contact unused foods. Even when the provider is of a higher caste than the receiver the general rule is that one should not accept human leftovers. Indeed, no caste or tribe admits to receiving such food from another in Torkotala. Nor were any castes or tribes observed to receive such food, though such exchanges probably do occur between persons of birth groups which vary greatly in rank, because just as humans are held to receive spiritual-cum-corporeal merit by eating food left for them by the gods, so are persons of lower ranking castes held to benefit similarly by accepting and ingesting the food left for them by persons of higher ranking castes. Then, too, persons of lower ranking castes may accept leftover foods because there is some economic necessity for doing so.

Of more common occurrence and what can be observed in Torkotala is the transaction which involves removing the used dining plate (*thala*) and cleaning it after eating. If the receiver of food is of a much lower ranking caste than the food provider, it is expected that he will remove his own plate and see that it is washed and cleaned. This occurs commonly when a cultivator gives his agricultural laborers partial payment in the form of cooked food. The laborer, after eating, removes and cleans his own *thala*. If the receiver of food does not have a much lower rank, more often than not the used plate will be left where it is as it is, and neither the giver nor the receiver of food will attend to it immediately. Perhaps a servant of lower rank than the food receiver will collect and wash the used plate. Or the food provider will wait until the food receiver has departed and then see to removing the *thala*. But however the transaction is ultimately handled, what is involved is the transfer of natural and moral qualities which attach to the plate. To accept the plate is to accept the imperfections which attach to it.

The leavings of gods and the leavings of humans are the kinds of food having the widest and narrowest exchange value, respectively. Other kinds of food all have an intermediate exchange value. For example, raw food stuffs (*sidha* or *kacha mal*) are freely exchanged between all castes and tribes in Torkotala, excepting the untouchable Hari, whose slightest contact is enough to transfer *tamasik* qualities. Otherwise, no natural or moral qualities are thought to attach to foods like whole grains, uncut fruit, milk and other items that are unprocessed and uncooked. Indeed, in one sense *kacha mal* are not foods at all. *Kacha* denotes that which is raw, unprocessed, uncooked. *Mal* denotes merchandise, wares, goods. *Kacha mal* are the physical source of culturally defined foods, but are not themselves food in the sense of that which is ready and fit for consumption. That which is ready and fit for consumption is referred to differently as *khabar*.

Jal khabar refers to a variety of foods that are eaten as a snack; the category includes, for example, puffed rice that may be eaten on rising in the morning (and which is prepared over a dry heat, with sand or small, fine stones preventing the rice from sticking to the heated cooking vessel). It also includes the sweet confections prepared with milk and taken as a snack in the late afternoon, and wheat preparations or vegetables fried in vegetable oils – preferably mustard-seed oil. Fruits are also included among *jal khabar*. In fact, the term *jal khabar* refers to any and all varieties of food which are not boiled in water and which are eaten as a non-principal food. The differences between a principal and non-principal food, and the significance of food being prepared in boiled water, becomes clearer when *jal khabar* is contrasted with *bhat khabar*.

The term *bhat khabar* is used by Bengalis to refer to food in general. Thus to ask if someone has eaten *bhat* is to ask if he has eaten at all. But the term also has a more restrictive usage – for present purposes a more revealing usage. *Bhat khabar* refers literally to boiled rice (*bhat*) food, the staple of the Bengali diet. It refers as well to the side dishes usually eaten with boiled rice: lentils and vegetable curries. Lentils are prepared in boiled water, vegetable curries may or may not be. Because it is cooked in boiling water, *bhat* is thought to have a shorter period in which it is fit for consumption than foods cooked in vegetable oils; its should be eaten during the same meal for which it is prepared. Even persons of lower-ranking castes who would otherwise accept freshly cooked *bhat* may not accept rice left over from another meal. Such leftover rice is usually eaten only by members of the same family.

When economic circumstances allow, every Torkotala family will eat *bhat* at least once daily, usually at midday, as its main meal of the day. This is one sense in which *bhat* is a principal food. There is another. Of all the foods that contribute as a material source of blood, boiled rice is the most important source, the principal source. To give or receive boiled rice is thus more important than to exchange any other kind of food because the exchange of boiled rice implies a greater intimacy and willingness to have one's own blood, the transmitter of all that is distinctive of a birth group, affected.

Served along with *jal khaber* or *bhat* or on its own is drinking water (*jal*). There is a sense in which water is not food at all. The term *khabar* is never applied to it, it is not processed in any way, and water is not taken to satisfy hunger or to appease an appetite. But as drinking water is ingested and does transfer natural and moral qualities, it is recognized as an important exchange medium. In Torkotala, as in other Bengali villages, water has an exchange value intermediate between *kacha mal* and *jal khabar*.

There are ritual occasions when neither *jal khabar* nor *bhat* is thought appropriate fare: the first rice-eating ceremony, the initiation ceremony, marriage and funeral rites, for example. On these occasions, in which persons of several castes may be present, *bhat* would not be appropriate because of its restricted exchange value, and *jal khabar* would not be appropriate because it is ordinary fare. As a result, on ritual occasions foods are prepared with clarified butter (*ghi*); and at least one dish of the meal will include a preparation of milk or milk products, perhaps mixed with sugar. Clarified butter, milk and milk products are among the most favored and most perfect of foods because of their cooling, *sattvik* effect on the body, and because eating them involves no injury to life forms. It is also the kind of food available to humans which most nearly resembles the food of gods. The mere presence of *ghi* thus transforms ordinary foods into special foods, and gives them a much wider exchange value. Foods prepared in vegetable oils are preferred over foods prepared in boiling water. But foods prepared in *ghi* are preferred over all.

The general rule that food is best exchanged between castes of equal rank – or, failing that, from a caste of higher rank to a caste of lower rank, but not the reverse – can now be qualified in noting that the actual exchange of foods between castes depends as well on their relative value as exchange media. The central importance of any food transfer remains its potential effect on the defining features, and thus the rank, of the receiving caste.

Like marriage and diet, occupation (*britti*) and the generalized life style (*jibika*) attendant on pursuing an occupation are acts by which the defining features and rank of a caste, first given by the natural circumstances of birth, are altered and transformed through life activities. A full discussion of the importance of occupation and life style must await a better understanding of why specific activities and substances are deemed *sattvik*, *rajasik* or *tamasik*. Still some general comments can be made now. Occupations and attendant life styles such as those of a priest or spiritual perceptor, which focus thought and action on realizing the essential truths of the universe, are *sattvik*, for through them men approximate their greatest human potential, and may even realize their essential unity with Brahma. The defining features of a caste are thus positively transformed. Occupations and attendant life styles like those of a scavenger, toddy maker, skinner or tanner of animal hides, or prostitution – which focus thought and action on satisfying those life needs which men share with animals or lower forms of life – are *tamasik*, for through preoccupation with hunger, procreation, force and violence, or with bodily processes like elimination, reproduction and death, humans approximate the nature and code of inferior life forms. The defining features of a caste are thus transformed negatively. Finally, the occupation and attendant life styles of artisans, agriculturalists or herders are *rajasik*, for these confirm and maintain the ordinary preoccupations of humans born to the temporal world of earth.

Whether participation in any specific occupation will positively or negatively transform the defining features and rank of a caste depends, of course, on its present nature and code. Thus for a caste of artisans to work as artisans only confirms and maintains their defining features, while the same work, if adopted by a caste of scavengers, refines and elevates their defining features. Conversely, for a caste of artisans to adopt the work of scavengers debases and lowers their features.

Summary and discussion

This chapter began with a description of the major worlds of the universe and the life forms which inhabit them. The several worlds of the universe are ranked according to their relative proximity to Brahma at the northernmost point in the universe, with the higher, more northerly worlds ranking above the lower, more southerly worlds. The six life forms – gods, humans, demonic beings, animals, plants and objects – occupy a place and rank in one of these worlds according to the extent to which their own defining features approximate those of Brahma, the apical being in the Bengali cosmos.

The same premise of ranked inequalities which informs Bengali perceptions of the cosmos was then seen to inform Bengali perceptions of the various birth groups (*jati*) into which humans in society are divided. The four *varna*, castes and the more highly differentiated groupings of *gotro*, *kul*, *bongso* and *poribar* can all be compared and ordered high and low. Clearly, therefore, a comprehensive ethnography of rank among Bengali Hindus must include the study of institutions beside caste, the usual focus of study, as well as those properties of rank general throughout the Bengali cosmos and society.

Several other conclusions and some general insights as to their importance for the study of systems of rank among Hindus can be drawn from the manner in which the Bengali cosmos and society is ordered by ranked inequalities.

First, the life forms and various human birth groups recognized by Bengalis are all defined and ranked by the same features of physical nature and behavioral code. Given their common source in Brahma, each is constituted of the same primordial matter, *prakriti* – or more specifically the three *gun* of which *prakriti* is constituted – and each has a behavioral code, or *dharma*, appropriate to its physical nature. To determine the rank order of life forms, as a result, does not entail comparing beings that are essentially different. All life forms are essentially similar, differing only in the way that their own nature and code approximates that of Brahma. Thus it is a property of rank general throughout the Bengali cosmos and society that all life forms can be placed in a unified series of ranked orders and ordered ranks.

Second, the physical nature and behavioral code by which each life form and human birth group is defined are viewed by Bengalis as a single, if duplex, criterion of rank. Thus the rank of any unit is determined by its physical nature, its disposition of *gun*, and its behavorial code, its *dharma*. One is but a reflection and realization of the other. It is in this sense that attributional, interactional and purity-plus-power theories of rank are unified by a cultural analysis which recognizes nature and code as cognitively non-dualistic features.

Third, because all human birth groups are ordered by the same premise of ranked inequalities, defined by the same features of nature and code, and ranked by the same criterion, in principle at least all birth groups of the same kind can be ranked in an inclusive ordering. In fact, Torkotala residents can only construct an inclusive rank ordering of the four *varna* and the castes of their localized, interactive community. Included within castes are the more highly differentiated *gotro, kul, bongso* and *poribar*, a limited number of which may be compared and ranked but for which an inclusive ordering of like units cannot be established by Torkotala residents.

Though not emphasized in the course of this chapter, the cultural definitions of *gotro, kul, bongso* and *poribar* which were provided bear upon the criticism that cultural analyses preclude the possibility of a comparative social science. In fact, the less ethnocentric ethnography towards which cultural analyses strive actually allows for more accurate comparative statements and more truly universalistic definitions as well. A *gotro*, to illustrate, differs significantly from a clan, given the usual definition of this term by anthropologists. Similarly, a *kul*, though often identified as a unilineal descent group, is not a descent group as such, for it includes in-marrying wives and excludes out-marrying daughters. And if a *bongso* is to be glossed as a patrilineage, then it must be recognized that among Bengali Hindus lineage membership, like certain other memberships, is not fixed and unchanging through time. Bengali women belong to the *gotro, kul* and *bongso* of their fathers before marriage, but to those of their husbands after marriage. In all of these cases does the more accurate emic provided by a cultural analysis allow for a better etic. Then, too, a cultural definition of the Bengali family raises yet another issue in cross-cultural comparison. For while universalistic definitions of the family usually stress the husband and wife as a minimal pair, or alternatively, follow Goodenough (1970) in emphasizing the central importance of the mother, the existence and duration of the Bengali family is defined culturally in terms of its male head, the husband/father, and is said to desist upon his death or permanent departure.

And fifth, the defining features, and thus the rank, of a human birth group, given initially in the order of nature, are not fixed and unchanging through time, but can be altered, for better or worse, according to activities in the order of culture, including marriage, diet, food exchanges and occupation. It is for this reason that a unified theory of rank is also transformational. In chapter 4 the transformational perspective will be applied to the politics of caste to account for how the Bagdis successfully advanced claims to higher rank, and how the Sadgops defended their present rank. But first it remains to consider the place and importance of individuals among Bengali Hindus, and to complete the development of a transformational theory of rank, for this will further clarify the broad sociocultural context in which Torkotala villagers act politically.

3. Lok

Des and *jati* are the two identifications by which Bengalis introduce and locate themselves in physical and social space. It is the ranking of *jati* within each *des*, plus the inclusive ordering of all *des* as but larger and smaller divisions of space, that lends a pervasive vertical organization to all of Bengali society. This said, the ethnography of Hindu rank can be extended still further with a discussion of the individual in Bengali thought and action.

The individual as a thinking, acting being is present in all societies. A conception of the individual as a unique being of intrinsic worth; a more or less autonomous, self-fulfilling being, with private interests, wants and goals; a being valued as the elemental social unit, is not similarly universal. As noted in the Introduction, Dumont argues that such a conception is peculiar to modern countries of the West, with their values of equality and liberty, and should not be attributed to more traditional societies. In Hindu India, Dumont (1970:1–20) writes, individual identities are submerged in the birth groups to which they belong while individual interests are subordinated to the society as a whole, which bears primary value. The individual only becomes an important unit in India in the person of the renouncer.

The evidence from West Bengal suggests an alternative evaluation of the individual in Hindu society. *Lok* refers to the several worlds of the universe. It also refers to the individuals who inhabit those worlds. As the discussion below will indicate, this double meaning of the term *lok* felicitously marks another premise of Bengali culture: that individuals are a microcosm of the universe at large, a *suksma-jagat*, a subtle or minute (*suksma*) world (*jagat*) in themselves. The same processes of development that are general to the universe are replicated in the physical-cum-moral development of individuals. The same premise of ranked inequalities which orders the various worlds, life forms and human birth groups applies as well to individuals. And like the birth groups in which they are included, individuals undergo transformations of their defining physical nature and behavioral codes, and thus their rank, in accord with their own life

81

activities. It is to detail these processes of individual development and
transformation as they are marked by a series of life stages and life-cycle
rites that this chapter is written. The closing section of the chapter will also
consider how individuals in Bengali society have an identity and ranked
social position, or situs, apart from their memberships in particular birth
groups.

The individual as microcosm

As noted earlier, Bengalis regard creation as the transformation of that
which already exists in latent form into that which is apprehensible as part
of the diverse phenomenal world. In creation all that already exists is made
manifest as various emanations from Brahma. From Brahma first
emanated *purusa*, the male principle of the universe in which is embodied
hard, structuring, but relatively inert matter. Then *prakriti*, the female
principle of the universe in which is embodied soft, energetic, but relatively
unstructured matter. From their union was created this phenomenal
world; all that exists within the world depends on their continued union
and reunion over time, and the way in which primordial matter is
differently combined and mixed by the structuring male principle.

Like all else in the phenomenal world, individuals originate from the
creative force of Brahma through the union of *purusa* and *prakriti*,
symbolized in the joining of male and female in sexual intercourse.
Individuals also develop in much the same way as all else in the universe.
From Brahma first emanated the structuring, sentient principle; then the
unstructured material principle. Among humans, too, the conscious,
sentient principles develop first. First evolves intellect, the faculty of
thought. Intellect gives rise to the principle of egoism, the faculty which
appropriates thought or regards it as one's own. Then are evolved further
aids to conscious, sentient life, the mind, the five sensory functions – taste,
touch, hearing, sight and smell – and the five motor functions – speech,
handling, walking, evacuation, and reproduction. The mind proceeds from
the *sattvik* ego because it aids individuals in perceiving the reality of the
phenomenal world. All of the sensory and motor functions proceed from
the *rajasik* ego.

In the fifth month after conception the foetus is endowed with
conscious, sentient life. From then until actual birth the limbs and members
of the physical body become increasingly more developed. In the eighth
month, after the foetus is conscious and has completed its basic physical
development, it becomes endowed with a soul (*atman*) that is fully
cognizant of its activities and experiences in prior lives, as well as its
essential unity with the universal soul, Brahma. This awareness, signi-

Table 5. *Basic substances of the Universe and of Man*

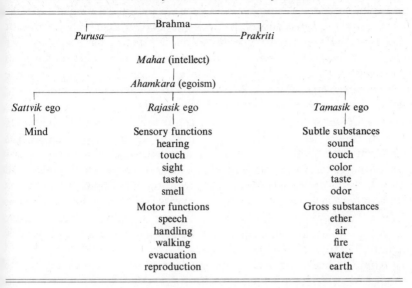

	┌──────Brahma──────┐	
Purusa──────────────┼──────────────*Prakriti*		
	Mahat (intellect)	
	│	
	Ahamkara (egoism)	
Sattvik ego	*Rajasik* ego	*Tamasik* ego
Mind	Sensory functions	Subtle substances
	hearing	sound
	touch	touch
	sight	color
	taste	taste
	smell	odor
	Motor functions	Gross substances
	speech	ether
	handling	air
	walking	fire
	evacuation	water
	reproduction	earth

ficantly, is lost during the pains of birth while passing from the mother's womb to the world outside. Life in the temporal world of earth thus is often described by Bengalis as an attempt to regain the perfection that was once.

Only after birth, on entering the temporal world, does an individual become involved with the *tamasik* aspect of being. The temporal world is composed of elementary substances having two phases. In their simple or subtle phase these substances are known as elemental sound, elemental color, elemental taste, elemental odor and elemental space. All are material in nature – everything in the phenomenal world is – but in a very refined, intangible, imperceptible way. In combination they form the five gross elements of the world that are perceptibly material. From elemental sound emerges ether. From that and elemental touch, air. From these and elemental color, fire. From them and elemental taste, water. And from them and elemental odor, earth. These subtle and gross elements represent the *tamasik* aspect of being because they emphasize or bring to fore the material quality of the world.

The gross elements of the universe – earth, water, ether, fire and air – together form the physical frame of the human body. Earth is present in the bones. Water in bodily fluids. Ether in the humors. Fire in the energy or activity of the nervous system. And air in the soul. The soul represents in humans the presence of Brahma and thus their essential spiritual identity. It is to free the soul from its physical housing towards which all *sattvik* activities are directed; to do so is to overcome the *tamasik* aspects of being that attach one to the temporal world and to satisfying material needs.

Actually the soul is housed in not one but two physical bodies. *Sarira* or *deha* are the Bengali terms generally used to designate a physical body. The outermost body (*sthula sarira* or gross body) consists of all five of the gross elements of the universe. Upon death and cremation, two of these five elements, earth and water, are destroyed. Fire, air and ether remain to form the *suksma sarira* or subtle body. A subtle body, like a subtle element, is also material, but in a refined, imperceptible way. It is the subtle body which houses the soul directly, and it is the subtle body which persists through the round of births and reincarnations endured by humans according to their activities in past lives. Thus is the gross body considered mortal, being destroyed after each life, while the subtle body transmigrates to be reborn in a new physical frame or gross body. The subtle body is not eternal, though, for when the religious quest is finally attained, its three elements of air, fire and ether are left behind and dispersed as the soul is completely freed to reunite with Brahma.

Attaining liberation requires freeing the soul from the gross and subtle bodies which house it. Different paths towards this end are recommended according to sectarian beliefs. Common to all Bengali Hindus, though, is the understanding that liberation from the round of births is a solo quest which requires developing the *sattvik* qualities over and in subjugation of *tamasik* qualities. Unborn offspring are fully aware of this necessity during their eighth month of life in the female womb. The same awareness is lost upon birth and entry into the temporal world, and thus must be learned anew as individuals develop during their own lives. To do so is to regain a past perfection.

A transformational theory of human development

⌐The individual as microcosm is an important unit of thought among Hindus because within the individual is seen mirrored the creation and ⌊order of the universe at large. As a knowing, responsible being who can effect, for better or worse, those features acquired through the natural circumstances of birth, and can even realize the ultimate religious quest, the individual is also an important unit of action and the normative subject of institutions. In chapter 2 we saw how castes and the more highly differentiated birth groups into which humans are divided are defined and ranked according to their physical nature and the behavior held appropriate to that nature; also how the defining features, and thus the rank, of a caste can be transformed for better or worse. Much the same is also true, significantly, of individuals. Upon conception a foetus is ascribed physical

and behavioral features appropriate to its parentage. Some of these
features are identical with those of the parents and others who actually or
putatively share descent, and provide the basis for ascribing the newly born
membership in a family, line and caste. Other features are unlike those of
kin or caste fellows, for Hindus regard no two individuals as ever being
exactly alike. Both sets of features exist initially only as naturally given
potential, a set of capacities which must be realized through an individual's
own life activities. Thus it falls upon every individual progressively to
develop, refine and improve the material qualities and behavioral codes
given initially in the order of nature (*prakriti*) through activities in the order
of culture (*sanskriti*). The extent to which this is done provides a basis for
individual rank or situs in this lifetime. It also affects one's *karma*, and thus
one's being and social memberships in future lives. Exactly how individuals
proceed in this normatively sanctioned task via a series of life stages and
life-cycle rites is here formulated as a transformational theory of human
development, which completes the transformational theory of rank begun
in chapter 2.

Life stages

Torkotala villagers do not generally describe themselves as being of a
certain age. Many do not know their exact age. Even among those who do,
age is not viewed criterially because acting in accord with the prescriptions
of Hindu life is held less a function of age *per se* than of passage through a
series of life stages.

    Textual sources list four life stages or *asramas*: studentship (*brah-
macharya*), householder (*garhasthya*), forest dweller or recluse (*vanap-
rastha*) and renouncer (*sannyasa*).[1] Each is described in turn, and then all
are contrasted with an alternative division of the human biography into six
life stages that has no textual basis, but which Torkotala villagers describe
as better reflecting local, popular understanding.

    The first *asrama*, studentship, is open only to males, and then only to
males belonging to castes of the Brahman, Kshatriya and Vaisya *varnas*.
Thus are persons of these *varnas* entitled the 'twice-born,' referring to the
second and spiritual birth (or rebirth) that marks their initiation into the
study of the Vedas and other religious texts under the guidance of a
Brahman preceptor. Neither women nor Sudras have the opportunity for
Vedic study because such study is thought unsuitable and inappropriate to
persons of their nature and code. Nor do women or Sudras wear the
sacrificial thread (*poita*) because receiving the thread is part of the
ceremony which initiates a youth into studentship.

    The Manu Dharmasastra (chapter 2, lines 36, 38) does state that a

Brahman youth should enter studentship between the years of 8 and 16, a Kshatriya youth between the years of 11 and 22, and a Vaisya youth between the years of 12 and 24. As understood by Torkotala Hindus, though, the ages specified are not intended literally; rather, they loosely designate a youthful period of life in which it is appropriate to learn of the first of four goals common to all Hindus: upholding *dharma* as it applies to the natural and moral orders of the cosmos, society, birth groups and individuals. That ages are specified at all suggests that youths of higher *varna* are more quickly able and ready to accept instruction in the sacred texts.

At the close of studentship the previously celibate student enters a second life stage by marrying and becoming a householder (*grihastha*), thus passing from a period of youthful learning to active, responsible adulthood. While a student, individuals repay a debt to the sages who first introduced men to Vedic lore and worships. Still other debts common to all Hindus can only be repaid after becoming a householder. This second *asrama* is open to persons of all *varna*; indeed, it is incumbent on all Hindus to marry and enter the stage of householder to better repay debts, first, to the ancestors by providing male progeny to continue the descent line and to perform ancestor worships after his own death; second, to the gods by using his position and wealth as a householder to offer worships; and third, to other humans and other life forms of the universe by offering hospitality and alms. Though not recognized as a debt of the same order, the householder is also best able to repay a debt to self by realizing the first three goals of Hindu life: upholding *dharma*, acquiring wealth and material gain (*artha*), and satisfying aesthetic and sensual, including sexual, desires (*kama*). For all of these reasons a householder has a special place of importance among Hindus, and is the person on whom members of the three other *asramas* are said to rely and depend. It is the householder and his wife who are the parents of future students. It is the householder, as creator of wealth, on whom students and teachers depend for material support, as do forest dwellers and renouncers.

In the third life stage the householder retires from active family and social life and seeks relative seclusion as a recluse (*vanaprasthin*; literally, forest dweller), passing from a period of active responsibility for family and social affairs to a stage in which his activities and thought are aimed more directly at attaining the religious quest (*mukti*), the fourth and last goal of Hindu life. Even while living apart from his family and community, though, the recluse remains available to them for advice and counsel. In the fourth *asrama* one renounces all family and social ties to concentrate thought and action wholly towards realizing liberation from the round of births in this lifetime. Though the stage of recluse is open to males of the Kshatriya and Brahman *varnas*, only Brahmans are held to have the

Table 6. *The four varnas and their asramas*

Varnas	Asramas			
(in ranked order)	brahmacharya	garhasthya	vanaprastha	sannyasa
Brahman	×	×	×	×
Khsatriya	×	×	×	
Vaisya	×	×		
Sudra		×		

appropriate nature and code to become a *sannyasin*, or renouncer. Table 6 indicates how the ranked order of *varnas* corresponds to the differential capacity to enter the four life stages.

Torkotala Hindus are aware of the four life stages described in textual sources. They do not, however, find them satisfactory for describing the human biography as they know it experientially, preferring instead to speak of six different stages, referred to popularly as *bayas*. Like the life stages described in textual sources, each of these popular life stages is defined not by specific ages, but according to the physical capacities and moral responsibilities of its members. Unlike the textual life stages, though, each of these popular divisions of the human biography is open to persons of all *varnas*, and applies to male and female alike. The textual life stages are described solely in terms of the male biography. These differences notwithstanding, Torkotala villagers do draw analogies between their own understanding of six life stages and the stages described in textual sources;

Table 7. *Hindu life stages: textual and popular*

Left stages (textual)	Goals of Hindu life	Debts incumbent on all Hindus	Life stages (popular)
			Infancy
			Childhood
Studentship	Learn *dharma*	To sages	Youth
Householder	*dharma*	To ancestors	Young adulthood
		To gods	
		To other men and beings of the universe	
	artha		
	kama		
			Middle-aged adulthood
Recluse	Begin to focus on *mukti*	To self	Old age
Renouncer	*mukti*	To self	

for however one divides the human biography, it is incumbent on all Hindus to repay at some time during their life the same debts and to realize for themselves the same life goals. (A schematic comparison of the various life stages, textual and popular, is presented in table 7.)

Torkotala Hindus think it curious that the texts describe studentship as the first stage of life. In their own experience there are two prior stages of life in which one is neither physically nor morally mature enough to follow the discipline required of formal schooling and instruction. These are the stages of infancy (*saisab-bayas*) and childhood (*balokal-bayas*), both marked by rapid physical growth during which the very young remain essentially unknowing of moral expectations and thus not responsible for living within them. It is during infancy and childhood that whimsical behavior, even errant behavior, is expected and tolerated of youngsters. Indeed, the mischievous child is often praised for its likeness to Lord Krishna, who was also a consummate prankster and breaker of rules while very young.

Children are not totally free of restrictions on their behavior, even as young boys or girls. But their own moral judgement is considered undeveloped as yet, and thus the very young are not held responsible for their own actions in the same way as are their seniors. The expectation of children is that they act in accord with the orders or instructions of persons in the more senior life stages.

The passage from childhood to youth (*koisor-bayas*) is marked by no special rite, but is generally described as occurring when a young boy or young girl is physically-cum-morally mature enough to receive formal instruction regarding what is expected of persons of a given sex, family, caste, village, etc. Such instruction may begin at different ages. For all youths such instruction begins in the home, when young girls are instructed how to assist and serve elder females in household tasks, and when young boys begin to accompany their fathers on village or extra-village outings, thus learning by example about male tasks. For the largest number of Torkotala youths this instruction is continued in the village primary school, where they learn basic skills in reading and writing and how to do simple arithmetical calculations; also local history and some religious teachings. Youth is also a period of other changes reflecting greater physical-cum-moral maturity. Dress habits change. Infants and young children, for example, are often seen without clothing of any sort, especially in warm weather months. Youths will always wear a lower garment, usually short pants, and when in school or other non-play situations, will also wear an upper garment. For males this consists of a simple shirt, for females a simple dress over their short pants. Particularly as young girls develop physically they are seen less and less without an upper garment, and increasingly trying to manage wearing a full sari. Then too, youths also have greater mobility in their comings and goings. The play of children is usually restricted to the household compound or that of immediate neighbors where they are never far from the watchful eye of a parent or elder brother or sister. Youths, by contrast, roam through the village freely, and play often takes them away from their own home and compound. Boys and girls may still play together as youths. But as they mature there is a gradual separation and parting of the ways so that young girls are seen spending more time with each other and more time around the home, while young boys spend their time moving freely about the village, and even outside it. A walk to the nearby Narayanghar Town or weekly market is a frequent outing for boys – but not girls – of the village.

Youth is viewed by Torkotala villagers as directly analogous to the *brahmacharya asrama*. Obvious differences are recognized regarding who studies, what is studied, and how that study is organized and imparted. What remains analogous is that youth is the life stage considered most appropriate for the disciplined instruction that will best prepare one for adult life.

The passage from youth to adulthood is marked by marriage, for upon marriage one assumes the adult responsibilities of repaying those debts incumbent on all Hindus, as well as being able to realize for oneself the goals of *dharma*, *artha* and *kama*. Thus is adulthood analogous to the *garhasthya asrama*, with one difference. A local distinction is made between householders who are young adults and those who are middle-aged.

Young adulthood (*jowban-bayas*) attains to those householders who are newly married, newly charged with familial responsibilities, and newly entered into the social and political affairs of the village as active participants. They are adult persons fully able to play a responsible role in family and village affairs; only they are new and relatively inexperienced in this role. Young adults do not usually exert decided influence in village affairs. Even in their own home a newly married couple may live under the authority of others, especially if the customary virilocal residence pattern is maintained. Middle-aged adults (*prowdya-bayas*) are householders who are both active and well experienced in their adult roles. They are in all but exceptional cases the active heads of their own households, and it is from among the male members of this life stage that village-level leadership is usually drawn. This said, it must be stressed again that the difference between young and middle-aged adults is not one of age, as counted in days or months or years. There is a general correspondence between age and inclusion in a specific life stage. Males identified as young adults are usually between 20 and 35 years of age, their wives being slightly younger. Males identified as middle-aged adults are usually over 35 years of age. But this general correspondence is viewed by Torkotala villagers as the incidental result of local customs regarding the proper time for males and females to marry. It is not criterial for defining life stages, which are otherwise distinguished by the differential capacity of their members for active leadership and responsible participation in family and social affairs, a capacity which comes only with life experience. The importance of experience over age *per se* is exemplified in the biography of MGD.

In 1971 MGD was 28 years old, married for less than five years. His coevals in Torkotala are all identified as young adults, whereas MGD is included among the middle-aged adults of the village. The difference is that MGD acts the part of a more experienced, responsible adult. He is the active head of his own household. He holds the weighty position of teacher in the village primary school, is the head of the village economic cooperative, and is the chief broker between the village and bank and government officials outside the village. Though not formally a member of the statutory village council, MGD is also invited to attend and participate in all council meetings, and usually acts as recording secretary. He is also invited to all *ad hoc* meetings of village leaders. Further, MGD leads what many in Torkotala consider an exemplary religious life, spending time every morning in private worship, materially assisting all village worships, and ungrudgingly giving rice to everyone who asks his help. For all of these reasons does MGD act the part and provide the kind of leadership usually associated with more senior persons; and thus is he included among the middle-aged adults of the village, though his actual years are not many.

When individuals are no longer able actively to head their own household or actively to participate in village affairs, they are regarded as of old age (*bardhakya-bayas*) and are referred to as old man (*bura*) or old woman (*buri*).[2] Again these terms do not refer to any specific age; only to the stage of life when individuals are physically unable to assume the roles expected of adults. Even when physically decrepit, though, it is the old of the village, experienced and worldly-wise in the ways of life, who are honored and respected as elder statesmen and consulted as repositories of local history and custom. The very terms *bura* and *buri* reflect this honored position; they mean literally 'increased' and are used euphemistically to avoid reference to advanced debility. The old are often compared with persons of the *vanaprasthya asrama*. Both have retired from active social life to concentrate on the religious quest. Yet both remain available to their family and the wider society for sage advice and counsel.

Old age is the sixth and last popular life stage, closely followed by death. Thus popular divisions of the human biography include no single stage that is directly analogous to the *sannyasa asrama*. Rather, Torkotala villagers hold that renunciation and a life directed wholly towards the religious quest is a prerogative of individuals at any and all stages of life. From infancy to old age one proceeds through a prescribed series of life stages. But that series can be interrupted at any time to follow the life of a renouncer. The biography of Phani Babu, a Brahman of Torkotala, is a case in point.

Phani Babu's first wife died about 19 years ago when he was approximately 40 years of age. Soon afterwards Phani Babu adopted the life of a *sannyasin* and for two years roamed the Bengal countryside living solely on alms. The life did not suit him, as Phani Babu now says, so he returned to Torkotala where his father's sister's son was managing the family lands. He resumed work as a cultivator and priest, remarried, and by 1971 had had eight children by his second wife. Phani Babu is presently the active head of his own household, and despite his relatively advanced age of over 60 is considered one of the leading middle-aged adults of the village.

Life-cycle rites

Every Hindu occupies a life stage commensurate with his physical-cum-moral development. The discussion above identified those life stages as they are described popularly and in texts. Left unmentioned thus far is that within these life stages Bengalis recognize even finer divisions of the human biography according to an individual's passage through a series of rites referred to collectively as *samskaras*.

Samskaras are rites by which individuals can refine, improve upon and positively transform the features of nature and code initially given them by the circumstances of birth. *Nitya karma* refer to those rites of this kind which are done regularly, even daily, like bathing or worshipping.

Table 8. *The Hindu population of Torkotala village by life stage, 1971*

				Life Stage			
Caste	Infancy	Childhood	Youth	Young adulthood	Middle-age adulthood	Old age	Total
Sadgop	12	19	52	18	34	6	141
Bagra-Khatriya	16	11	29	22	17	2	97
B-K Boisnab		4	7	4	2	1	18
Bagal	1	5	7	8	5		26
Jogi	1	2	6	4	6		19
Kayastha	1		5		4		10
Tantoby			4		3		7
Brahman		2	6	1	2		11
Rajok		1	2	1	2		6
Mahisya Boisnab	1	1			2		4
Hari	1				2		3
Mahisya					1		1
Totals	33	45	118	58	80	9	343
% of total	11	13	34	17	23	3	100

Table 9.   *The performance of life-cycle rites by caste*

Caste	Rite										
	1	2	3	4	5	6	7	8	9	10	11
Brahman	+	+	+	+	+	+	+	+	+	+	+
Sadgop	−	+	+	+	+	+	+	+	−	+	+
Kayastha	−	+	−	+	+	+	+	−	−	+	+
Mahisya Boisnab	−	+	+	+	+	+	+	−	−	+	+
B-K Boisnab	−	+	−	+	+	+	+	−	−	+	+
Bagra-Khatriya	−	+	−	+	+	+	+	−	−	+	+
Jogi	−	+	−	+	+	+	+	−	−	+	+
Tantoby	−	+	−	+	+	+	−	−	−	+	+
Rajok	−	+	−	+	+	+	−	−	−	+	+
Hari	−	−	−	+	+	+	−	−	−	+	+

Key to rites: (1) *garbhadana*, (2) *pum-savana*, (3) *simantonnayana*, (4) *jat-karma*, (5) *nama-karana*, (6) *annaprasana*, (7) *cura-karana*, (8) *karna-vedha*, (9) *upanayana*, (10) *bibaha*, (11) *sraddha*.

Naimittika samskaras refer to those rites of this kind that are done irregularly, or even once in a lifetime, like marriage. What defines all of these rites, regular or irregular, as of a kind, is the common goal of providing for the gradual development and refinement of those features given initially upon birth in the order of nature through the systematic performance of acts in the order of culture. The irregular *samskaras* also mark and provide for the gradual social incorporation of an individual into the universe, society and ascribed groups which he enters naturally by birth. They may be typed, following van Gannep (1960), as 'life-cycle rites' or rites of passage between culturally defined divisions of the human biography.

Textual sources list as many as 40 life-cycle rites for Hindus (cf. Pandey 1969:15–24). Torkotala Hindus, by contrast, recognize only 10 principal rites, and among villagers there is variation in the way these common rites are performed, if they are performed at all. This variation is due in part to differences in caste, with the higher castes celebrating more life-cycle rites and in more elaborate fashion (see table 9); also to differences in the manuals used by officiants when performing the rites. Among families of the same caste, variation in performance is due in the main to differences in wealth, which affects not only the elaborateness of those rites performed, but also the number of life-cycle rites celebrated and whether individual rites are performed on separate occasions or several rites are combined on one occasion. This said, for present purposes the further discussion of life-cycle rites will focus less on their ritual content and variations in performance than on the effect of each *samskara* upon the individual who undergoes it.[3]

The first life-cycle rite is *garbhadana* or conception; yet marriage, the tenth rite, is held to begin the developmental cycle of an individual because marriage provides the appropriate context for conception. As described in texts, *garbhadana* ideally consists of a husband and wife receiving the blessings of a Brahman before intercourse. The rite is considered obligatory for all householders, for without offspring one of the proper goals of marriage cannot be met. In Torkotala, only Phani Babu, the village Brahman, has ever observed the rite, and then only prior to his first child.

Once conceived, the sex of an offspring is determined by the relative quantity of semen and uterine blood. If the quantity of semen is greater, the offspring will be male. If the quantity of uterine blood is greater, the offspring will be female. The actual mix of semen and uterine blood is thought influenced by specific acts on the part of individuals. The likelihood of male offspring, for example, is enhanced when conception is on even-numbered dates of the lunar month, and especially on the even-numbered dates of the bright half of the lunar month, when the moon is waxing. The likelihood of female offspring is enhanced when conception is on odd-numbered dates of the lunar month, and especially on odd-numbered dates of the dark half of the lunar month, when the moon is waning. The conception of male offspring is also held more likely if sexual intercourse occurs during the night rather than the day, with the later portions of the night being more auspicious than the earlier portions.

The second life-cycle rite, *pum-savana*, is performed some time between the second and eighth month after conception in the hope of receiving a healthy male offspring by strengthening the female in whom it is being nurtured. The rite consists of dressing the expectant mother in a new sari having a red border, symbolizing fertility, and feeding her culturally valued foods, like fish and rice preparations with milk and clarified butter in addition to whatever other foods she may crave. No Brahman priest is required for this rite. It is performed by persons of the household, with the husband's mother taking primary responsibility for serving the expectant mother, who eats first. Only later will the rest of the household eat. This honors the expectant mother by reversing the usual order of eating and service. Ordinarily, all males of the household will eat before any females do, and the elder females of the household, including the husband's mother, will eat before the younger females who serve them.

The *pum-savana* rite directly honors the expectant mother; it indirectly honors the offspring she nurtures, for a pregnant woman is physically and spiritually linked with the offspring inside her womb. The needs and longings of one are the needs and longings of the other. Thus to feed the mother and to satisfy her desires is to feed and satisfy the desires of the offspring at the same time, for they are one and the same. Not to do so could prove injurious to both.

A third rite, *simantonnayana*, is performed some time before the actual birth of the child, ideally before the eighth month of pregnancy, to further strengthen the mother in the hope of an easy delivery. Like the *pum-savana* rite, it is a family affair that requires no priest as officiant. And like the *pum-savana* rite, it consists in the main of honoring the expectant mother and child with a special feeding. In addition the expectant mother is informed of certain precautions required to ensure an easy and successful delivery. Older women of the house will caution the expectant mother to reduce her physical activity, not to bend deeply, not to carry heavy loads, and to take care in the foods eaten so that the offspring will have proper and sufficient material sustenance. The expectant mother will be cautioned as well about walking about where malevolent spirits are known to live, plus other local folkways regarding childbirth. In Torkotala the rite is most often performed for women in their first pregnancy, and may be combined in one occasion with *pum-savana*.

The fourth life-cycle rite, *jat-karma*, is a turning point in the physical development of the offspring. Whereas the three previous rites provided for the proper conception and growth of the offspring within the female womb, emphasizing the essential unity of mother and offspring, the *jat-karma* rite involves the parturition of the child and its physical separation from the mother with the cutting of the umbilical cord. The *jat-karma* rite and all later rites will now emphasize the development of the child as a separate identity apart from its mother.

The *jat-karma* rite can be performed just after delivery of the offspring but prior to the cutting of the umbilical cord; or it can be performed just after the umbilical cord is cut. At either time the rite consists of several parts in which the father places clarified butter or gold on the child's body and recites invocations asking that the child develop with intelligence, long life and bodily strength. Then the mother is praised for the successful bearing of a child, and is especially praised if the child born is a male. All of the life-cycle rites up to this point are identical for male and female children. But all are done in the hope of receiving a male offspring.

Upon any birth the entire household is affected with birth impurity. During the impurity period no worships will be performed in the house, and no alms or hospitality will be offered to outsiders. Excepting the mother and newly born, all other members of the household, including the father, will otherwise carry on their normal routine of life after first bathing. The mother and newly born, by contrast, observe the full impurity period, usually 10 days. During the whole of that time they are ideally confined to a special room or area of the house, where their bodily needs are ministered to. This is a period of rest and recovery, a regaining of strength for the mother and a first gaining of strength for the infant. On the tenth day after birth the soiled clothes are removed, the confinement area is cleaned, and the mother and child are ceremonially bathed. This frees them from the special impurity of birth. On the eleventh day they and the family will resume the full round of daily activities, including the performance of worships and providing hospitality to beggars and others.

Especially for the infant child does the period of confinement after birth have a special importance beyond the mere gaining of physical strength. A newborn is a welcomed addition to the family, particularly if it is a male. But it is at the same time suspect as a newcomer that may not stay. Only as the physical fitness of the infant to survive becomes clear is the child gradually introduced to and included into the universe and society in which it was born. Not until the sixth day after birth, for example, is the child first welcomed to the universe. On that day the goddess Sasthi, the protectress of children, is worshipped, and an oil lamp is lit on behalf of the child and placed in the doorway to welcome the male god who will come that night to write the fate of the child on its forehead. On the eighth day after birth other children of the village are fed on behalf of the newly born. These children, in turn, welcome the newcomer by singing songs and beating the air with sticks to keep malevolent spirits away from their infant friend. On the eleventh day after birth, when the mother and child have left the confinement area, the child is presented to the moon god, Candra, and through him to all the other gods as well. Even now the child is not fully included as a member of the family or descent groupings into which he was born, though, and will not be until after several other *samskaras* are performed.

The fifth life-cycle rite, *nama-karana*, further separates the infant from its mother by providing the infant with his own named identity, consisting of a surname and one or more personal names. The surname (*paddhabi*) is common to all members of the patriline, including females who marry into the line. Personal names usually consist of a proper or good name (*bhalo nam*), and a second, more informal, colloquial name (*dak nam*). If a formal horoscope is made recording the exact timing of birth, an individual will also have an astrological name (*ras nam*). Each of these personal names is to be whispered to the infant by his father on the tenth night after birth. The astrological name should never be made public; the other personal names usually are not announced publicly (and may not be decided) until the sixth life-cycle rite.

The sixth rite, *annaprasana*, marks another turning point in the independent growth of the infant. It is held some time between six months and one year after birth and consists in the main of feeding the infant solid food – boiled rice (*bhat*) – for the first time. This begins the process of weaning the infant from the mother's milk, its sole source of nourishment until now, and represents the first time the infant has not been directly dependent upon its mother for sustenance, Several other parts of the rite require special mention. Worship to the goddess Sasthi is performed again.

Also, before the infant is fed, a Brahman priest offers prayers and oblations to the infant's ancestors in his name. This represents the first time that the infant's name is announced to the ancestors and marks his formal inclusion into the male descent line. Following this ancestral worship, the infant is fed boiled rice for the first time as a symbol of family unity and family membership. Then the infant is presented with gifts by persons related through his mother and father, and by friends of the village as well, who will later all be feasted as part of the celebration. These gifts may vary somewhat, but will include a full set of eating utensils (a plate, bowl and glass), a cloth or two, usually short pants and a shirt for males or short pants and a dress for females, and some coins, representing wealth. Among some families the gifts may also include a small wooden seat used while eating. Taken together these eating utensils, clothes and coins represent the minimal necessities of social life; it is on the occasion of *annaprasana samskara* that the developing infant first receives them.

The first six life-cycle rites are common to both males and females. For females there is but one other principal rite, marriage. During the intervening years it is expected that females will mature physically and will be instructed practically and morally in preparation for the adult responsibilities of a wife, a householder, and a future mother. No separate rite marks this intervening life stage for females.

For males the period between first feeding and marriage is marked by three other rites. *Cura-karana* refers to the first ceremonial cutting of the infant's hair. This may not be the infant's first hair cutting, but it is the first tonsure done as a ceremonial offering to the gods. The rite is done by a person of the barber caste, while the offering is made by the infant. The rite aims at securing a long and healthy life for the infant by offering the hair at the top of the head – which protects a vital junction of the body – in the hope of securing more powerful divine protection.

An eighth rite, *karnavedha*, or the ceremonial piercing of the ears, also aims at securing the long and healthy life of the infant. In this instance, though, longevity and health are sought by flawing the infant's body because an imperfect body is thought less attractive to malevolent spirits and other demonic beings.

The tonsure and ear-piercing rites are often combined and both are best performed before the infant finishes the third year of life, which loosely marks the beginning of childhood. It is then that the chances of the newborn to survive are less suspect, and an offspring's eventual death will be recognized ritually in the same way as the death of any other more senior person of the descent line. To explain more fully, if an infant dies before celebrating the tonsure rite, it is buried rather than cremated, which is the more common and more honored way of disposing of the dead among Hindus. Also, the impurity associated with the death of an infant before the tonsure rite is much reduced. In the instance of an adult Brahman, for example, death impurity ordinarily lasts for 10 days. If a Brahman offspring dies while still in its mother's womb, only the mother must observe a period of death impurity, and then only for as many days as months elapsed after conception. Neither the father nor other relatives observe any impurity period at all. If the offspring dies after birth but before celebrating the tonsure rite, the mother, father and near lineal relatives (*sapinda*) all observe but one day of impurity. Both the practice of burial and the reduced impurity period observed on the death of a child who has not celebrated the *cura-karana samskara* reflect on the tentative and suspect status of the newly born as a member of the birth groups into which he was born. Only after celebrating the tonsure rite does the death of a child result in three days of impurity for lineal relatives and is the child cremated rather than buried. Only after initiation for a male or marriage for a female is a full period of death impurity observed.

Upanayana is the ninth life-cycle rite. Whereas the first eight rites address the physical growth and development of the offspring from conception through infancy to childhood, *upanayana* initiates a male youth into a formal period of instruction and learning. The physical body having developed so far, as it were, initiation now emphasizes the moral development of a youth. Though open to males of the three highest *varna*, in Bengal today only Brahman youths commonly observe this rite, and then only Brahman youths from families who actually serve as priests. In other Brahman families the initiation rite is more closely associated with being included among the twice-born, and with receiving the right to wear the sacrificial thread.

Bibaha or marriage is the tenth and last of the principal life-cycle rites. It is common to both males and females, and represents for both the passage from youth to adulthood. Marriage marks the point of physical-cum-moral maturity when individuals are expected to participate as responsible adults in family and social affairs, and to realize the various debts and personal goals described earlier as common to all Hindus. This does not mean that marriage and adult status mark the final development in the human biography. No rites mark the passage from young adulthood, to middle-aged adulthood, to old age. Yet Torkotala villagers do distinguish between adults according to their differing capacities and responsibilities while actually participating in family and village affairs.

There is another life-cycle rite not included among the principal ten because of its inauspicious nature: death and the ancestral worships (*sraddha*) done to honor the dead. Death rather than marriage marks the final and complete separation of an offspring from its parents, and truly completes the developmental cycle of an individual. Upon death and cremation a person's physical frame is destroyed, freeing the subtle body and the soul it houses to travel to the world of the ancestors (*pitrilok*) – located above the earth in the upper regions of the atmospheric world – where it will reside until reborn at a later time in another physical body appropriate to its past actions. Souls that have led a more uplifting, meritorious life – a *sattvik* life – remain in the blissful world of the ancestors for a longer period of time. Souls that have led a more non-meritorious life – a *tamasik* life – rest among the ancestors for a shorter period of time before again experiencing the pains of rebirth and life on earth.

All souls do not go to the ancestral world, and even those that do, do not go directly. Still other cultural acts are required progressively to transform the subtle body so that it and the soul it houses can successfully pass from earth to the upper regions of the atmosphere to be reunited there with other ancestors of the descent line. Immediately after cremation the subtle body travels to the lower regions of the atmospheric world where it hovers until the first ancestral worship is performed. If no *sraddha* rite is performed, the subtle body remains in the lower atmosphere forever, perhaps occasionally visiting the earth as a malevolent spirit or ghost. When the first ancestral worship is performed, by contrast, the subtle body passes from the lower to the upper regions of the atmosphere. Then its visits to earth are usually beneficial and will occur regularly when a yearly *sraddha* is performed or when a special *sraddha* is performed on the occasion of auspicious rites like first-feeding, initiation or marriage. Before each of these life-cycle rites a special worship is performed to ask for the blessings of the ancestors, who, though now separated from their descendants on earth, remain intimately bound to them through ties of common blood.

The individual as a unit of rank

The individual as the normative subject of institutions in Hindu society is particularly evident when tracing the human developmental cycle and the behavior appropriate to individuals as they pass through a series of life stages and life-cycle rites. Also evident is a standard for the relative valuation of individuals: namely, senior persons who have more fully realized their naturally given potential and are best able to act in accord with the prescriptions of Hindu life rank above their less fully developed, less capable juniors. The local reasoning informing this standard can be summarized thus: every *jati* is defined by physical and behavioral features which all members of the birth group share in common; or more correctly, all members of the birth group share the potential to develop the same features in full. Not all do. Thus, whether they actually do or do not becomes a criterion of individual rank or situs among persons who are otherwise apparent equals in belonging to the same birth group, be it a family, a caste, or the genus Man.

For an individual to realize the full potential of the nature and code given by the circumstances of birth depends on his own life activities, including the proper performance of life-cycle rites. Each rite both helps an individual pass through a division of the human biography, and at the same time marks that passage. Individuals in the latter, more senior life stages rank above persons in the earlier, more junior stages because they have realized the greater capacity to act as mature, responsible Hindus. Age is not at issue here. Only the gradual, but progressive development of an individual's capacity to act as a responsible Hindu.

Associated with seniority are expectations of behavioral dominance. Seniors are esteemed as preceptors and guides, as *gurus*, and it is expected that they will direct the activities of their less experienced juniors. Juniors, in turn, are expected to follow the direction and example of their seniors. The behavior appropriate to individuals of different physical-cum-moral maturity, and its implications for interpersonal relations within a birth group, will be detailed in chapter 4 when discussing the politics of family life. For now, we will consider further how individuals can be ranked apart from their membership in particular birth groups.

Differences in seniority are associated with still other differences in power (*sakti*), knowledge (*jnana*), wealth (*dhana*) and respect or honor (*sanmana, maryada*). These are the personal attributes assumed to come with passage through the several life stages. They are also the specific criteria used to justify the asymmetrical relations between preceptor and disciple (*guru/sisho*), patron and client (*sardar/rayat*), a large landholder (*jotdar*) and his sharecropper (*bargadar*) or hired laborer (*mojur*), and landlord and dependent (*zamindar/praja*). The individual ranks established through personal ties, significantly, may contravene those expected on the basis of group membership alone. In Torkotala, for example, Sadgops rank above Bagra-Khatriyas. Yet in ranking by opinion male heads of households it was clear that Kagendro Dolai, a B-K, stood above Baneshor Dey, a Sadgop, thus inverting caste and individual rank.

Kagendro and Baneshor both married into Torkotala about 26 years ago. At the time neither man owned any land in his native village, and both men took up residence in the home of their wife's father. Upon the death of their fathers-in-law, Kagendro and Baneshor each became the head of his own household and assumed the management of three acres of family land. In these respects are the recent biographies of the two men similar. In other respects their biographies vary critically, for during his years in Torkotala Kagendro purchased six acres of agricultural land in his own name, began a successful business in raising goats for sale, and periodically earned additional income by making or repairing wheels for bullock carts.

Baneshor owns no land of his own, and the three acres controlled by his wife are insufficient to provide year round for a family of four. When compared with Kagendro, Baneshor is a poor man, and he is a less powerful man in the sense of having less control over his own activities and those of others. Kagendro is able to employ others to plow his fields. Baneshor must do his own plowing, and more degrading still he must work the land of others to supplement the meager yield of his own fields. In the past Baneshor supplied such service only for Sadgops of the village, but in recent years he has also plowed the fields of Kagendro Dolai, thereby contravening the general practice of higher caste persons being served by but not serving persons of lower caste. It is this asymmetrical relationship between Kagendro as landholder and Baneshor as laborer which Torkotala villagers cite to explain why an individual Bagra-Khatriya ranks above a Sadgop.

The comments of Torkotala villagers while ranking Kagendro and Baneshor and other heads of household reveal that, quite apart from ranking individuals on the basis of seniority, there is another and crosscutting system of rank which is based on considerations of individually achieved wealth and power and life style. In a peasant economy centered on rice agriculture, the primary source of wealth is agricultural land. Villagers thus distinguish initially between individuals who own some land, and are appropriately termed *chasi* or farmers, and others who are landless. In Torkotala 18 of 65 heads of Hindu households (28%) are landless and must work exclusively in the employ of others. To do so entails wide-ranging political as well as economic dependency, for there is a surplus of agricultural labor in Torkotala that makes it difficult to find any work let alone move from employer to employer because of personal differences. The landless and their families are thus not only impoverished individuals, but individuals of little power whose life style reflects the exigencies of a hand-to-mouth existence. It is the landless who live in the smallest huts, wear the coarsest clothes, and have the most meager diets. It is among the landless that women of a family work outside their own household, a practice Hindus avoid when possible in order to insulate their wives and daughters from interaction with unrelated males.

Among landholders, Torkotala villagers further distinguish between *chasi* who are rich men (*dhani lok*) and have more than enough wealth to satisfy their wants; poor men (*gorib lok*) like Baneshor Dey who do not and thus are forced to labor some of the time in the employ of others; and those like Kagendro Dolai who are among the middle class (*majhari lok*). The rich include those individuals who have enough wealth so that they and their family members can avoid all physical labor in the field, compound and home by employing others to work in their stead. It is said that there are no rich men in Torkotala today, perhaps because the rich are thought to have

Table 10. *The distribution of agricultural land in Torkotala by caste and household, 1971*

Households by caste	Size of landholdings in acres																					Households		Total land Acres % of total	
	0	1	2	3	4	5	6	7	8	9	10	11	12	13	14	15	16	17	18	19	20	No.	% of total	Acres	% of total
Brahman										1												1	2	9	3
Sadgop	2			6					2	1		2	1	2	1		1				3	21	32	188	64
Kayastha			2																			2	3	4	1
Mahisya	1																					1	2	0	0
Mahisya Boisnab		1																				1	2	1	<1
B-K Boisnab		2	2		1																	5	7	10	3
Bagra-Khatriya	9	1	1	1		2		2	3	1	1											21	32	73	25
Jogi	1	3																				4	6	3	1
Bagal	3	1		1																		5	7	4	1
Tantoby	1	1																				2	3	1	<1
Rajok		1																				1	2	1	<1
Hari	1																					1	2	0	0
Totals																						65	100	294	100

101

Table 11. *The distribution of Hindu households in Torkotala by class, 1971*

Class	Households	
	No.	% of total
Landless	18	28
Poor		
(1–7 acres)	27	41
Middle class		
(8–20 acres)	20	31
Rich	0	0
Total	65	100

Note: this table summarizes data presented in table 10.

accumulated their wealth through dubious, even dishonest, means. Also, with government enforced land ceilings of 20 acres per family, even the largest landholders are not as wealthy as men of the previous generation – Radhanath Mahabarto or Tijendro Pal, for example – who were not similarly constrained in their landholdings.

Within the middle class are counted those heads of households who are neither so wealthy as to avoid all physical labor nor so poor as to require laboring in the employ of others. They have sufficient wealth to hire laborers to do the more onerous physical tasks required in the field and compound, thus freeing themselves and their family members from such *tamasik* activity, but do need to economize by performing less onerous tasks on their own. Such persons are identified as the true *grihasthas* or householders of the village. It is upon them that the landless rely for employment. Counted within the middle class are the heads of 20 out of 65 Hindu households (31%), including the only Brahman in Torkotala, 13 out of 21 Sadgops, and 6 out of 21 Bagra-Khatriyas. In Torkotala middle-class households own from eight to twenty acres of land.

The poor include those minimal landholding individuals who cannot avoid the more onerous and demeaning physical tasks of farming or housework by employing others to work in their stead and of necessity work in the employ of others some of the time. The men of such families, for example, typically plow for themselves and for others, which is not only dirty and demanding work but involves one with the *tamasik* activity of taking the life of those animals that live in the soil. The women of such families also work on family lands during the peak labor season of harvest. It is uncommon for women of this class to work in the fields of others, which would put them under the direct supervision of an unrelated male. But it is not uncommon for them to do housework for a middle-class family under the supervision of another female. Counted among the

Torkotala poor are the heads of 27 out of 65 Hindu households (41%). They own from one to seven acres.

It is the ranking of those individuals who are heads of households, and by extension the ranking of households which share corporately the personal qualities and material resources of their head, that provides the basis for distinctions of class within a caste society. Classes can be defined, in a Marxist fashion, in terms of property relations, which would divide agriculturalists in Torkotala initially into two: the landholders and the landless who are laborers. Class divisions among landholders would then be distinguished according to differences in the size of agricultural landholdings. This Marxist scheme seemingly suits the Torkotala material, for Torkotala residents do make an initial distinction between landholding farmers and landless laborers, and do associate each class of landholders with a certain amount of agricultural land. In Torkotala the poor own from one to seven acres of agricultural land, while those households counted among the middle class own from eight to twenty acres, as noted in table 11. But for Torkotala residents an exclusive focus on property relations, even when refined by an attention to the size of agricultural landholdings, defines classes too narrowly.

Classes also can be defined, following Weber, in terms of property relations and the kind of economic services provided. This is closer to the conception of class held by Torkotala residents and allows for distinctions among Torkotala landholders according to the labor done for themselves and others. But as the discussion above suggests, local conceptions of class are multidimensional in integrating with wealth considerations of power and life style that Weber held distinct from class as a strictly economic phenomenon. For Torkotala residents the economic is not distinct and separate from other social domains. The ranking of individuals by class thus emphasizes differences in landholdings, the primary source of wealth in an agricultural economy. But it includes as well an assessment of power, for the control over land entails the control over persons, one's self and others. Differences in wealth and power, in turn, are associated with the social correlates of life style conveyed by the contrast between *bhadralok* and *chotolok*.

The term *bhadralok* came into usage among Bengalis at the beginning of the nineteenth century as a sanskritized synonym for the English term 'gentleman' and carries such connotations as cultured and restrained of manners, civilized, learned, of superior quality and cultivated taste (Sinha and Bhattacharya 1969:50). It is applied to those individuals who have sufficient wealth to be included among the middle class, plus sufficient taste and manners to live in a comfortable dwelling, to lead a relaxed, regulated, *sattvik* life, to use polished language, to wear fine clothes, to be knowing of civil manners and to be properly educated as a good Hindu and as a man of some worldly experience. Brahmans, Kayasthas and Baidyos are the *bhadralok par excellence* in Bengali society, but as inclusion in this category is defined by an achieved life style, individuals of any caste can acquire the status.

Chotolok are stereotypically landless or minimal landholders who by necessity work in the employ of others, dwell in very modest, perhaps dilapidated quarters, look lean and even malnourished, wear coarse clothing and in other ways too reflect a life of poverty. In addition, *chotolok* are stereotyped as lacking the initiative, diligence and intelligence required to improve their lot. In contrast with the *sattvik* traits of the *bhadralok*, *chotolok* are characterized by *tamasik* traits of laxity and lethargy. The term is usually reserved by Torkotala villagers for persons of the lowest castes, but it is applied as well to individuals of high caste who have not realized the full potential of their birth. Baneshor Dey, though of relatively high caste, is counted by Sadgop and non-Sadgop alike as among the village *chotolok*.

That a Bagra-Khatriya, Kagendro Dolai, is included among the Torkotala middle class, while the Sadgop Baneshor Dey is not, documents how the class rank of individuals can invert caste rank. The same point can be generalized for other Torkotala residents as well. For as indicated in table 10, it is not uncommon for persons of different castes – high and low – to belong to the same class, or for persons of the same caste to belong to different classes. When Torkotala was first founded, the caste and class of its settlers were congruent. All landholders were higher-caste Sadgops. All agricultural laborers were lower-caste Bagdis, who were landless. Such congruency no longer exists, but that caste and class continue to coexist in Torkotala today evidences that the two forms of sociation and inequality are not incompatible.

In elaborating the multiple referents of the term *jati*, it was useful to distinguish between birth groups like *varna* that are categories or conceptual aggregates of individuals who share certain attributes but are not tied to each other as interacting members of an organized social unit, and those *jati* like families and castes that are true sociological groups. The same distinction between categories and groups provides the analytic key as to why caste and class are not incompatible forms of sociation. Classes are categories, and inclusion in a conceptual aggregate need not conflict with membership in an organized, interactive group like caste. Indeed this has been the experience of Torkotala villagers. This said, it can be added that inclusion in a class may become a conscious identification and class interests may provide an orientation for collective action. When individuals of a class do organize around common economic interests, they act as a third type of social unit, an association formed along class lines. In chapter 5 discussion of the Torkotala labor dispute will document a rare instance of class competition that for some participants was conflictual because of their caste membership. But aside from the rarity when an association is formed along class lines, caste and class in Torkotala are not incompatible forms of sociation.

Caste rank is based on ascribed inequalities of birth. Class rank is based on individual achievement. Yet these two forms of inequality coexist in Torkotala without contradiction, given a transformational theory of human development. All members of a caste share by birth the same potential to develop certain features in common. But not all caste members realize that potential in full, or have realized it equally at any given time. Consistent with a transformational perspective, individuals can thus be ranked apart from their membership in a caste according to the extent to which they have developed their full human potential. To do so is to rank individuals on the basis of individual achievement, be it the physical-cum-moral maturity that comes with passage through the various life stages and life-cycle rites, or those individually achieved differences in wealth and power and life style that are the basis of class.

Summary and discussion

This chapter began by extending an earlier definition of the term *lok* to include not only the several worlds of the universe, as described in chapter 2, but also the individuals who inhabit those worlds. The double meaning of the term *lok* felicitously marks the premise that individuals are a microcosm of the universe at large. What is true of the universe, and its several worlds, is true as well of the individuals who inhabit those worlds.

It was then described how the physical-cum-moral development of individuals replicates certain processes of development that are gerneral to the universe. Individuals, like all else in the universe, originate through the union of *purusa* and *prakriti*, as symbolized in the union of male and female in sexual intercourse. Like all else in the universe, individuals also develop from the same basic substances, altered or transformed over time. Developing first are the *sattvik* aspects of being, including intellect and mind, which help individuals perceive the essential reality of the world. Only later are the *rajasik* sensory and motor functions developed. Later still are manifested the subtle and gross elements representing the *tamasik* aspect of being. In this the development of an individual parallels the development of the universe, as it was the more structured, sentient principle of *purusa* which first emanated from Brahma, followed later by the more unstructured, material principle of *prakriti*.

Prior to birth, while still within the female womb, an individual has full and perfect awareness of all past lives and of his essential identity with

Brahma. This is lost upon entry into the temporal world, and thus must be learned anew as individuals develop and mature during the course of their lives. Marking this process of gradual development are a series of life stages. Textual sources known to Torkotala villagers describe four such life stages, the four *asramas*: student, householder, recluse and renouncer. From their own life experience, Torkotala villagers speak of six life stages, popularly referred to as *bayas*: infancy, childhood, youth, young adulthood, middle-aged adulthood, and old age. Yet both textual and popular divisions of the human biography are premised on the same assumption, namely, that each life stage is defined not by age, as counted in days or months or years, but the differing capacity and responsibility of individuals for upholding the prescriptions of Hindu life as they develop physically and morally.

It is to help individuals refine, improve upon and positively transform the features of physical nature and behavioral code given them at birth that there exists among Bengali Hindus a series of rites known collectively as *samskaras*. Some of these rites are performed regularly, even daily. Others are performed irregularly and correspond to what are commonly termed life-cycle rites. All of the *samskaras* serve to mark and provide for the gradual development of an individual's physical-cum-moral capacities. In addition, they mark and provide for the gradual incorporation of individuals into the universe, society and groups which they enter naturally at birth, and from which they depart at death.

The discussion throughout this chapter suggests why, contrary to Dumont's argument, the individual is an important unit of thought and action among Bengali Hindus. As noted earlier, Dumont holds that while the individual as a thinking, acting being is present in all societies, the individual as normative subject is not, but is peculiar to modern countries of the West, with their values of equality and liberty, and thus should not be considered a universal unit of comparison. In Hindu India, Dumont holds, individual identities are submerged in the birth groups to which they belong, while individual interests are subordinated to those of society as a whole, which bears primary value. The individual, as a result, is not an important unit except in the person of the renouncer, who, paradoxically, realizes his individuality in the effort to extinguish it and merge with Brahma. Under all other circumstances it is the various birth groups to which an individual belongs, say his family, line or caste, and not the individual as such, which are the normative subject of institutions in Hindu society.

There is ample evidence of the importance of the various birth groups into which humans in Hindu society are divided. But there is also evidence that individuals retain a personal identity, pursue individual interests, and are the normative subject of institutions quite apart from their membership in particular birth groups. This is especially evident with regard to the human biography and the behavior appropriate to individuals of the several life stages; also in the manner in which an individual's defining features may be transformed by his life activities. For Bengali Hindus, if not for Dumont, individuals are knowing, responsible actors whose individual self (*atman*), radical substances (*gun*) and behavioral code (*dharma*) are the normative subject of institutions, not only in this lifetime, but also through the round of rebirths occasioned by one's own activities and the resulting *karma*.

Much the same point can be made in another way, which reflects as well on a final aspect of Dumont's argument. Dumont (1965a:91) holds that the smallest normative unit in Hindu society is that in which order or rank is present, and that an individual Hindu is not such a unit. Yet it is clear that individuals in Bengali society occupy ranked social positions that are distinct from their status as a member of a birth group. Individuals are ranked on the basis of relative seniority. And they are ranked according to differences in individually achieved wealth and power and life style that are the basis of class.

In chapter 2 a transformational theory of rank was developed in discussing how the defining features and rank of a family, line or caste can be altered for better or worse according to the life activities of its members. In this chapter the transformational perspective was extended further to include a theory of human development and to account for how individual Bengalis can be ranked according to the extent to which they realize their full potential as mature, responsible, accomplished human beings. To focus in this way on the individual as the normative subject of institutions and as a unit of rank is not to deny the overriding importance of the birth groups in which Hindus are included. But it does point to why the individual among Bengali Hindus remains an important unit of thought and action, even in group-oriented India. Still further support for this conclusion will be evidenced in the discussion of Torkotala politics, to which we now turn.

4. Gramer kaj

Des and *jati* are the two identifications by which Bengalis locate themselves in physical and social space, respectively. *Lok*, and the associated concepts of *asrama, bayas* and *samskara*, are identifications of another sort, referring to the physical-cum-moral development of an individual through time. In combination these sets of concepts pertain to the ordering of Bengalis along two planes. *Des* and *jati* pertain to the spatial plane of social and cultural organization wherein each individual and birth group occupies a place and rank in the cosmos and society according to their defining physical nature and behavioral code. *Lok* and its associated concepts pertain to the temporal plane. According to their own life activities, individuals experience a number of lifetimes in which they move towards or away from the ultimate religious quest, release from the round of rebirths in the temporal world in favor of an essential unity with Brahma. Life itself is organized in its individual and social aspects by movement along these two planes, by the movement of individuals through the ranked orders and ordered ranks of the Bengali cosmos and society.

Chapters 2 and 3 have described how the Bengali cosmos and society are ordered by a system of ranked inequalities. This and the following chapter examine how the Bengali concern with rank and the behavior appropriate to ranked social units generates a variety of political competitions, and how those competitions in turn variously maintain or alter, support or challenge, an inequalitarian social order. In both chapters the purpose is partly to detail patterns of competition in rural West Bengal today and to account for why they occur. It is also to relate individual competitions – whatever the immediate bone of contention – to an issue that is not strictly limited to the domain of politics. Namely, what is the right and proper ordering of Hindu society, now and in the future? Towards these ends, the discussion of Torkotala administration begun in chapter 1 is renewed and extended in this and chapter 5.

In highlighting the conjunction of rank and rivalry, an additional aim is to advance a holistic style of analysis that integrates the study of political

108

structure and process with an attention to that complex assemblage of shared ideas, concepts and understandings that constitute political culture. Already the discussions of *des, jati* and *lok* in the first half of this study have described in part the cultural context of Torkotala politics, especially as it is defined by those considerations of rank and inequality that also inform activity in other social domains. This and chapter 5 further the description of Torkotala political culture in detailing the ideas and understandings particular to the domain of politics.

As noted in the Introduction, Torkotala residents refer to politics as *sason*, or rule, and then distinguish between two forms of rule: village politics (*gramer kaj*) and government politics (*sorkari kaj*). Government politics refers ultimately to the activities of the central government in New Delhi, but also to its more immediate extensions in the West Bengal capital of Calcutta, the district headquarters town of Midnapore, and Narayanghar Town, the local site of many district-level offices. It refers as well to the activities of government officers and agents who work in the most localized administrative units of the state and nation, villages like Torkotala. According to their goal orientation, non-government personnel, like political party workers, are also referred to as doing the work of the government. But whatever the specific reference, government politics is identified by Torkotala residents with policies and programs that originate outside of Torkotala and yet aim to alter life within the village. Government politics is in that sense innovative. It aims to level, if not completely eliminate, the existent system of inequalities supported by Hinduism in favor of a polity, society and view of the cosmos ordered on the premise of equality. This goal is defined in relation to the Indian constitution and legal system, which also establish politics and religion as formally separate domains in a secular India.

An extended discussion of government politics is presented in chapter 5. This chapter focuses first on *gramer kaj*, the work (*kaj*) of the village (*gram*), or village politics. The distinctive contrast between these two forms of rule is not the structure of political teams, the personnel involved, or even the processual events by which competition is waged, though differences in these regards do exist. The contrast rests instead on the culturally defined goal of political acts. Both village politics and government politics are identified behaviorally with rivalries over rank. Only in the context of village politics, the many family, caste and factional competitions aim to uphold and protect a polity, society and view of the cosmos ordered on the premise of inequality. This goal is defined in relation to the religious framework of Hinduism, which posits the natural and moral order of society as divinely given and thus beyond the agency of human change.

This and chapter 5 begin with a discussion of the premises which constitute the theme of village politics and government politics. Then the interaction between theme and events is examined through a documentary analysis of various competitions. This is the same procedure as was used without explication in chapters 2 and 3 to explore how the premise of ranked inequalities is evident socially in patterns of marriage, diet, food exchange, work and ritual performance. It is formalized here to clarify how politics also can be studied as a form of symbolic action, As noted in the Introduction, in fitting theme to events there is no assumption that either systems of meaning or action are primary in some determinative sense. The attempt is only to integrate social, structural and cultural analyses by taking into account both what actors do and what actors say as explanation for why they do what they do. To proceed in this way is also to illustrate by example how politics can be studied as two-dimensional: as singular, instrumental acts and as embodiments or paradigmatic examples of a system of meaning which informs a number of different, ostensibly unrelated acts occurring at discontinuous points in time.

Polity, society and cosmos

In the epic Mahabarta, as in the Dharmasastras, the Hindu universe is described as passing through an interminable series of long cycles, each consisting of four ages (*yuga*), and as now being in a phase of decline, the Kali Yuga. In the three earlier ages *dharma* was upheld to a greater extent. Both individuals and birth groups acted in greater accord with their behavioral codes, thereby earning merit and at the same time maintaining the divinely given natural and moral orders of the cosmos and society. Indeed, in the Golden Age *dharma* walked on four legs, meaning that behavioral codes were upheld in their entirety, while in the succeeding Silver and Bronze Ages *dharma* walked on three and two legs, respectively. In the present Iron Age or Kali Yuga *dharma* hobbles along on only one leg. Increasingly people act in disaccord with their behavioral codes, and increasingly the natural and moral orders of society are disrupted. It is written that as the Kali Yuga progresses there will be a continued dissolution of *dharma* resulting, finally, in a world of anarchy where people act not in accord with natural and moral laws, but out of narrow self-interest. Then the 'law of the fish' will prevail. Just as in every pond big fish eat little fish, so in every *des* strong men will dominate and exploit weak men. With what result? With the eventual dissolution of the known universe, thereby completing a cycle of four ages, and the subsequent creation of another universe in which *dharma* is once again maintained in its entirety.

It was to uphold *dharma* and to prevent anarchy that kings and the institutions of rule are said to have first appeared in Hindu society. During the first three ages the presence of a king and institutions of rule were unnecessary. Men upheld *dharma* of their own accord. But when this was no longer so in the Kali Yuga there appeared kings enjoined to maintain and uphold the natural and moral order established by Brahma for the good of all. This injunction was itself a *dharma*; the *dharma* appropriate to kings. It consists in part of protecting a given territory and people, a *des*, the kingdom, from external threats to life, property and customary practice. It consists in part of protecting the kingdom from similar threats originating from within. But above all it consists of protecting and maintaining *dharma*, for if *dharma* is upheld all other conditions for the material prosperity and moral development of a people will perforce also be present. Thus is a Hindu king, charged with ruling over the worldly affairs of men, also an agent of moral growth and liberation. Through rule which[7] maintains and upholds *dharma* a king secures the material and social conditions conducive to the moral development of all within the realm. In doing so the king also forwards his own moral development, for in the exercise of royal power and the judicious use of force and punishment he acts in accordance with his own behavioral code. The moral growth and liberation of the ruler and the ruled are thereby linked, for both depend on upholding the natural and moral orders of the cosmos and society through activities which are themselves in accord with those orders.

Torkotala Hindus do not claim to know precisely when kings first appeared among men. But consistent with textural sources read within the village, including the Manu Dharmasastra and popularizations of the Mahabarata, the appearance of kings and institutions of rule among Hindus is attributed to the failure of individuals and birth groups to uphold *dharma* on their own. Neither kings nor institutions of rule, as a[7] result, are viewed by Torkotala Hindus as entirely desirable. Yet they are recognized as entirely necessary, at least in the Kali Yuga. Simply, kings maintain *dharma*, prevent anarchy, forestall the 'law of the fish,' where ordinary persons cannot. Consistent with this view, many of the Bengali terms for politics refer to the activities or powers of kings, or more generally, to the practice of rule: *rajadharma*, the dharma of kings (*raja*); *rajasastra*, the science or practice (*sastra*) of kings; *ksatra-vidya*, the exercise (*vidya*) of royal (*ksatra*) power; and *rajniti*, the customs (*niti*) of rule, are all examples.

All of these terms are known to Torkotala villagers, but none are used commonly. In their stead Torkotala villagers use the general term *sason*, or rule, which better reflects their understanding of the nature and aim of politics. Village politics represents a particular model of proper rule or administration. To elaborate the consciously held premises of that model is also to define the theme of village politics.

Politics is the administration of dharma
The Bengali polity, society and cosmos are not considered the product of a haphazard, fortuitous concourse of elements; all are organized in accord with a common set of natural and moral laws, *dharma*. Further, the natural and moral order common to polity, society and cosmos is viewed as an objective, divinely given one inherent in the material nature of the universe. It is not for persons to change this order, but to understand, guard and protect it. Thus when kings first appeared they acted as regents and executors of *dharma*, not as innovators or legislators of a new universal order. Their task was to maintain and uphold the given orders of the cosmos and society, *dharma* writ large, by maintaining the specific behavioral codes, *dharma* writ small, appropriate to ranked individuals and birth groups. It is this protective function of rule which Torkotala villagers emphasize in saying politics aims at the administration of *dharma*.

Politics is (ideally) moral activity
From the first premise follows a second, that the means to a moral end – the administration of *dharma* – should themselves be moral. Torkotala villagers recognize that political activity is at times guided by pragmatic evaluations of relative effectiveness quite apart from normative considerations of right or wrong, but ideally political acts aimed at the administration of *dharma* should themselves be guided by *dharma*.

Politics is the shared responsibility of all
Kshatriyas and Vaisyas are not held indigenous to contemporary Bengali society. Torkotala villagers nevertheless regard the king – whatever his actual *varna* – as Kshatriya-like, and look upon him as the exemplary political figure. It is the king who is enjoined as part of his behavioral code to exercise royal power (*ksatra*) and to use force and punishment (*danda*) in exercising that power. Yet politics is not held the sole responsibility of kings, or named officials, or of exceptional individuals; nor is it the sole responsibility of specific birth groups, like the Kshatriya *varna*, nor, in the Torkotala context, of the dominant Sadgop caste. Rather, Torkotala villagers hold that the work of administering the village through moral activity in accord with *dharma* is the shared responsibility of all within the village.

Chapter 1 described how each of the physical divisions of Torkotala village, like those in the wider Narayanghar kingdom and Midnapore district, are also social divisions, so that compounds are identified with the families who occupy them, neighborhoods with lineages, hamlets with Hindu castes or the tribal Lodhas or Mundas (but not a mixture of these groups), and the village with all persons who accept the authority of the traditional headman, the *Mukhya*. To this can be added that each of these physical-cum-social divisions of the village is also viewed locally as an administrative division. Each has a recognized head and each head is charged with overall responsibility for upholding the *dharma* appropriate to his administrative unit. Each head replicates the function of a king, as it were, within a more limited realm. The same is true of individuals. Each individual is his own king and rules over himself, in the sense of bearing responsibility for adhering to his personal code for conduct (*svadharma*). Individuals and groupings of individuals at every level of social organization are thus seen as replicating royal functions, as being single or collective political actors, each concerned with the common aim of maintaining and upholding *dharma*.

Politics is subordinated to and inseparable from dharma
Politics is subordinated to and inseparable from *dharma* in the sense that it takes its ultimate ground of authority, its definition of goals, and its definition of moral means towards those goals, from this concept. Specifically, politics aims to uphold the natural and moral orders of the Bengali cosmos and society by upholding the behavior appropriate to ranked individuals and birth groups. The means towards this end should themselves be in accord with *dharma*.

This underscores the lack of native boundary between politics and religion. It also points to the limitation of identifying politics in Hindu society solely with the pursuit of *artha*, or worldly gain. Like marriage, diet, food exchanges, work and ritual performance, politics is itself a form of symbolic action which reflects and realizes the natural and moral order of society. Politics is also integrated within the broad goals of life common to all Hindus. That is, *dharma* is held to regulate the pursuit of other goals. Both worldly gain (*artha*) and sensual, including sexual, pleasure (*kama*) are recognized as necessary to life – no one can live without acquiring some goods and without enjoying those goods to some extent – but these pursuits are best controlled by considerations of *dharma*, and must themselves contribute to the administration of *dharma*. How is this possible?

Artha literally refers to 'thing, object, substance,' and applies to the whole range of tangible objects that can be possessed, enjoyed and lost, and which are required in daily life for the upkeep of a household, the raising of a family, and the discharge of religious duties. *Artha*, in brief, refers to the material goods or wealth required for the virtuous fulfilment of life's obligations, *dharma*. Sponsoring worships, whether as the ruler of a kingdom, or the head of a household, requires a certain measure of wealth. So does the fulfilment of obligations to preceptors, ancestors, family members, other men, and to one's self. *Artha* is valued as providing the necessary means for all of these acts, for providing the means to maintain *dharma*. In addition, as the second of four goals of life common to all Hindus, *artha* has a certain value in and of itself. But that value is always subordinated to the value placed on upholding *dharma*. Similarly with *kama*. Learning, aesthetic sensibilities and sexual involvements have a certain value in themselves, but their pursuit is always to be regulated by considerations of *dharma* and then *artha*. To marry and bear offspring especially sons, for example, is recognized as pleasurable in itself. But these acts are transvalued because householders are the major economic supporters of persons in the three other life stages, as well as the primary sponsors of worships, and because sons provide for the continuance of the descent line and the future worship of ancestors. In all of these ways is a pleasurable act also an act which contributes to the maintenance of *dharma*, even while being informed by *dharma*. *Mukti*, the fourth goal of Hindu life, aims at entirely freeing an individual from temporal concerns and life on earth. Yet it too can only be attained through activity in accord with *dharma*.

These four premises constitute the theme of village politics. Consider now how this theme fits a variety of ostensibly unrelated competitions all identified locally as instances of village politics. The politics of family life, the politics of caste, and factional politics will each be discussed in turn.

The politics of family life: *matabbori*

Studies of the Hindu family often include a description of the interpersonal relations among family members – what Dube (1955) terms the 'web of family ties' – and some even detail the strains between specific family members (see Sarma 1951; Srinivas 1952; Dube 1955; Gough 1956; Mayer 1960; Ross 1961; Madan 1965; Mandelbaum 1970). From these accounts it is evident that competitions within the Hindu family are not unusual features of life in rural India, at least not in any statistical sense. But as yet there is no account that relates competitions between specific dyads of the family to each other, and all to a generative model that suggests when and why interpersonal competitions within the family will recur in predictable fashion. In addressing such questions, the evidence from Torkotala is used here to document how individual competitions between family members – for all their singularity – are systematically related to the Hindu concern with ranked inequalities.

The Bengali family is defined culturally in terms of its male head, the husband/father, and consists of his wife, their unmarried daughters, and their sons, whether married or not. During his lifetime the male head of household (referred to as *malik*, chief, or *korta*, doer) is the symbol of family unity and in principle exercises mastery and authority (*adhikara* over all affairs of the family; internally with regard to the interactions between family members, and externally as spokesman for the family in all public affairs. The male head is also primarily responsible for maintaining the behavioral code appropriate to the family as a whole and to its individual members. Thus he is compared to a king, who is similarly charged with maintaining *dharma* within his realm. Like a king, the male head of household is held the regent of family customs and practices and the chief arbiter and final judicial authority within his unit of social organization. Like a king, the male head of household is also held responsible for securing those conditions which allow for the material prosperity and moral development of all within his charge.

This homology between the head of a household and the head of a kingdom can be extended still further. Both the family and the kingdom are defined culturally with respect to their male heads, and are said to terminate upon his death or permanent departure. Simply, there can be no family without a male head of household, and there can be no kingdom without a king. In each case is the male head considered the active, responsible agent on whom the existence and well-being of the entire social unit depends, both materially and morally. Further, a king is often described as the parent (*ma-bap*; literally, mother and father) of his people, while all persons within the kingdom are termed his offspring (*praja*). *Praja* is also used to describe the offspring of a family, while the male head of household is said to rule like a king. Both exercise *adhikara*. And both are said, in the local idiom, to lord it over (*prabhutra kora*) others.

There can only be one king in a kingdom and only one male head in a household. But the ambition to be a king, or to be the male head of a household, or at least to act as if one were, is not limited in the same way. Indeed, it is this ambition to rule over others, resulting in myriad interpersonal competitions, which Torkotala villagers identify as the generalized source and content of the politics of family life. Even more specifically, the politics of family life is identified with interpersonal competitions as to who will exercise mastery and authority over the other, who will lord it over the other, who, in short, will be recognized as head, leader, chief – as boss (*matabbor*).

Within the family seniors rank over their juniors, who are thought far less knowledgeable, experienced and able in the day-to-day affairs of social life. Males rank over females for the same reason, in addition to the general dependency of women and the more highly valued social contributions of men in this patrilineal society. Associated with distinctions of rank, significantly, are also expectations of behavioral dominance. Persons of higher rank, that is, are esteemed as preceptors and guides, and it is expected that they will direct the activities of persons of lower rank. Persons of lower rank, in turn, are expected to follow the directions and example of those who rank above them. Who directs whom is thus interpreted locally as a demonstration of rank and behavioral dominance.

When persons of higher rank justly merit the status of preceptor and guide, interpersonal competitions within the family are not anticipated and indeed rarely occur. Distinctions of rank go unchallenged, and for a person of higher rank than another to judiciously direct the activities of the latter will more often engender respect than ill-will, compliance rather than competition. When the expected association between rank and behavioral dominance is unsupported by the realities of daily life, so that one's senior is not more knowledgeable or able, then interpersonal competitions within the family are anticipated and do occur most often. Distinctions of rank are challenged, and for one person to direct the activities of another will more often engender ill-will than respect, competition rather than compliance. The pattern of such competitions is described below; afterwards an explanation of the processes which generate that pattern will be suggested.

'Bhai-bhai jhogra'

Bhai-bhai jhogra refers to that form of rivalry (*jhogra*) which is common, even anticipated, between brothers (*bhai*). Torkotala villagers expect that brothers will be close, intimate friends and supporters in all that they do throughout their lives. This is consistent with the ethic of shared responsibility and gain, or loss, that defines the family as a single social unit. It is also the ideal social relationship towards which brothers are expected to strive.

While young, brothers may approximate to this ideal behavior. If young brothers occupy the same life stage, for example, friendship, intimacy and sharing is evidenced in being constant playmates and companions, in wearing the same clothes, in possessing toys or games or secrets in common, in leading the same regime of eating, bathing and sleeping, and so on. If brothers occupy different life stages the same friendship, intimacy and sharing is evident in the elder brother looking after and instructing his younger brother much as a father does his son.

It is as the brothers mature, and especially after the younger brother marries and enters the life stage of young adulthood that fraternal amity usually wanes and fraternal rivalries, though unwelcomed and regarded as undesirable, occur increasingly. The specific bones of contention which spark fraternal rivalries vary, of course. But as Torkotala villagers perceive them fraternal rivalries occur most often when the younger brother begins to chafe at and question his elder brother as senior, and especially his perceived disadvantage as junior. 'Why must I always do (*kora*) and not cause to do (*koran*)?' is a frequent expression of this plaint.

While their father remains alive and active as the head of household, whatever rivalries may exist between brothers will usually remain muted under his unquestioned authority and firm disciplinary hand. Brothers may harbor ill-will for each other, but the active presence of their father, and the threat of his strong sanction if the behavioral code expected of brothers is violated, is usually enough to inhibit any overt rivalry between them. It is when this clear line of leadership and authority breaks down upon the death or permanent departure of the father that fraternal rivalries tend to surface openly, or where none existed, to be first engendered. This was the case in the relationship between Khudi and Satya Dolai.

Khudi and Satya Dolai are brothers, approximately 60 and 55 years of age respectively (in 1971). When their father died, about 35 years ago, the brothers were living in the same household with their mother and their wives as a single family unit. Neither brother had any children as yet. Both Khudi and Satya, like other men of the Bagdi caste, worked as agricultural laborers for Sadgop landholders of the village. What income they earned in this way was pooled in a common purse which the brothers vowed in the presence of their mother to use for their mutual support and benefit. In the presence of their mother, the brothers also vowed to use their pooled income 'as if of one mind.'

Within three months of his father's death, Satya decided to work alongside an outsider to the village as a carpenter's assistant. An argument (*jukti*) ensued over this decision between him and Khudi. Khudi's position was that carpentry would take Satya outside the village and away from his agricultural work. Carpentry was also something that no one of the Bagdi caste had done before so there was no way of knowing how others in the village, especially the Sadgops, would react, though Khudi expected the worst. It was his opinion that Satya should give up the idea. Satya argued that the income earned as a carpenter's assistant was greater than, and thus preferable to, that earned as an agricultural laborer. Carpentry was also preferable work because a carpenter is not bossed like a field laborer. Further, Satya saw no conflict between his work as a carpenter's assistant and his work as an agricultural laborer. He could do both, he thought, because carpentry is seasonal work done when people are not busy in the fields.

Satya worked as a carpenter for some months when another argument arose as to how the income earned in this way should be spent. At first Satya spent his income procuring needed tools. But then he began to buy clothes and other niceties for himself and his wife. Khudi objected, reminding him of their vow to pool all income and to use that income as if of one mind. 'Only the shrimp swims backwards,' Khudi scolded, reminding Satya that one who goes back on his word is as small and insignificant as a shrimp. Satya was eventually persuaded to repeat his vow, again in the presence of their mother, but this time also witnessed by certain other Bagdis. In front of their mother and caste fellows Khudi and Satya also publicly stated that the brothers would use Satya's new carpentry skills and some of the income earned through those skills to build another room onto the family house. Additional space was needed as children were expected soon.

It was towards the end of the first year after their father's death that the seeds of rivalry were planted. Others in the village began to refer to Khudi, the elder brother, as *malik*, or male head of household. It was to Khudi that notice of village meetings was sent, and it was from Khudi that villagers enquired about agricultural work the brothers would do in tandem. Khudi also began to act the role of *malik*, taking it upon himself to direct Satya's work activities in ways that he had never done before. This annoyed Satya and one day, when Khudi directed him to finish plowing a field while he sat in the shade of a tree, a shouting match erupted. Initiated by Satya, soon both brothers were shouting verbal abuse (*gala gali*) at each other. This ended only when Satya walked away from the field saying that he and Khudi were no longer brothers, meaning they no longer acted like brothers.

For the rest of that rice-growing season Satya refused to work alongside Khudi in order to avoid having to take orders from him. Instead, Satya arranged to work on his own for different Sadgop families. The brothers continued to live in the same house and to eat at the same time, but they hardly spoke to one another. This persisted for several months until, under the pressure of jointly harvesting their own small rice crop, they decided to make a public announcement to all villagers (though the announcement was actually heard by some Bagdi caste fellows only) to the effect that Khudi and Satya had the best possible relationship between brothers; they were friends and partners. It was also announced, much as a dictum, that villagers should not speak of one brother as having more honor than the other, or of one brother being *malik*. In their family, Khudi and Satya stated, there was no head of household aside from their father, now dead. With these statements the rivalry between Khudi and Satya Dolai was resolved.

Not all fraternal rivalries are resolved so amicably, or resolved at all, which is why, perhaps, this particular rivalry is often recalled by Torkotala villagers, including Khudi and Satya Dolai, to explain the common root of all fraternal rivalries. Namely, whenever one brother dominates over another there is potential rivalry. When brothers are widely separated in experience and knowledge, so that the cultural valuation placed on seniors over juniors is supported by the sociological reality, the potential for rivalry may never eventuate in something like the shouting match between Khudi and Satya, for then the differences in rank seem warranted. But when brothers are closely matched in experience and knowledge, so that the cultural valuation placed on seniority is unsupported by the events of daily life, then the widespread ambition of family members to be boss, in combination with a sensitivity to being bossed, is likely to eventuate in fraternal rivalry. In this light the content of the pronouncements by Khudi and Satya are particularly interesting. They explicitly state that there is no living head of household in their family, that neither brother should be referred to as *malik*, and that the brothers are of the same honor, that is, rank. In doing so they seek to resolve their rivalry by denying the commonly understood cause of rivalry: distinctions of rank. The language of claims by which Satya justified his verbal abuse of Khudi is also significant. In pulling rank and acting like a boss Khudi was not acting as a brother should, Satya said. Brothers should be friends and partners. It was to correct this transgression of the behavioral code between brothers, and thereby uphold *dharma*, that Satya claimed the moral right to precipitate a rivalry with Khudi.

Fraternal rivalries are common, even anticipated, among Bengalis because of the strain between the cultural premise that seniors rank above their juniors, and another that enjoins brothers to act as intimates and partners. Fraternal rivalries also occur because the younger brother to such a competition usually has little to lose and much to gain. Like Khudi and Satya, the brothers may find an amicable resolution to their rivalry, thereby reaffirming and renewing their fraternal amity. Failing that the two brothers can decide to establish separate households, in which case the younger brother immediately realizes his ambition of becoming head of his own household. Far more fraternal rivalries are 'resolved' in this manner than by a reaffirmation and renewal of fraternal amity. The rivalry between Atul Mahabarto and Pulin Mahabarto provides a case in point. It also highlights the material interests which commonly spark fraternal rivalries.

Atul and Pulin are brothers, ages 48 and 37 respectively (in 1971). After their father, Guru Prasad Mahabarto, died about ten years ago, the brothers continued to live together with their wives and children in a single household as one large family unit. Atul had five children; Pulin three. The brothers and their families lived together for less than one year before the decision was made to partition all ancestral lands and property and to establish separate households.

While Guru Prasad lived he made all decisions regarding when to plant the rice crop, what kinds of seed to use, when the young seedlings should be weeded and what kinds of fertilizer should be applied, when the crop should be harvested, how much of the paddy should be sold for cash, how much retained for family consumption, and so on. These decisions were most often communicated to Atul, the eldest son, along with instructions as to which laborers to hire, how much to pay them, and so on. Atul, with the help of Pulin, would then see to implementing his father's directions.

Usually the brothers worked in tandem, both brothers supervising the laborers in the field, for example, or both brothers driving the rice to market in a bullock cart. Occasionally Atul delegated work to Pulin. In this way there was established a chain of command from father to eldest son to younger brother.

During the first rice-planting season after the death of their father, Atul and Pulin disagreed on how the family rice lands, about 40 acres in all, should be planted. Atul wanted to plant the rice seeds broadcast as Guru Prasad had always done. (Using this method the rice seeds are scattered by hand over prepared soil and then plowed under.) To Atul's surprise, Pulin suggested that they plant their rice in a nursery bed until ready for transplanting by hand in prepared soil to form straight rows and columns. This method required more labor, and thus greater initial expense, but promised a higher yield per acre than rice grown by the broadcast method. Harsh words passed between the brothers on this issue. Atul rejected using the transplant method because even though recommended by the local agricultural extension agents, few in Torkotala had any experience of planting rice this way. As a new method, it was for Atul also a suspect method. Pulin forced his hand, though, with the threat of demanding a formal partition of all ancestral lands if at least some rice was not grown by the transplant method he favored.

A compromise was reached when Atul and Pulin agreed to broadcast rice seeds on those paddy fields lying furthest from the family compound and a secure source of irrigation water, while planting fields nearer to the family compound and a deep pond that never ran dry by the transplant method. This allowed the brothers to keep a watchful eye on those fields in which they invested greater labor and expense, while also ensuring a ready source of water if the monsoon rains failed, or were late. (Rice seedlings are best transplanted in water-soaked fields and the task cannot be postponed once the seedlings have reached a certain growth.)

After the rice was harvested and the work of turning paddy into eatable rice begun, another rivalry was sparked between the brothers because of words passed between their respective wives. Pulin's wife complained that she, the junior wife, was being given more than her fair share of work to do by Atul's wife, who bossed others while herself remaining idle. Pulin's wife also accused Atul's wife of hoarding a disproportionate amount of rice for her own husband and children, and – playing on the premise that village politics is the shared responsibility of all – spread gossip (*baje khobor*; spoiled news) to other women of the village about the impropriety of such behavior. She also complained to other women of the village about the inequity of sharing rice with a woman who had five children when she had only three. If their husbands did equal work, Pulin's wife petitioned, why should Atul's wife receive a larger share of the product? Pulin soon took up the same plaint and spread a rumor (*uro khobor*; flying news) that Atul was making large profits by selling hoarded rice to shopkeepers in Narayanghar Town. Upon learning of this, Atul walked up to Pulin one morning and said, 'Our friendship is broken; a rivalry has been struck.'

The strained relationship between them and their wives convinced Atul and Pulin that their own differences could not be settled amicably, at least not for long. Therefore it was prudent for the brothers to effect a formal partition of their patrimony. Each brother would receive about 20 acres of farm land, other household effects would also be divided equally, and the brothers would establish separate households. This decision to partition their patrimony and to establish separate, entirely independent households went against the injunction that brothers should live and share together as friends and partners throughout their lives. But such decisions are the most frequent result of fraternal rivalries.

'Where it is brother/brother, there it becomes place/place.' As this Bengali proverb insinuates, the mutual friendship and intimacy of brothers is seldom of long duration. Out of 65 Hindu households in Torkotala in 1971, only 3 (5%) of a possible 13 households (20%) included brothers living together with their wives and children as a single family unit. Of the remaining 62 households, 23 (37%) had male heads who never had this opportunity, either for lack of brothers, or because brothers had died or permanently left home before the death of their father. In another 38 households (61%), the male head had once lived with a brother as part of a single family unit, but no longer did so. Of these, in only 7 cases did this separation result from the natural cause of a brother's death. In the remaining 31 cases (82%) the single family unit reportedly was dissolved over fraternal rivalries, though some of these fraternal rivalries, like that between Atul and Pulin, were probaby aggravated by competitions between other family members.

Why should the incidence of brothers living together as a single family unit be so low when the value placed on fraternal solidarity is so high? Put another way, why should fraternal rivalries result so frequently in the dissolution of joint family units in favor of separate, independent households?

The strain between the cultural valuation placed on seniors ranking over their juniors, and the ethic of shared responsibility and gain between brothers, has already been cited. It has also been noted that a younger brother hardly stands to lose from a formal partition of ancestral property, for through partition he realizes the ambition of becoming head of his own household. In addition, the low incidence of brothers living, or continuing to live, as a single family unit, as well as the timing of the dissolution of single family units, is related to material interests governed by the customary pattern of inheritance and succession to property in Bengali society.

Inheritance and succession to property in West Bengal is formally regulated by codified law upheld by the judicial courts of the state and nation. Yet the actual inheritance and succession to property, as well as the pattern of partitioning ancestral estates, in rural West Bengal continues to follow an older pattern of customary law known locally as Dayabhaga. It is this Dayabhaga law, referring to the division or partition (*bhaga*) of property (*daya*), that operates *de facto* if not *de jure* in Torkotala village, and so will be discussed here. It must be noted, however, that if co-sharers of an inheritance are not satisfied with the way ancestral property is divided in accord with local customary law they always have recourse to the system of state-supported judicial courts and their brand of law. This recourse is taken by Torkotala villagers infrequently, and when taken may be pejoratively labeled by third parties as an instance of *sorkari kaj*, or government politics. But the recourse does exist, and the possibility that a slighted heir may appeal to the law courts of the state operates to ensure that brothers do, in fact, divide their ancestral property as fairly as possible under the provisions of customary law.

Under Dayabhaga law the father has sole rights over all ancestral property, whether immovable property such as land, or movable property such as livestock and household effects. He can dispose of this property during his lifetime, allotting it according to will, but this is his decision alone and he cannot, in principle, be forced by his wife, sons or daughters.

Upon his death, the father's property should succeed in equal shares to the surviving sons. Sons have no claim on ancestral property as a right of birth, as in those parts of India governed by Mitaksara customary law. Their claim exists as a right of survival only. Women, whether as daughters, wives or widows, have no similar claim to ancestral property; only the right of maintenance, which in practice usually depends on their continued residence in the family household. Thus daughters, upon their marriage, come under the protection and maintenance of their husbands, even while retaining the right to return later to their natal household. A widow who leaves her husband's village for her natal village in effect renounces the right to benefit from her husband's property.

It is because a son's claim on ancestral property exists as a right of survival, and not as a right of birth, that the partition of family lands in Bengali society usually follows rather than precedes the death of the father. In none of the 65 Hindu households in Torkotala were family lands partitioned, nor did brothers establish separate households, before the death of their father. Fraternal rivalries are timed, as it were, to the possibility of partitioning ancestral property.

When partitions do occur, they are themselves often the cause of additional fraternal rivalries because what constitutes an equal share of the patrimony is not always beyond dispute. Consider again the rivalry between Atul and Pulin Mahabarto, this time after the decision formally to partition their patrimony.

Within a year after their father died, Atul and Pulin decided to partition all of the farm lands, about 40 acres, as well as all household effects and livestock. It was also decided to partition their physical household, using dividers of woven thatch, until new and separate homes could be built for each brother and his family. These new homes would be located in a vacant part of the family compound, with soil for the mud walls being obtained by digging deeper into the present pond, which always ran dry in the rain-free winter months.

Work on the new buildings began soon after the decision to partition. Eight acres of rice land were sold to gather ready cash for building materials and labor expenses. Additional cash was available from the savings left by Guru Prasad. Work proceeded apace through the dry winter months until the rains began, when it was suspended. It was during the rainy season that Atul and Pulin decided to economize by joining their separate homes with a common dividing wall. This would save labor costs and the expense of additional materials. But as the common wall would be built without a door or passageway it would not alter the original plan for each brother to have an entirely separate, self-contained home. As part of the decision to build separate homes with a common dividing wall, it was also agreed that Atul and his family would occupy the house which fronted southwards towards the main village road, while Pulin and his family occupied the house facing northwards, away from the main road, opening onto the pond being dug as earth was removed to build the new homes.

The new homes were completed during the second winter building season. Afterwards Atul went to the government land office to formally register a deed recording the partition of family lands between him and Pulin. Atul took this task upon himself as the elder brother, the presumed head of household in the absence of Guru Prasad. Pulin did not question Atul's right to do this, and did not accompany him to the registry office, assuming that the remaining 32 acres of farm land would be divided between the brothers equally. Even in competition it was expected that Atul would act in accord with customary law. In fact, Atul wrote the deed so that he received 20 acres of land, leaving Pulin with only 12 acres. Upon learning of this, Pulin was enraged, confronted Atul with verbal abuse (*gala gali*) and took to beating him (*mara mara kora*) with his fists. An open quarrel (*bibad*) had been struck.

Fellow Sadgops recall that Atul once justified his claiming 20 acres to Pulin's 12 because as the elder brother it was primarily his responsibility, and his expense, to provide for yearly ancestral worships and to support a widow of the line, Amodini. The extra land was claimed to offset the extra expense. Nowadays Atul and Pulin no longer publicly discuss the unequal partition of their patrimony. By 1971 the brothers had resolved whatever differences once separated them – 'now we are truly brothers,' says Pulin – and lament the fact that they once decided to establish separate households. Other Torkotala residents do discuss this past rivalry, though, recalling it as an object lesson. Namely, politics is ideally moral activity, but it is often difficult to follow what all recognize as a just and moral practice: that brothers inherit ancestral property equally.

Villagers regard the partition between Atul and Pulin as unequal from the start because it is preferable that one's house face southwards, where the winter winds are milder, and where it will open onto the main village road. To occupy the side of the house facing northwards is less desirable because of the cold winter winds, and because it means occupying the back part of the structure. The back part of any structure is less desirable than the front part. If the doors of both homes faced southwards, frontwards, villagers reason that the two homes still would not be equally desirable. The home standing on the right side of the other as a visitor approached from the main road would have the better location, for the right side of a physical structure, like the right side of the human body, is valued above the left side. Carrying this reasoning still further, it is held that even if the two homes were freestanding, with no common wall between them, they would not be equally desirable, because they would be differently located in the family compound, and no two locations are without important differences. The same can be said of rice lands. Even if Atul and Pulin did divide the 32 acres evenly, 16 acres each, one of the brothers could always claim he was slighted by receiving the less fertile, or less well watered, or less conveniently located acreage.

The point to draw from this kind of argumentation is that no two persons, objects, locations, or anything else, are ever entirely identical, and thus are never valued in exactly equal measure. If brothers have a mind to, as a consequence, they can always find cause to argue, rival or quarrel over inequalities. To do so is to engage in the politics of family life: *matabbori*.

'Bon-bon jhogra'

Like rivalries between brothers, rivalries between sisters (*bon*) recur predictably among Torkotala villagers.

There is no expectation that sisters, like brothers, will live and share together as a single family unit throughout their lives. After marriage sisters generally leave their natal home and village to live in the home and village of their respective husbands. Residence in Bengali society is usually virilocal. For the daughter of a village to be married to a son of the village, though not proscribed, is an infrequent occurrence. For sisters to be married into the same village is also exceptional. Given these patterns of marriage and residence, married sisters tend to live at a distance from one another. Separate and distant residences do not preclude sororal rivalries, however. Indeed, it is after their respective marriages that rivalries between sisters occur most often.

While unmarried and still living in the home of their parents sisters generally share a common style of life, follow the same routine of work and play, have similar diets, wardrobes, ornaments, and have much the same opportunities for study and travel. Minor differences exist, of course, according to the life stage and individual propensities of each sister. But the material circumstances of their lives are essentially similar. And much like young brothers, young sisters of the same life stage tend to be close friends and companions, while a senior sister will often look after her junior sister with all the protective custody of a mother.

Marriage markedly disrupts this relationship between sisters, for upon marriage in Bengali society a female changes more than her residence. The new wife is identified with and incorporated into the birth groupings of her husband, and comes to share the living circumstances of her husband and his family as well. It is when sisters compare their new social identities and living circumstances that sororal rivalries may be sparked, for the circumstances and rank of the family each sister enters upon marriage will invariably differ, and any difference becomes a ready basis for invidious comparison. Comparisons are commonly made, for example, between the wealth of the two families into which sisters have married, as this points to the relative comfort and ease in which the sisters will live. Also compared are the personal qualities of each sister's husband. Is he educated or illiterate, mild-mannered or temperamental, healthy, strong, handsome, sound of body, etc? If the husband of one sister becomes the head of his own household, the second sister may feel an unjust inequality in having to continue living under the authority of her husband's father and his wife. This is so because a wife's rank in the household is defined largely in terms of her husband's rank. A similar logic informs a sister's boast that her life circumstances are better because she married the eldest son of the family while her sister married the youngest son. To be under the mastery and authority of an elder brother's wife is held an even worse fate than having to accept direction from a husband's mother. Then, too, sisters compare themselves in their status as mothers. If one of the sisters bears children while the other does not, or if one of the sister bears male children while the other only has female children, this too can become a basis of inequality and likely rivalry.

As in fraternal rivalries, inequalities and the concern with rank are the generalized source and content of sororal rivalries. Where sororal rivalries differ is in the manner in which they are pursued. Unlike brothers who ideally live together throughout their lives and come to share common property, sisters live apart from each other after marriage and usually hold no property in common. Their rivalries, as a result, are less about material interests or bossing each other directly, than the more intangible property of honor and name or reputation. News (*khobor*), rumor (*uro khobor*: flying news), gossip (*baje khobor*: spoiled news), stories (*golpo*: created news or fiction), lies (*mithya kotha*), criticism (*dosa dosi*) and invidious comparisons are the usual means of competing for honor and name. Secrets (*gopon*) are another less open, more selectively circulated type of message towards the same end. Any or all of these kinds of messages can be employed to detract from the honor or name of one's sister and her new family, and thereby elevate one's own honor and name by comparison. This said, it must be emphasized that sororal rivalries are not without material and behavioral consequences. Marriage in Bengali society is a test of family rank, for while the families and lines allied through marriage are presumed ritual equals, they are not necessarily political or economic equals. With a more favored marriage, a sister may claim that she did more than another to uphold or advance the rank of their natal family. A more favored marriage can then provide the basis for still other claims to preferential treatment when gifts are sent, as is customary, by the bride's family to their married daughters. Rather than distribute gifts equally, one daughter may be shown preference in order to cultivate affinal ties. The same logic also suggests why a brother may favor the sons of one sister over those of another, less well married, sister.

Beyond the immediate prize of competition, sororal rivalries also differ from fraternal rivalries in being pursued more irregularly, in fits and starts, as the mails are delivered, messengers travel, or visits are made. Such rivalries nevertheless persist over extended periods of time, even when interaction is indirect and infrequent, because sisters share similar expectations, hold similar goals, assess their attainments and those of their marital families against one another, and seek favored treatment from the same relatives. Sororal rivalries and fraternal rivalries differ in yet another way. If no amicable settlement can be reached otherwise, brothers can always agree to disagree, as it were; to partition ancestral lands and to establish separate, independent households. Married sisters already live apart, and visit the other in their own home only rarely, if at all. They have so little direct contact with each other that there is little, if any, opportunity to actually check and confirm the news, gossip or rumors that they hear about each other. All sisters can effectively do to resolve their rivalry, as a result, is to desist in making the comparisons by which inequalities are judged. This decision may be made in open, explicit agreement. More often it is made tacitly as a gradual result of each sister, over the years, assuming additional responsibility in her own household, and becoming increasingly preoccupied with the affairs of her own family, and less so with those of her sister. When resolved at all, sororal rivalries are most often resolved by default.

'Ja-ja jhogra'

Ja is the reciprocal reference term used between the wives of brothers. *Ja-ja jhogra* refers to those rivalries which are typical between the wives of brothers, especially when living together in one household.

Within the Bengali family the principle of seniority and rank extends to the relationship between brothers' wives, albeit with a slight modification. The wives of brothers are not compared directly, but according to the rank of their husbands. Thus the wife of an elder brother is considered senior to the wife of a younger brother, regardless of her actual age. As discussed in chapter 3, seniority among Bengalis is not measured by age *per se*, but according to an individual's physical-cum-moral development and the subsequent ability to handle the responsibilities of adult life in Hindu society. The wife of the elder brother is senior by this logic because she was the first to marry and enter the life stage of an adult female; she is the more experienced. (Assumed is that an elder brother will marry before his younger brother, which is almost invariably the case. In Torkotala there is but one exception to this in the last two generations, and in that instance the younger brother married only after his elder brother announced that he would never marry.)

It sometimes happens, although rarely, that the wife of an elder brother is actually less experienced and knowledgeable than the wife of the younger brother. Rivalries may then result if the wife of the younger brother will not willingly defer to or accept direction from a woman as her senior and guide when the cultural expectations seem unwarranted by the events of daily life. The rivalry between Usa and Lokkhi, who live in a village near to Torkotala, provides a documentary example.

Giresh and Charu Dey are brothers, 30 and 27 years of age respectively (in 1971). They and their wives live together as a single family unit. Giresh married some 12 years ago while his father was still alive. His bride, Usa, is five years his junior, making her (in 1971) 25 years of age. Charu was a student when his father died, and with his elder brother's consent decided to continue his schooling through high school before marrying and taking on full-time responsibilities as an agriculturalist on family lands.

Charu finished high school. Then he decided to again delay his marriage in order to study at the college in Karagpur. Giresh acquiesced to this plan, knowing that Charu's education would cost him additional expense for city clothes, books, bus fares, teas, etc. He also knew that having a college-educated brother would bring honor to the family, and Giresh expected eventually to benefit materially from Charu's education. Charu was a student of agriculture, which would be useful when he began working the family lands. Also, Giresh expected to receive a substantial dowry when his brother, a college graduate, finally did marry.

During Charu's last year in college Giresh sought and found for him a suitable bride, Lokkhi. Although a year younger than Usa, who is not schooled and cannot read or write, Lokkhi had finished high school before her marriage.

When Lokkhi entered the family, Usa was already established as the female head of household (*ginni*), the mother of Giresh and Charu having died several years earlier. Lokkhi's relationship with Usa was cool and impersonal from the start. The brothers' wives rarely spoke to one another When directed to do some household chore, Lokkhi received her instructions and went about her tasks in a sulky, sullen manner that was more insulting than if she had openly refused to accept direction. To other women of the village Lokkhi gossiped that Usa beat her, thereby playing on the shared responsibility of all villagers to help redress an unjust situation Usa, for her part, criticized Lokkhi to these same women for not knowing how to cook or to clean house, and for being too weak to carry water from the pump well. Rarely were the two brothers' wives seen in each other's presence. Eventually, their relationship became marked by mutual avoidance.

Torkotala villagers attribute the rivalry between Usa and Lokkhi to their closeness in age and experience, and to the fact that Lokkhi, the junior wife is better educated than Usa, the senior wife. Lokkhi does not willingly defer to Usa as her preceptor and guide, calling her unschooled, and trying to avoid receiving instructions whenever possible. Usa does not overlook the slight implied by such behavior, concluding that Lokkhi is schooled in the wrong ways, and does not know the behavior appropriate to a younger brother's wife. Being unable to change Lokkhi's errant behavior on her own, and finding Lokkhi unmindful of the reprimanding comments of other women in the village, Usa ultimately petitioned her husband, the acknowledged head of household, to remedy this transgression of family *dharma*.

The competition between Usa and Lokkhi documents how family politics aims to maintain the behavior appropriate between ranked family members, including the wives of brothers. This is explicit in Usa's claim that Lokkhi does not know the behavior appropriate to the junior wife of a household. It is also evident in Lokkhi's own language of claims. Lokkhi never disputed Usa's right as the senior, more experienced wife to direct her activities; she claimed only that Usa beat her for not minding those directions, which to Lokkhi was itself a transgression of the behavior appropriate between brothers' wives. For both women, significantly, their language of claims centered on family politics as the administration of *dharma*, as aimed at insuring the behavior appropriate between ranked family members. The competition between Usa and Lokkhi also documents how family politics is the shared responsibility of all within the village, at least potentially, for all are held responsible for acting in accord with their own behavioral code and ensuring that others do the same. It is for this reason that it was not considered unusual for Usa or Lokkhi initially to appeal their cases to other women of the village, or for Usa ultimately to petition her husband as male head of household to remedy a perceived transgression of family *dharma*.

The number of situations in which *ja-ja jhogra* are attributed to wives being close in experience and knowledge is relatively few. Far more frequent are those rivalries that result from the actual or presumed preferential treatment which one brother's wife receives from others in the household, and especially from her husband's mother.

On marrying and entering her husband's family, a new bride comes under the authority of her husband's mother. Typically there are strains as the husband's mother instructs the bride in the customs and practices of her new family, and in her new role as wife. These strains are themselves a source of a particular kind of rivalry between mother-in-law and daughter-in-law discussed below. They also give rise to rivalries between the brothers' wives as each tries to win the affection of their new mother-in-law and, perhaps, her leniency regarding certain of the more unpleasant, onerous household chores. The assignment of the majority of chores, or the least favored chores, is thus interpreted as a sign of favoritism and becomes a likely bone of contention and rivalry between the brothers' wives. How often a bride is allowed to visit her natal home, and how long she is allowed to stay there, are still other likely bones of contention.

Whatever the specific courses, rivalries between brothers' wives are rarely settled to their satisfaction as long as the father of their husbands remains alive, for only after his death can the women successfully prevail upon their husbands to partition ancestral lands and establish independent households, in which they no longer live under the authority of another female. Not to be the female head of one's own household, impugns one Bengali proverb, is to be 'a nose-pierced cow' – to move always at the will of another.

'Sasuri–bou ma jhogra'

Sasuri and *bou ma* are the reciprocal reference terms for mother-in-law and daughter-in-law respectively. Rivalry between these persons stem from the former's position as female head of household, which includes the role of task master and disciplinarian for incoming brides. Especially if the new bride is a poor worker, is coarse or ill-bred in her personal habits, or is unwilling or unable to accept her new responsibilities as an adult, will the relationship between her and her husband's mother be strained and rivalrous. It is for the mother-in-law to introduce her new daughter to the customs of the family. From her point of view a bride who is slow or unwilling to accept instructions is a bothersome, if welcomed, addition to the family. From the bride's point of view anything that her mother-in-law requests of her is an imposition, or at least a new demand, because in her natal home she was but a youth who was not expected to shoulder adult responsibilities.

Even when a bride cannot be justly faulted in her work or personal habits, or in her willingness to adapt to the life ways of her new family, the relationship between her mother-in-law and herself may still be rivalrous because the two women vie with each other for the affection and loyalty of the same person, a son to one and a husband to the other. A wife's presence in the household should not disrupt or alter her husband's relationship with other members of the family, including his mother. Thus the newly married couple are expected generally to avoid each other during the day while each does allotted tasks. In the evening and night, too, it is expected that the husband and wife will not spend all of their time together. The husband, as a result, will usually sleep in a room or area of the house shared by other males of the family, while the wife generally retires to a room or area of the house shared by other females of the family. The husband and wife, strangers to each other before marriage, nonetheless do come to have shared interests, affections and loyalties that strain their relations with other family members. *Sasuri–bou ma jhogra* is a frequent result of that strain.

Structure, process and meaning in the politics of family life

Still other interpersonal competitions between family members could be mentioned, but like the rivalries already described they would affirm that the politics of family life is identified by Torkotala villagers with interpersonal competitions over rank and the behavior appropriate to ⌐persons of different rank. These competitions do not challenge the ∟hierarchical order of the Hindu family; only the proper place and rank of individuals within that order. Precedence in rank is the prize, the valued end towards which interpersonal competitions within the family aim. Each competitor wants to exercise mastery and authority (*adhikara*) over others, to lord it over others (*prabhutra kora*), to be recognized as head, leader, chief, as boss (*matabbor*).

This suggests the first of several propositions towards a model of how the observed pattern of interpersonal competitions between family members in Torkotala is generated. Specifically, in the interaction between family members, who directs whom both demonstrates and determines rank. A person of higher rank than another will direct the activities of the latter more frequently than the reverse. A person of lower rank than another will accept direction from the latter more frequently than the reverse.

Precedence in rank is the ultimate prize of family politics. Yet this first proposition suggests why the ultimate prize of rank also entails the immediate prize of behavioral dominance or the control over people. Rank also entails the control over material resources. In the documentary cases presented, for example, the immediate bone of contention which sparked interpersonal competitions included control over the kind of labor done, the distribution and use of joint family income, the spoils of favoritism, and the less tangible property of honor or reputation. It is this intersection of prizes which reveals the relation of ideas and interests in the politics of family life. That is, as defined within a transformational theory of human development, the rank of individual family members is a situs realized through behavior – including the control over people and material resources. Behavioral dominance and material interests are prized in their own right. But in the context of family politics they are also transvalued as reflections of rank.

Rank is the ultimate prize of family politics. Yet competitions for that prize are sometimes in conflict with a value of support, friendship and partnership which defines the ideal relationship between siblings of either sex. The rivalry between Khudi and Satya is an example of this conflict of values, and also of the fragility of sibling solidarity alongside the premise of inequality. The rivalry between Khudi and Satya, and especially the language of claims which accompanied its resolution, suggests a second proposition.

The more frequently family members interact with each other in a manner where neither person directs the activities of the other, the greater will be the equality between them, and the less the likelihood of interpersonal competitions.

This proposition suggests why competitions between brothers and between sisters will be less frequent than competition between brothers-in-law or sisters-in-law, or between mother-in-law and daughter-in-law, who do not share an ethic of sibling solidarity. There are still other family members between whom interpersonal competitions are not anticipated, and indeed rarely occur, as between father and son, father and daughter, mother and son, mother and daughter, husband and wife, brother and sister, and grandparents and grandchildren. Considerations of rank are not absent from these relationships, but in each instance the expected association between rank and behavioral dominance is usually supported by the events of daily life, and thus beyond challenge. In rural West Bengal, where formal education is not yet extensive and practical education is truly a matter of life experience, a father ordinarily is more knowledgeable and sophisticated than his son, a husband more than his wife. Under such circumstances, for the person of higher rank to judiciously direct the activities of another engenders respect and compliance more often than ill-will and competition. This suggests why the converse of the second proposition does not necessarily follow. Namely, when a person of higher rank merits the status of preceptor and guide, his directing the activities of another rarely leads to interpersonal competitions. When cultural expectations and sociological reality are not similarly matched, however, as in the relationship between Usa and Lokkhi, for one person to direct the activities of another often engenders ill-will. Thus a final proposition.

When the interaction is between family members whose differences in rank are supported by the realities of social life, respect and compliance are likely. When the interaction is between family members whose differences in rank are not supported by the realities of social life, ill-will and competition is likely.

It is this proposition which suggests why every interaction between ranked family members does not result in actual competition. Simply, some differences in rank are viewed as perfectly warranted and thus beyond challenge. Moreover, to be the subordinate in a relationship is not necessarily degrading or even disadvantageous. A son does benefit from the experienced direction of his father, as a wife does from that of her husband, or a younger brother from that of his elder brother. Then, too, rank and behavioral dominance is never divorced from the complementary expectation of responsibility and obligation towards those for whom one is preceptor and guide. This proposition also suggests what Simmel (1955:38–43) would term the 'realistic' nature of family politics in rural West Bengal. That is, interpersonal competitions between family members are usually not a mere acting out of hostilities between ranked persons. Most often they are occasioned and purposely directed towards redressing an actual or perceived inconsistency between rank and the behavior held appropriate to that rank. In that sense are interpersonal competitions between family members generated by efforts to correct an imperfect fit between order perceived culturally and realized socially. That correction is possible underscores the nature of competition as a transformational act. It also underscores that the rank order among family members is not, as it may appear, fixed or static. What is apparently static is but continually renewed, and sometimes adjusted, through rivalries over rank.

Those competitions between family members which do occur, however frequently or infrequently, take three principal forms. When the competition is a matter of occasional disagreement, as when Khudi and Satya disputed the use of income held in common, it is referred to as *jukti,* or argument. Less frequent, but potentially far more divisive, are those competitions which take the form of open quarrels (*bibad*) in which the competitors seek a clear and immediate decision to their respective claims. War (*juddho*) is not a recognized form of competition in the politics of family life. Yet when open quarrels are most virulent, they are often likened to wars. Between argument and open quarrel is another form of political competition, rivalry (*jhogra*), in which competitors test each other, but do not pursue their competition to a clear or immediate conclusion. Rivalries are confrontations, not encounters (Bailey 1969:94). They are by far the most frequent and characteristic form of family strife. They are also a form of political competition which can be pursued over extended periods of time, or recurrently at different times, without threatening family dissolution. Rather, they usually reaffirm the ordered ranks of the family and the behavior appropriate to its competing members.

Interpersonal rivalries are a chronic feature of Hindu family life, but they are not condoned. The family as a social unit is bound by moral as well as natural ties, and any competition between family members is viewed as a transgression of family *dharma*. If each family member acted in accord with his own behavioral code, it is held that there would be no competitions. Given this perspective, the only acceptable justification for rivalry is the moral claim to be acting to maintain or restore the behavior appropriate between family members. That competitions may also be pursued in the hope of establishing a new and more favorable rank order is not, supposedly, the end towards which family members compete. In its language of claims, and often in fact, the politics of family life is the enactment and protection of moral order. Not rank alone but morality too is at stake.

The politics of caste

It is now well agreed that the caste system is an organic system of complementary, interdependent units in which constituent units – individual, named castes – do not exist and cannot be properly understood as social isolates. Understanding caste as an organic system thus requires understanding the relations between castes. There is no similar agreement on what the organic nature of the caste system implies about political relations between castes. Leach (1960:7), for example, observed that whenever castes compete with each other, 'they are acting in defiance of caste principles.' Bailey (1963:121) once described castes as groups 'which co-operate and do not compete,' though he did allow that a locally dominant caste may act as a corporate political unit in relation to subordinate castes of the village. André Beteille (1969), in critiquing Leach and Bailey, noted that to view castes as non-competitive units is to confuse the ideology or values of the caste system with the material interests which actually govern the interaction between castes. Thus he writes of the 'politics of non-antagonistic strata,' pointing to the actuality of competition between castes which in principle are not competitive. The evidence from Torkotala is used here to argue that caste competitions are not – as Leach, Bailey and Beteille each conclude – contrary to the nature of caste as an organic system. Rather, recurrent competitions between castes are consistent with a transformational perspective in which the defining features and rank of a caste are continually open to change, and thus also continually open to challenge. This is not to deny or underestimate the importance of material interests in fueling specific caste competitions; only to suggest why the politics of caste is a common, even anticipated, feature of life in rural India precisely because of the value placed on rank and the premise of inequality by which the caste system is ordered.

Like the politics of family life, the politics of caste is identified by Torkotala villagers with competitions over rank and the behavior appropriate to ranked units, albeit with characteristic differences. In the politics of family life competition is a matter of interpersonal rivalry. In the politics of caste competition it is between corporate groups, and the prize sought is to be recognized as the caste having the more *sattvik* features of physical nature and behavioral code, and thus higher rank as well. The politics of caste, therefore, is largely a matter of inter-caste competitions, but not exclusively so, for within each caste are occasionally found members whose individual actions threaten the defining features and rank of the entire corporate group. In dealing with such backsliders the politics of caste also has an intramural face. Both inter- and intra-caste competitions will be examined in turn with an eye towards the processes which generate the politics of caste.

Inter-caste competitions

Inter-caste competitions focus on attempts by one caste to improve its rank in the local caste hierarchy – to 'caste-climb' as Bailey (1968) terms it – and attempts by one or more castes to block the success of any such climb. 'The prosperity of an enemy is a cause for sorrow.' By the logic of this maxim, for one caste to gain in rank is for all others to lose. Those below the climbing caste lose because the relative distance between them in the caste rankings is made still greater. Those above the climbing caste lose because the relative distance between them is made smaller. Immediate to the climbing caste in the hierarchy is usually another which has suffered the direct loss of having its relative rank reversed, so that it is now below a caste it once ranked above. Thus do inter-caste competitions involve not only the active competitors but, at least indirectly, all other castes in the local hierarchy as well.

The process by which castes climb in a local hierarchy has been described by M.N. Srinivas as Sanskritization. In his study of the Coorgs of Mysore, Srinivas found that lower castes sought to improve their position in the caste hierarchy by imitating Brahmans in matters of dress, food and ritual, while also giving up some of their own customs, like meat-eating and animal sacrifices, which the Brahmans considered demeaning. To denote this process Srinivas first used the term 'Brahmanization.' Later the term 'Sanskritization' was substituted to indicate a more general 'process by which a "low" Hindu caste, or tribal or other group, changes its customs, ritual, ideology and way of life in the direction of a "high", and frequently, "twice-born" caste' (Srinivas 1966:6). Caste-climbing, in other words, is an imitative process by which lower-ranking castes alter their generalized life style or *jibika* to be more like that of higher-ranking castes, and then make claim to higher rank on the basis of those changes. The imitative process can persist for generations before arrival is conceded, if at all. A caste of any *varna* can be the object of imitation, not just Brahmans. In Torkotala, for example, Bagdi efforts to be recognized as Bagra-Khatriyas were oriented toward a Sudra model of Sanskritization fostered by the locally dominant Sadgops. A description of those efforts is presented below, and then a generative model for advancing claims to higher rank is suggested.

Until about 30 years ago, Torkotala Bagdis typically worked as agricultural laborers for landholding Sadgops of the village. Some of this work was done on a daily or short-term basis. More often individual Bagdis were retained by a Sadgop family throughout the year, and did whatever work was required seasonally. This pattern changed when several Bagdi families acquired lands of their own for the first time by clearing outlying areas of the village of scrub jungle. Others did the next best thing in arranging to sharecrop lands. Having thus acquired rights to their own land, the Bagdis stopped working in the employ of Sadgops entirely, or, as was more common, combined their work as agricultural laborers with work on their own lands as well. In the context of Torkotala village life, for Bagdis to work their own lands and to be at least partially independent of serving Sadgops represented a significant refinement in their life style.

Sadgop landholders of the village reacted to the new economic independence of the Bagdis by employing in their stead tribal Lodhas and Mundas who had previously worked their fields only as migrant laborers during the peak of the rice harvest. In years past these Lodhas and Mundas had returned to the hilly tracts of their native *des* in western Midnapore when the harvest season ended. Now they were offered permanent employment in Torkotala, and land to settle on as well.

From the early 1940s to the mid 1950s the Bagdis used their new economic wealth and independence to attract other caste fellows to Torkotala, thereby increasing their numbers. In 1941 there were four compounds of Bagdis, five households. Persons in all but one of these households owned their own lands and were at least partially self-employed. By 1951 there were eight compounds of Bagdis, 9 households, in Torkotala. Persons in all but two of these households owned their own lands and were at least partially self-employed. By 1971 there were nine compounds, 21 households of Bagdis: 12 households owned their own land and 6 were entirely self-employed.

As their landholdings and numbers grew, the Bagdis soon were able to employ others to do the kinds of agricultural labor they once did for the Sadgops and later did for themselves. In this way the Bagdis came to have economic clients and political supporters of their own. Like their previous employers, the Sadgops, the Bagdis also took to supervising agricultural work rather than doing such physical labor themselves. This, too, represented a significant refinement in life style, as to refrain from direct physical labor is to refrain from involvement with the more *rajasik* and *tamasik* aspects of life. Still other changes followed. In the late 1950s Bagdi youths first refused to accept the scholarship aid available to persons of Scheduled Castes and Tribes on the grounds that the Bagdis were not a Scheduled Caste. Individual Bagdis also adopted a middle name after the pattern of higher castes. Khudi Dolai referred to himself as Khudi Ram, for example. Satya Dolai referred to himself as Satya Chandra Dolai. In many Bagdi families children were given a middle name at birth. Some Bagdis also substituted the surname Dolopati for Dolai. Dolopati, or 'group leader,' is held a higher, more refined form of Bengali speech, and therefore a preferred surname.

Accompanying this complex of changes in life style and naming pattern was the Bagdi claim to be Bagra-Khatriyas, a Kshatriya (in Bengali, Khatriya) caste. Sadgops of the village pointedly ignored this claim. Neither did the Sadgops recognize other Bagdi claims, like having middle names or the surname Dolopati.

The Bagdi do not admit that they were ever without the ritual services of a Rajok, Napit or Brahman. Other evidence suggests that it was not until 1960, or very shortly before, that the Bagdis began to receive the ritual services of the same washerman and barber as serves the Sadgops and other high-ranking castes in Torkotala. Soon afterwards the Bagdis also secured the services of a Brahman priest, though not the same priest that serves others in the village. To this day Torkotala Sadgops discredit the importance of these additional changes in Bagdi life style by saying they are the product of a 'black arrow,' an arrow that travels by indirect, clandestine, morally suspect paths. (A 'white arrow' travels directly, openly, and without need of morally suspect paths.) In support of this argument Sadgops explain that the village Rajok was forced, out of poverty, to serve as washerman for Bagdi families at the threat of losing side income as an agricultural laborer for Khudi Dolai. That the Bagdis were able to secure the services of a Brahman is also explained by Sadgops in terms of the black arrow of wealth. 'With money one may procure tigers' milk,' i.e. that which is most unattainable. In addition, the Brahman who serves the Bagdis as priest is labelled as fallen (*potita*), and his services discredited as not being those of a true (*sat*) Brahman. His real work, Sadgops claim, is fixing bicycles under the giant banyan tree along the trunk road to Narayanghar Town.

In spite of all the refinements in life style the Bagdis had already effected, in 1960 they still had not won recognition from Torkotala Sadgops or others in the village as Bagra-Khatriyas. Recognition was not to come until another set of events, originating in the broader environment of Torkotala, made its effect on the village.

In 1957 the West Bengal state government, acting under directions from the federal government in New Delhi, passed legislation for the establishment of statutory councils (*panchayats*), including village councils, throughout the rural areas of the state. Participation in these councils would be open to all citizens through free and recurrent elections in which every adult had the right to vote. The actual organization and establishment of Panchayati Raj, as this system of rural self-government became known, proceeded at a very uneven pace throughout the state, so that in 1960 there still were no statutory councils in the Narayanghar area. Councils had been organized, and elections had occurred in other parts of the state. Torkotala residents were aware of this, and anticipated the time when a statutory council would be organized in their village, too. Whenever established, it was expected that a Sadgop would be elected as council head, as *Adhyaksa*. Far less certain was which Sadgop would be elected *Adhyaksa*, as both Atul Mahabarto and Anil Pal wanted the position.

Campaigning for the position of village *Adhyaksa* began well before any government officials ever entered Torkotala to organize the first statutory village council. The Sadgop caste was divided in its support of Atul and Anil. Both men canvassed for decisive support among non-Sadgops of the village, and especially among the Bagdis, who represented the second most populous caste in Torkotala, and also the second most influential caste in the number of economic clients counted within their political following.

While Atul and Anil were trying to win support for their selection as

Adhyaksa, Khudi Dolai was making final preparations for the marriage of his daughter. Part of those preparations, significantly, included indirect soundings as to whether or not certain leading Sadgops of the village, including Atul and Anil, would accept an invitation to his daughter's wedding feast. No Sadgop had ever accepted even drinking water from the hands of a Bagdi. Yet Khudi was now asking if a wedding invitation, which carried an implicit agreement to accept food served as part of the wedding feast, would be accepted. Sadgops who did accept the invitation, it was rumored, would receive Bagdi support when the new statutory village council was formed, and the support of all Bagdi clients as well.

To Khudi's soundings, Anil was at first noncommittal. Atul – voicing a goal of government politics – immediately let it be known that he favored breaking down all social barriers separating castes of the village. To do so would contribute to village unity, and was consistent with the aims of Panchayati Raj. Not to be outdone, Anil was soon heard making similar statements. Other Sadgops of the village, in reaction, called a meeting of the caste council to decide whether Anil and Atul should be allowed to accept Khudi's invitation, as they said they would. Should the Sadgops not defend themselves against another of Khudi's black arrows? Those present at the council meeting debated this question for some time, but in the end none remained opposed to Anil or Atul, not even Haripado Bhunai. It was Haripado, speaking as *Mukhya*, though, who suggested that Khudi's invitation should only be accepted if he agreed to have the wedding food cooked and served by a true (*sat*) Brahman, and if he agreed to contribute 50 rupees to the village fund for the honor of having Sadgops attend his daughter's marriage. By this plan the Sadgops could attend a Bagdi wedding feast, as Khudi wanted, without acting in disaccord with Sadgop *dharma*, as Haripado wanted, for there was no Sadgop injunction against accepting food from a true Brahman. Also, by this plan the Sadgops could attend a Bagdi wedding feast, as Khudi wanted, without violating the established social order between castes of the village, as Haripado wanted, for in agreeing to make a contribution to the village fund the Bagdis were, in effect, honoring Sadgops as a higher ranking caste.

Khudi accepted the Sadgops' conditions. He agreed that the Sadgops could arrange for the service of any Brahman cook they wished, and to contribute 50 rupees – which was collected from all Bagdi families of the village – to the village fund. The Sadgops, in return, attended the Bagdi marriage feast as promised, and persuaded persons of other high-ranking castes in the village to attend as well. Phani Babu, the village Brahman, was away from the village at the time, some say purposely, but did send his eldest son as proxy.

During the marriage feast Atul conspicuously addressed several Bagdi men using their middle name. Khudi Dolai was addressed as Khudi Ram.

His brother, Satya, was addressed as Satya Chandra. It was also·Atul who, for the first time ever, publicly referred to Khudi, Satya and others of their caste as Bagra-Khatriyas. The surname Dolopati was never used by anyone attending the marriage feast, and presently is no longer used even by Bagra-Khatriyas.

Bagdi attempts and eventual success at being recognized as Bagra-Khatriyas are interesting for several reasons. The object of Bagdi imitation, and the principal audience for Bagdi claims, was the locally dominant Sadgop caste, belonging to the Sudra *varna*, and not the single Brahman family represented in Torkotala. Local Sadgops eventually did recognize Bagdi claims to be known as Bagra-Khatriyas, but not, significantly, Bagdi claims to be a Kshatriya caste. In their eyes, as in the eyes of other villagers, the Bagdis remain a Sudra caste, only now they are known by a new (and somewhat misleading) name. Bagdi attempts to caste-climb are also interesting for the length of time and the sequence in which changes in life style were made and claims advanced before recognition was finally granted by local Sadgops, and then others. Three decades passed before the complex of changes effected by the Bagdis finally resulted in their gaining recognition as Bagra-Khatriyas. At first the Sadgops saw no need to oppose Bagdi efforts to secure rights over their own land by clearing the scrub jungle or by arranging to sharecrop. They did not object when individual Bagdis stopped working as agricultural laborers on Sadgop lands. Neither did they actively oppose other changes in Bagdi life style, as when Bagdis took to supervising the work of others rather than doing physical labor themselves, or when individual Bagdis assumed a middle name. Indeed, these changes and any accompanying claim to higher rank were treated so lightly as to be generally ignored. Only when the Bagdis procured the services of the same ritual specialists as served the Sadgops could their claims no longer be ignored. Then they had to be undermined and discredited.

To ignore the claims of a competitor or to try and undermine and discredit and thereby actively oppose those claims are two common strategies in the politics of caste. The former is to avoid a competition by not recognizing the claim-maker as a legitimate competitor. The latter is to recognize a claim-maker as a legitimate competitor but to oppose the claims made. That the Sadgops first ignored, later actively opposed and ultimately granted recognition to Bagdi claims illustrates another feature of the politics of castes, namely, that the effects of inter-caste rivalries can be cumulative. Small gains at one point in a rivalry provide the basis for larger gains later. Thus the Bagdis could use their new landholdings and economic independence to attract increasing numbers of caste fellows to settle in Torkotala; increasing numbers to acquire still more landholdings and economic independence; wealth and numbers to hire others in their employ; having others in their employ to change their working habits; a change in working habits, dress, diet, and so on, to secure the ritual services of a Rajok and Napit; and the services of these ritual specialists to secure the services of a Brahman. In this sequence of changes effected by the Bagdis, each previous change provided the basis for a later one, and taken together all of the changes represented a gradual but progressive refinement of Bagdi life style in the direction of making it more and more *sattvik*. Changes in life style then provided the basis for claims to higher rank.

The changes in life style effected by the Bagdis, in combination with other accounts of caste-climbing (cf. Gough 1959; Silverberg 1959; Marriott 1968; Bailey 1968), suggest a three-phase processual model for advancing claims to higher rank. Namely, (1) a change in occupation and/or economic independence and wealth (2) is used to refine caste patterns of dress, diet, food exchanges, service, naming, ritual practices, etc.; (3) a refined life style is then used to claim an appropriately higher rank.

In this processual model actual material changes in life style are critical, but are not themselves explicable apart from the cultural importance given by Hindus to behavior as an outward reflection of inner physical nature. The Hindu preoccupation with rank as a cultural value is also critical to this processual model, but higher rank is unattainable apart from material changes in life style. Put differently, because the generalized life style of a caste is deemed both a reflection and realization of its rank, it is difficult to argue that either the push of an improved life style or the pull of rank as a cultural value is the prime mover of the politics of caste. Any reductionist account of the material and cultural considerations at issue is additionally problematic because the success of efforts at caste-climbing are also contingent on a certain amount of happenstance. Three decades ago there were ample uncultivated lands surrounding Torkotala for the Bagdis to clear, which they did without impediment from local Sadgops, perhaps because there was an ample number of tribal Lodhas and Mundas to replace the Bagdis as the principal agricultural laborers of the village. Recognition of the Bagdis as Bagra-Khatriyas also depended in part on preparations for the marriage of Khudi Dolai's daughter happening to coincide with the extension of Panchayati Raj into the Torkotala area and the willingness of leading Sadgops to bargain recognition of Bagdi claims for election support as council head.

The processual model suggested identifies the likely phase development of a successful effort at caste-climbing, and the material and cultural considerations at issue. The duration of each phase in the transformation of a caste's defining features is unpredictable and, as with Bagdi efforts to be recognized as Bagra-Khatriyas, can be spread over generations. More predictable is that inter-caste competitions are timed to redress an actual or perceived inconsistency between the life style of a caste and its rank. In that sense do such competitions aim to uphold and maintain the natural and moral order of society. That is, Bagdi efforts to improve their rank did not challenge the caste system *per se*; only their position in the local ordering of castes. Indeed, far from challenging the caste system, the cumulative effect of caste-climbing efforts over time is to affirm the principle of ranked inequalities around which castes are organized by dramatizing and seeking to correct an imperfect fit between order culturally perceived and order socially realized. In that sense does caste-climbing evidence how an apparently static caste system is not static at all, but continually renewed through rivalries over rank. Consider now how the temporary disorder of intra-caste competition can also lead to a lasting sociocultural order.

Intra-caste competitions

Though the lead in pressing for recognition as Bagra-Khatriyas was taken by only a few Bagdi families, and especially by Khudi and Satya Dolai, all Bagdis benefited from their activities. It is for this reason that Khudi felt justified in collecting the 50 rupees paid to the village fund for the honor of having Sadgops attend his daughter's marriage from all of the Bagdi families of the village. Simply, it is the nature of castes as political teams to be corporate; what one team member does benefits all. For the same reason, the activities of any member of the team can also cause loss to the entire caste. It is in dealing with backsliders, persons who do not uphold the defining features of the caste, and thereby threaten its rank, that the politics of caste also assumes an intramural face. An occasion when the Bagdi caste council met some 15 years ago to judge an alleged affront against the entire caste provides a documentary case in point.

A young widow of the Bagdi caste returned to Torkotala from the village and house of her recently deceased husband. She stayed with her father for some months, then left to live in Calcutta, where she went alone and without knowing anyone who could help her settle. While in Calcutta the widow did not write to her father, nor to anyone else in Torkotala, so no one knew where she was living or what work she did. Two years passed. Then the widow returned to the village unexpectedly and again took up residence in her father's house. But whereas she had left for Calcutta in poverty, she returned to Torkotala with many new ornaments, fine saris and other costly objects.

The newly acquired wealth of the widow occasioned much rumor among Torkotala residents, for no one could imagine how the widow acquired such wealth, at least not honestly. Gossip had it that the widow's wealth came through a 'loss of character,' i.e. through prostitution, and therefore she should be outcasted for not acting like a true Bagdi.

The widow returned to Torkotala at a time when her father was deathly ill, so no one was willing to raise publicly the question of outcasting her just then. Soon after the father's death, though, a Bagdi council was called for that purpose. At the council meeting, attended by Bagdis of several villages, it was decided that there was no proof of the widow's activities in Calcutta, only suspicion. Yet suspicion that the widow earned her wealth in ways that violated caste *dharma* was so strong that it was also decided she should undergo a penance for whatever wrongdoings may have occurred while she was in Calcutta. The widow was informed of this decision before the entire caste council, and at the same time given a public lecture as to the *dharma* of the Bagdi caste, of widows, of females, and of Hindus. The widow was also asked to pay a fine to the caste, which she did.

The meeting of the caste council, reported by the (now) Bagra-Khatriyas, was narrated in such a way as to indicate a clear object lesson: that Bagdis behave just like the higher ranking Sadgops. Specifically, the Bagdi widow was compared to Jogi Pal, born to the Sadgop caste in Torkotala, but later outcasted for consorting with Lodha females. If the Bagdi widow did prostitute herself, she would have been outcasted like Jogi Pal for not acting in accord with caste *dharma*. 'No one will touch him/her who forsakes the right way for the wrong, not even with a stick,' warns a Bengali proverb.

Another case of backsliding that was a focus of intramural caste politics, this time among Torkotala Sadgops, involved Baneshor and Kennaram Dey.

Baneshor Dey married into Torkotala about 26 years ago. His younger brother, Kennaram, married his wife's younger sister about 23 years ago, and also took up residence in Torkotala. The two brothers and two sisters lived together in a single compound but maintained separate households. As expected of all newcomers to the village, soon after taking up residence in Torkotala Baneshor and Kennaram each honored other Sadgops of the village with gifts of areca nut and betel leaf. Thereafter whenever either of the brothers or members of their family celebrated a life-cycle rite they also honored the village Sadgops with areca nut and betel leaf, sweets, a feast, or with whatever was appropriate.

Baneshor and Kennaram had lived in Torkotala for 13 years and 10 years respectively, when the father of their wives died. Because they could not afford to do so, the brothers provided no feast to caste fellows and others of the village at the end of the death-impurity period. When Baneshor's wife died two years later, again no feast was given to caste fellows or others of the village at the end of the death-impurity period.

Other Sadgops of the village knew that Baneshor and Kennaram were not well off economically. They held no lands of their own, and the lands held in the names of their wives were minimal. To maintain himself and his family Baneshor even worked as a day laborer during the plowing season for Kagendro Dolai, a Bagra-Khatriya, thereby contravening the general pattern of higher ranking caste persons being served by but not serving lower-ranking castes with their physical labor. Nonetheless Sadgops of the village met and decided that Baneshor and Kennaram had not acted properly when they failed to feast their caste fellows and others of the village on not one, but two, occasions. As punishment it was also decided that the Napit and Rajok who served other Sadgops of the village would be prohibited from serving Baneshor and Kennaram. The brothers were thus forced to walk to Narayanghar Town, where several Napits and Rajoks worked on a cash basis, whenever the services of a barber or washerman were needed.

This situation persisted for almost two years. Then negotiations began for Baneshor's second marriage. On learning of these negotiations other Sadgops of the village threatened to spoil them unless Baneshor and Kennaram paid a fine of 40 rupees to the Kali Puja committee, headed by Sadgops of the village, for their past errant behavior, and promised to invite all the Sadgops of the village to a marriage feast. Baneshor and Kennaram agreed. Not long afterwards Baneshor and Kennaram once more began receiving the services of the village Napit and Rajok.

Why were Sadgops of the village so upset by not being feasted on two occasions, especially when well aware that Baneshor and Kennaram Dey were truly impoverished? In part this is because poverty is not thought to excuse one from acting in accord with personal or caste *dharma*. In part it is because of what other villagers said in reprimanding Baneshor and Kennaram, and by extension, all Sadgops. Providing a feast at the end of the death-impurity period is not considered optional for family members. It is obligatory because the presence of invitees accepting food indicates that the family of the deceased, previously in a state of impurity, is once more able to resume a normal social life without restrictions of diet, activities or social contacts. Not to provide a feast is to fail in one's moral obligations, to act in a way that belies one's defining features and rank. Since village politics is presumed the shared responsibility of all, it also provides others in the village an occasion to say that the Sadgops do not know, or worse yet, know but do not follow, Hindu *dharma*; which is exactly what the Bagdis, at the time still pressing their claims to be Bagra-Khatriyas, did say. As the activities of any caste member reflect on the entire caste, Sadgops felt required to respond to such criticism by censuring Baneshor and Kennaram. Moreover, in the specific means selected for that censure Torkotala Sadgops evidenced that they indeed knew what was proper or moral behavior for all Hindus. Both the denial of ritual specialists and exposing potential marriages as improper are well established among Torkotala Hindus as means towards outcasting in the absence of reform.

Structure, process and meaning in the politics of caste

While the cases presented above stop well short of illustrating the full range of competitions which Torkotala villagers identify as instances of the politics of caste, they do suggest some of its general features. The politics of caste aims at actively improving one's caste rank in the local hierarchy, to caste-climb, or to maintain defensively one's present rank by opposing the caste-climbing efforts of others while also upholding those features of physical nature and behavioral code by which a caste is uniquely defined, and its rank established. Whether on the offensive or defensive, whether trying to caste-climb or merely maintain one's present position in the local hierarchy, castes in competition all aim at the same political prize: precedence in rank.

What merits the ultimate prize is defined within a transformational theory of rank. Namely, precedence in rank goes to the caste whose defining features are recognized as more *sattvik*. The life style or *jibika* of a caste is both a reflection and realization of those defining features, and thus also a means by which the defining nature and code of a caste and its rank can be altered for better or worse. Indeed, any change in the life style of a caste provides a ready basis for competitions over rank, which is both the generalized source and content of the politics of caste.

This conjunction of rank and rivalry suggests why – contrary to arguments by Leach, Bailey and Beteille – competitions between castes are not inconsistent with the nature of the caste system. It also suggests a general proposition about competitions between and within castes. Specifically, the politics of caste is generated by inconsistencies between the life style of a caste, understood as a reflection and realization of its defining features, and its rank. In inter-caste competitions this inconsistency results from actual or perceived refinements in the life style of a caste. Competition over claims to higher rank is advanced on the basis of refinements in life style. In intra-caste competitions the inconsistency between life style and rank results from actual or anticipated action by a backsliding member which threatens the corporate whole. Competition aims to rectify or forestall acts by individual caste members that would debase the defining features and rank of the entire caste.

The politics of caste can result in actual positional changes within a local caste hierarchy. Such changes of caste rank, or even attempts at the same, are not frequent occurrences in Torkotala in the sense of happening weekly or monthly or yearly. But neither are they uncommon or unanticipated, given a transformational perspective in which the features of a caste are continually open to redefinition. This points to why group mobility within a local caste hierarchy is always a genuine possibility, both in principle and in fact. It also underscores the realistic nature of the politics of caste, for the rank order of castes in a local hierarchy is indeed maintained or altered through competition. And it underscores the nature of competition between and within castes as transformational acts of the same order as, say, marriage.

Precedence in rank is the ultimate prize in the politics of caste. Yet as in family politics, the politics of caste also involves other more immediate and more material goals of control over people and resources. This is evident in the sequence of material changes in life style the Bagdis parleyed into control over ritual specialists and later into recognition as Bagra-Khatriyas. It is also evident in intra-caste competitions, where control over sexual access to women, the imposition of fines, the restriction of ritual services, and the provision of feasts were variously the immediate prizes at issue. The instrumental value of alliances in the politics of caste is also relevant here. Bagdi attempts to be recognized as Bagra-Khatriyas were successfully opposed for as long as they were only because of the united efforts of many Torkotala castes, high and low, all of which stood to lose if Bagdi efforts to caste-climb were successful. Bagdi recognition as Bagra-Khatriyas was finally won only when Sadgops of the village, the keystone of that opposition, felt the need to ally with the Bagdis to gain an immediate goal of their own – leadership of the anticipated statutory council. The value of alliances is also evident in intra-caste competitions, as when the Bagdis of several villages combined to censure the young widow suspected of a 'loss of character,' or when the Sadgops of Torkotala put aside their factional differences collectively to censure Baneshor and Kennaram Dey for ritual lapses which reflected negatively on the entire caste.

The politics of family life and the politics of caste are alike in consisting of competitions over rank. They differ somewhat in the way that competition is structured and the manner and means by which it is pursued. The politics of family life is almost exclusively a matter of intramural competitions. Competitors are individual family members and the ultimate prize is relative rank within the family. It is the nature of castes as political teams, on the other hand, to have two political faces, one looking outwards to competition between castes, and one looking inwards to protect against backsliders whose individual activities handicap the caste as a whole in that competition. It is the outward face that leads to inter-caste competition, the inward face that leads to intra-caste competition. The rank of a caste depends, of course, on both faces of the politics of caste.

Families are led by a single leader, the male head of household. Castes may be effectively led by a single, extraordinary person, but in principle are led by a collective leadership comprised potentially of the heads of all families within the caste. Both families and castes are political teams in which members are bound to each other by multiplex natural and moral ties. Recruitment to each team is by ascription, through the circumstances of birth. But in a family all members of the team are not only the supporters of its male head, they are co-sharers in all that he is and does. They constitute a morally committed core of supporters whose tie to a leader is not easily subverted. In a caste, by contrast, the ties between its collective leadership and supporters are not as strong. Entire sections of a caste may decide that the direction of its collective leadership does not suit them, and seek to disassociate themselves from it. New castes may even form in this way. Or an entire section of a caste may seek material rewards for the continued support they would not give freely. They may seek, in other words, a transactional bond to reinforce or even supplant the natural and moral ties which already exist between persons of the same caste. The demand for transactional bonds to reinforce natural and moral ties was evident amongst certain members of the Sadgop caste when Atul Mahabarto and Anil Pal let it be known that they would accept a Bagdi marriage invitation. Other Sadgops in the village questioned why they should allow Atul and Anil to proceed in this manner when no Sadgop had ever accepted food, or even drinking water, from a Bagdi. In calling a caste council and requiring Atul and Anil to justify their chosen course of action, these Sadgops were acting not as a core group of committed supporters, but as a following whose continued support had to be bargained for and won. Unlike their position in families, in castes as political teams supporters are often distinguishable, in Bailey's terms (1968:44–9), as core and following.

The politics of family life and the politics of caste also differ in the specific activities by which they are pursued. Family politics is almost entirely a matter of rivalries; any open quarrel between family members being a rare and untoward occurrence that receives the opprobrium and negative sanction of all. Open quarrels are a more frequent form of caste competition, especially within castes, and when they do occur are less often the object of extreme opprobrium than the subject of careful scrutiny as to whether open quarrel is at the time and under the circumstances a wise choice of political tactics. In intra-caste competitions open quarrel often takes the form of a caste-council confronting a backsliding member directly. In inter-caste competitions the more prolonged, less openly divisive rivalry is the characteristic form of competition. It is a form of competition particularly well suited to a caste-climbing process that may extend over decades, as in the Bagdi case.

Like intramural competitions within a family, it is expected that intra-caste rivalries and quarrels will be guided by normative rules. The same expectation also applies to inter-caste competitions, but it is recognized that when competitors belong to different castes they will more often proceed by pragmatic rules which advance tactics and stratagems as being most effective under the given circumstances quite apart from whether or not they are morally right or wrong. This is not to say that inter-caste competitions are entirely unguided by normative rules – they are not – but to emphasize the additional reliance on pragmatics. Thus Torkotala Sadgops might criticize the Bagdis for advancing their claim to be Bagra-Khatriyas through the black arrow of wealth, but it did not surprise them that black arrows were used. The politics of caste, like family politics, is ideally moral activity. In the competition between castes, however, fewer holds are barred.

Whether pursued through black arrows or white, Torkotala Hindus regard the politics of caste as ultimately avoidable. All caste competitions are deemed the unnecessary result of human misconduct because if each individual and caste acted in accord with their own behavioral code there would be no basis for competitions within or between castes. Given this perspective, the only acceptable reason for engaging in caste competitions is the moral claim to be acting to maintain or restore the behavior appropriate to ranked castes and their individual members, to administer *dharma*. Like the politics of family life, in its language of claims, and often in fact, the politics of caste is the enactment and protection of moral order.

Factional politics: *dola doli*

A *dol* is a flock or herd, a side or team. Competition between *dol* is described by Torkotala villagers as *dola doli*, and can be glossed as factional competition or factional politics. It is this kind of competition which has received the most attention from students of Indian politics.

From the mid 1950s to the present, the study of factional politics has proceeded in three directions. On the one hand are studies focused on the consequences of factional activity. Beals and Siegel (1960a; 1960b), for example, conclude that factionalism is overt, unresolved conflict within a community which interferes with the achievement of community goals, and thus is dysfunctional. Factional competition is undeniably disruptive and divisive, and to be labeled a factionalist – one who engages in *dola doli* – is for Torkotala villagers a pejorative term of abuse. Yet as Oscar Lewis concluded from his study in a north Indian village, factions also 'carry on important social, economic and ceremonial functions in addition to their struggles against each other' (Lewis 1954:503; see also Dhillon 1955:30). In the discussion of Torkotala factional politics of particular note will be the role of factions in advancing village betterment projects and in linking individuals (sometimes in very personal relationships) who are otherwise distanced by the *jati* divisions of society. Like all village politics, factional politics also serves to uphold *dharma*, and thus the right and proper order of Hindu society.

A second set of studies emphasizes the internal organization of factions and the manner in which they are recruited. Perhaps the first benchmark for these studies was the symposium on factions in Indian and overseas Indian communities. The papers presented in that symposium, collected and edited by Firth (1957), suggest that factions are political groups, though not part of the formal structure of government; factions are opposition groups; factions are impermanent groups mobilized for specific competitions; factions are organized around the role of leader and member; faction members are recruited by diverse religious, economic, kinship and patron–client ties, or by any combination of these; faction membership is voluntary and easily changed according to shifting personal advantage; factions can be composite groups in which allied factions nonetheless preserve their separate identities; a faction may promote the goals of its membership above those of the society as a whole; and factions may serve as the vehicle for individuals to achieve their personal goals. Some of these features are present in a more concise, formal definition of factions by Ralph Nicholas, who writes: 'Factions are conflict groups... factions are political groups... factions are not corporate groups... faction members are recruited by a leader... faction members are recruited on diverse principles' (1965:27–9). This definition, developed in part from Bengali materials, applies perfectly well to factions in Torkotala.

Most recently a third research direction has moved from the study of factions *per se*, the structure of which is now well defined, to a study of factionalism. At issue are the political processes internal to a faction, say at times of recruitment or mobilization, and the process of competition between factions. Bujra (1973) provides an early statement of the problems raised in viewing factions dynamically. The conference papers on factionalism collected and edited by Silverman and Salisbury (1977) provide a first set of generalizations. It is evident that factional ties are most often created through transactional bargains of a sort which exchange patronage for clientage; factional ties based on short-term exchange relations are unstable bases for political alliances; faction leaders try to convert relatively unstable transactional ties with supporters into ties of generalized loyalty and moral commitment; when the same faction members are mobilized on several occasions this action-set may be transformed into a quasi-group, or even take on permanence and corporate features characteristic of a party; through competition it is usual for one faction in a community to emerge as the strongest and come to represent an in-group establishment against one or more out-group opposition factions; factional competition usually concerns only the interests of the leader and his elite group; yet involvement in factional politics can provide an opportunity for faction members outside the elite to assert themselves as a group.

To this recent interest in factionalism can be added an attention to the context of meaning in which factional competitions occur. What is the prize of factional politics? What are the qualities deemed to merit that prize? How are factional competitions scored as won or lost? These are among the questions raised in adding a cultural dimension to the study of Torkotala factional politics. It is a dimension needed to clarify the dynamic which fuels factional politics in an Indian setting.

Like all village politics, Torkotala factional politics aims at the ultimate prize of rank. Factions are not themselves ranked social units, but their respective leaders are. As defined within a transformational theory of human development, individual Hindus can be ranked apart from their membership in a caste, line or family on the basis of personal power (*sakti*), wealth (*dhani*), knowledge (*jnana*), honor (*saman*) and name or reputation (*nam*). These are the qualities of a big man (*boro lok*), and it is among big men that factional competitions are waged. Indeed, factional politics is identified by Torkotala villagers with competitions among big men, teamed with their supporters, to be recognized as the biggest of big men, as *the* leader (*neta*).

The process by which big men as factional leaders are compared can be termed, paraphrasing Moore, 'selection for rank' (Moore and Myerhoff 1975:109–43). That is, factional leaders are ranked via a series of competitions which have the cumulative effect of sorting out big men as more or less behaviorally dominant, as having those personal qualities of power, wealth, etc. required successfully to complete a project once undertaken, or to oppose successfully the completion of projects undertaken by other big men. Every factional competition is thus a test of those personal qualities by which individuals are compared, with recognition as the biggest of the big being the cumulative result of many factional wins. Being the biggest of the big is an achieved status. As such it is also a status open to challenge and requiring occasional defense. This lends factional politics an open-ended or serial quality as competition breeds competition in a continuing selection for rank. The pattern of such competitions is described before returning to a discussion of the process which generates that pattern.

Selection for rank

The major factions and factional leaders in Torkotala were identified in chapter 1 as part of a discussion of local history and administration. As noted then, there are two major political cleavages in Torkotala. There is the cleavage between the Sadgop caste as the first settlers and largest landholders of the village and all other castes and tribes, which provides the vertical axis to village politics and rests, in the main, on Sadgops as a caste being the economic patrons of the village and also the primary regents of natural and moral order. Secondly, there is the cleavage within the Sadgop caste between the three factions led by Haripado Bhunai, the village *Mukhya*, Anil Pal, the village *Raj Mukhya*, and Atul Mahabarto, the village *Adhyaksa*, respectively. The competition between these men and their respective supporters provides the horizontal axis of village politics. Whereas the vertical cleavage between Sadgops and non-Sadgops of the village gives rise to the politics of caste, it is the horizontal cleavage within the Sadgop caste which is the primary source of factional politics in Torkotala. Though the membership of each faction has varied over the years, the competition between Haripado, Anil and Atul has been a constant in village politics for decades, and has roots even further back in time.

In Torkotala the office of *Mukhya* has been held by males of the Bhunai line from the very founding of the village. Thus the Bhunai have always had a prominent place in Torkotala village life. The prominence of the *Mukhya* and his line has diminished sharply in this century, though, since the declining fortunes of the Pal Rajas described in chapter 1. As the active rule of the Pal Rajas over their kingdom diminished, the *Mukhya* could no longer rely on the Raja to support his leadership of village affairs, and was left to compete for influence with other men of the village on the basis of personal resources that could be mobilized to attract and retain a political following. Rich men (*dhani lok*) began to rival the *Mukhya* as the effective head of Torkotala, for in Torkotala economic dependency implies wide-ranging political dependency as well.

Among the richest and most influential men of the times were Biswananth Maiti and Radhanath Mahabarto. These men were not coevals, but their lives did overlap. Biswanath was the elder of the two and had already amassed a large landholding and political following by the time Radhanath married and entered the life stage of young adulthood. Towards the end of his life, Biswanath saw Radhanath supplant him as the richest and most influential man in Torkotala. Biswanath viewed Radhanath as a brash upstart who maneuvered by ill means to be appointed tax collector for the British Raj. To him this discredited whatever wealth and influence Radhanath attained. It did not diminish Radhanath's actual influence over Torkotala village affairs, however.

The rivalry and strong animosity felt between Biswanath and Radhanath is retained in the relationship between their descendants. Why this is so is explained locally as the expected result of shared descent. Just as a man inherits the nature and code of his father, so too does he inherit his rivals. That the descendants of two rivals should pursue their own rivalry with vigor and determination is attributed to the ill-will, in thought and deed, engendered over time through specific competitions. The rivalry between Anil Pal and Atul Mahabarto, to illustrate, is considered the natural and moral consequence of their parentage (see figure 8). That these men should harbor the great ill-will for each other that they do is attributed to the specific events surrounding Kamala's marriage.

Kamala is Anil Pal's elder sister, his only sister. Some 25 years ago she was given in marriage by Anil's father, Tijendra Pal, to Radhanath Mahabarto, who stands to Atul in the relation of father's elder brother. This was the first marriage ever between the Mahabarto and Maiti–Pal lines, who already had a history of ill-will separating them because of the competition between Radhanath Mahabarto and Biswanath Maiti.

Kamala's marriage to Radhanath came at a time when Radhanath was already a very old, even sickly, man who had outlived two previous wives. Anil objected to the marriage on the grounds that Kamala would be a bride and a widow within the same year. He also objected because, as all in the village knew, when Biswanath died he and Radhanath were not on speaking terms with one another. It was wrong, Anil reasoned, that Kamala be given in marriage to Biswanath's rival.

For quite different reasons, Atul had equally strong objections to Kamala's marriage. Radhanath amassed a large amount of land during his lifetime. As his only son, the first in line to inherit these lands, was dead, this left Atul and his younger brother, Pulin, next in line of inheritance. It was to guard their interests in this inheritance that Atul objected to Kamala's marriage. That is, Atul suspected Tijendra Pal of using his daughter's marriage to gain control over Radhanath's land and to divert some of it into his own possession. That Tijendra entered Torkotala as a husband living in the house of his wife's father, and later maneuvered to acquire title to some of Biswanath's land after his death, lent credence to Atul's suspicions. Tijendra, as described by Atul and others, was a man who used his knowledge in sneaky-clever ways.

Anil and Atul were very close, even intimate friends as children and youths. Anil is three years senior to Atul, but as the two went through primary school in the same classes this seniority was never emphasized. After Kamala's marriage, Atul accused Anil of being in collusion with his father and of trying to divert some of Radhanath's land from him. Villagers now say this accusation was probably true to some extent. 'No tree shakes without a breeze,' meaning suspicions are seldom altogether groundless. That Tijendra and Anil were unsuccessful in their efforts to gain control of Radhanath's land was due in the main to the vigilance of Atul and Pulin, who seized all of Radhanath's land records immediately upon his death. Such suspicion and active opposition further exacerbated the ill-will between the Maiti–Pal and Mahabarto lines. Following Kamala's marriage Anil and Atul both claimed the other harbored the ill-will of their ancestors, intending thereby to continue their rivalries as well.

152

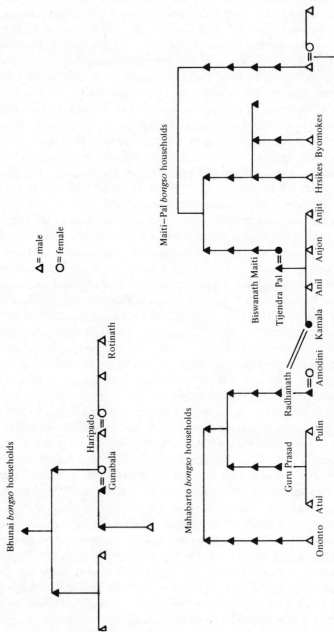

Fig. 8. Partial genealogies of the Bhunai, Mahabarto and Maiti–Pal *bongso*

Whereas the events surrounding Kamala's marriage account for the specific ill-will between Anil and Atul, the rivalry between each of them and Haripado Bhunai is attributed to a more general set of circumstances. Haripado thinks that the village *Mukhya* no longer receives the honor and respect once given to holders of this traditional office. This is due, as Haripado explains it, to the growing influence of rich men, like Anil and Atul, who are able to mobilize a greater number of economic dependents as a political following.

Involved in the competition between Haripado, Anil and Atul, and what expands their interpersonal rivalries into factional rivalries, are the core and following of each. These supporters are drawn from within the Sadgop caste and from without, and are recruited by a combination of kinship, neighborhood, religious and economic ties. The core supporters of each faction leader are nevertheless identified primarily with one of the three neighborhoods into which East Hamlet is divided. Specifically, the core supporters of Haripado, Anil and Atul come primarily from families of their line, all of whom live together in separate neighborhoods of East Hamlet. The factional alignments in Torkotala thus have their physical representation in the settlement pattern of East Hamlet.

In 1971 there were 21 Sadgop households in Torkotala. Six of these households belong to the Bhunai line and support the faction headed by Haripado Bhunai. Six households belong to the Maiti–Pal line and support the faction headed by Anil Pal. Four households belong to the Mahabarto line and support the faction headed by Atul Mahabarto. The remaining five households belong to other smaller lines, which do not constitute a factional grouping of their own, but divide their support and loyalties among the factions led by Haripado, Anil and Atul on a basis other than kinship ties.

The size of the Bhunai, Maiti–Pal and Mahabarto lines affects the recruitment activities of their respective leaders. That is, as the Mahabarto line consists of only four households, Atul has looked beyond his own kin for additional support to counter the larger Maiti–Pal and Bhunai factions. Atul's early recognition of Bagdi claims to being Bagra-Khatriyas was an obvious bid to win the favor and support of village Bagdis, for example. After being selected head of the statutory village council, Atul used his position as *Adhyaksa* to win still other supporters among the Lodhas and Mundas of the village through council projects which sunk tube wells in the tribal hamlets and improved roads between the Hindu and tribal hamlets.

Through his work as *Adhyaksa*, Atul has successfully attracted a political following that is not based on kinship or economic dependency *per se*, but on the promise of patronage spoils that can be distributed through the office of statutory council head. Anil's following, by contrast, consists by and large of economic dependents who work in one capacity or another for the various families of the Maiti–Pal line. The following gathered around Anil in this way is not small, as the Maiti–Pal line is collectively the largest landholder and employer of the village. But when compared to Atul's following, Anil's following is much more unstable. As individuals enter into and out of the employ of the various Maiti–Pal households they often switch their factional loyalties as well. Regarding Haripado's political following, beyond his own kin it counts but two or three persons in the direct employ of Haripado. The Bhunai line is not small, and includes six households. But the Bhunai families have the least landholdings. Also, the office of *Mukhya* no longer has patronage spoils to distribute aside from the personal support of the *Mukhya* himself. As a consequence, Haripado's faction is the smallest of all. Recognizing this, Haripado adopts for himself and his faction a kind of third-party position in which he stands aside from competitions between Anil and Atul in order later to play a mediating role, or to mobilize his own supporters later as a swing group to shift the balance of support in the particular direction he favors. In doing so Haripado describes himself as acting solely with the desire to maintain village unity and the proper administration of village affairs. He adopts an explicitly moralistic stance which emphasizes the proper aim of politics as rule in accord with natural and moral order, thereby justifying his own factional activities while indirectly reprimanding both Anil and Atul for precipitating factional competitions in the first place. This is not to say that Haripado and his supporters do not pursue factional goals of their own, which they do; only that Haripado is extremely careful not to be viewed as the initiator of factional competitions.

The organization of factional teams in Torkotala, and the manner in which they are recruited, suggest no features not already recognized in the definition by Nicholas cited earlier. Less often recognized is that beyond the apparent divisiveness of factional competitions, factions also play an integrative role in bringing together into one team individuals of different castes and tribes, some of whom may have no other personal tie with each other. The activities of factions over time also reveal how the leadership, core support and following of these teams can endure with little change over relatively long periods, and even across generations. The incidents of the club house and school will document how seemingly unrelated factional competitions, occurring months or even years apart, are identified by Torkotala villagers as the continuation of a single factional rivalry and how this continuing rivalry is part of a general process in which competitors are sorted out into ranked winners and losers. Note, too, the pattern of continuing competition, in which the loser in a specific competition is prone to renew the competition in order to reverse his fortunes, and rank.

The club house incident

On October 3, 1960 an *ad hoc* village meeting called by Atul Mahabarto met to discuss the establishment of a society (*samaj*) for Hindus of Torkotala. Both the Lodhas and Mundas of the village, with the encouragement and aid of the Tribal Welfare Officer, had already formed their own societies and since then were able to secure government aid for several development programs. The Mundas had built a club house in one of their hamlets with government money. The Lodhas secured government money to build a storehouse, so they would not need to sell their rice immediately after harvest when prices were lowest.

With the success of the Munda and Lodha societies in mind, Atul suggested that Hindus of Torkotala could organize their own society, to be known as Hitarthi Sangho. He suggested as well that the program of the new society could include, among other things, building a village club house, and establishing a village library. Those present at the meeting agreed to form such a society, and a temporary steering committee was selected immediately. Ononto Mahabarto was selected president; Bhakto Krishna Bhunai, vice-president; Atul Krishna Mahabarto, secretary; Satya Chandra Dolai, treasurer; and Pulin Bihari Mahabarto, member.

All the officers of Hitarthi Sangho were factional supporters of Atul Mahabarto, and all but Satya Dolai, a Bagra-Khatriya, were Sadgops. Not represented on the steering committee, nor present at the village meeting, were Anil Pal and Haripado Bhunai, nor were any of their factional supporters. Word of the business of the meeting had leaked out, and both Anil and Haripado boycotted, to indicate that they would not support one of Atul's projects.

That Atul looked upon the new society as an important personal project was confirmed for Anil, Haripado and others by the distribution of society offices. To their minds the nominations received from the body of the meeting were not unplanned. They suspected that Atul met with his core supporters before the meeting was announced publicly to decide what the name of the society would be, its program, and first slate of officers. It also did not surprise Anil or Haripado that Atul was nominated and confirmed as secretary of the Hitarthi Sangho. To be the secretary of a society is to be its active, responsible agent. President and vice-president are but titular, honorary positions.

During the first year of the Hitarthi Sangho, Ononto Mahabarto, who stands to Atul in the relation of father's elder brother's son, donated land at the western edge of East Hamlet on which a club house was soon built. On an adjacent piece of land, also owned by Ononto, a playing field was cleared during the first year as well. All these activities were formally reported on October 2, 1961, at the first annual meeting of the Hitarthi

Sangho. At that meeting it was also announced, name by name, who contributed in cash or labor to the building of the new club house and the clearing of the new playing field. Thus were all of Atul's supporters publicly identified and all those who opposed the work of the Hitarthi Sangho, or at least did not actively contribute to it, were also duly noted. Included among those who had not supported the society were Anil Pal, who opposed every project Atul had undertaken since Kamala's marriage, and Haripado Bhunai. Lodhas and Mundas of the village both gave their labor to the club house project.

During the first annual meeting a permanent steering committee was also formed. All past offices and officers remained as before. To them was added the office of assistant secretary, filled by Hrsikes Maiti. As Hrsikes was a kinsman of Anil, and an acknowledged member of Anil's faction, his acceptance meant that Atul had subverted one of Anil's core supporters. Why should Hrsikes choose to lend his support to one of Atul's projects? Public opinion had it that Hrsikes was personally ambitious. He was already a rich man; now he wanted to become known as a big man, a man of power and honor and name or fame.

On October 4, 1962 the Hitarthi Sangho convened its second annual meeting. Activities of the past year were reviewed. Then Atul proposed that the society sponsor a football (soccer) tournament. The BDO had recently been encouraging villages to cooperate in joint activities, and a football tournament, Atul argued, provided an excellent way to do this. The body of the meeting agreed to Atul's suggestion, and a games committee was appointed directly. Adi Patro, the headmaster of the village primary school, was appointed president. Hrsikes was appointed secretary. Atul's brother, Pulin, was appointed captain. After the committee was formed, Atul announced that a widow of his line, Amodini, had donated 25 rupees for a shield to be given to the tournament winner. The tournament would be named the Amodini Shield Tournament in her honor. Atul also announced that Gunabala, Haripado Bhunai's widowed sister, had donated money for a running cup to be given as a consolation prize. This piece of news was received with particular joy because it meant that Haripado, through his sister, was finally indicating his support for the Hitarthi Sangho. Previously Haripado had not attended any of the society meetings, nor spoken publicly in support of the society.

One of the original programs of the Hitarthi Sangho was to establish a village library. It was not until July 30, 1962, though, that first steps towards establishing a library were actually taken. On that day Atul sent a letter to the District Social Education Officer (DSEO) describing the activities of the Hitarthi Sangho and the success of its recently begun football tournament, and asking for money to buy library books for the club house. Within the week, accompanied by one of his supporters, Atul paid a visit to the Block Social Education Officer (BSEO) for the same purpose. The BSEO told him that government money would be available later if the villagers first raised some money of their own to start the library.

Within one week after his visit to the BSEO Atul raised 200 rupees, all from his factional supporters, and used the money to purchase books. On August 24 a letter from the BSEO was received, asking for a detailed proposal describing how the library would be used, managed, organized, and so on. Atul took this letter to an outsider to the village known to have wide experience with government officials, who wrote the proposal as requested. Eight months later, in March 1963, a non-recurring grant of 500 rupees was received from the BSEO for purposes of establishing a village library.

Through these and other activities of the Hitarthi Sangho Atul became very well known throughout the Narayanghar area. People began to speak of him as a famous man (*nam kora lok*). Hrsikes, too, became well known for his management of the successful Amodini Shield Tournament. Even Haripado received some measure of fame for being the headman of a model village. Anil, for his part, gradually removed himself from participation in village affairs. Especially after losing the election for *Adhyaksa* in 1962, Anil spent more and more of his time outside Torkotala. He began a rice business on the road to Narayanghar, and a second business trucking sugar-cane cuttings to other parts of West Bengal. Responsibility for the family rice lands was left entirely to Anil's younger brothers, with whom he lived as joint family. Torkotala villagers viewed Anil's business ventures outside the village as smart moves economically: 'one cannot make a good living as a rice farmer any more'. The same ventures were interpreted by some as meaning that Anil, defeated in the election for *Adhyaksa*, and unable to undermine the activities of the Hitarthi Sangho, had surrendered village leadership to Atul. In fact, Anil was only waiting for the right opportunity to renew his rivalry with Atul, as soon became clear in the incident of the school.

The incident of the school

On November 7, 1963, a meeting of the statutory village council was held, presided over by Atul Mahabarto, *Adhyaksa*, at which repair of the primary school building located at the east end of East Hamlet was raised. All present agreed that the primary school building was quite small and did not allow for internal divisions which would separate the children by classes. Also, the wood beams of its roof structure had begun to rot. For these reasons, the villagers decided, it was wiser to replace the primary school with a new one rather than continually repair the present building. Atul then suggested that the new primary school be located in the area adjoining the new club house and playing field. Members of the council agreed to this plan, but suggested that Atul notify the head of the area statutory council, the *anchal pradhan*, of their decision before actually relocating the primary school from its present site.

Though a member of the village council, Anil long ago had stopped attending its meetings, and thus was not present when the decision to transfer the primary school was taken. Hrsikes, because he was not a council member, was also not present. But as secretary of the village primary school, Hrsikes was angry at not being given an invitation to attend the council meeting, or at least consulted about the school transfer before the meeting. Thus Hrsikes immediately opposed the school transfer plan when he did learn of it. Anil was also opposed to it. He opposed all of Atul's projects. But beyond this, he and Hrsikes both had another reason for their opposition. To them Atul's plan to transfer the primary school to the west end of the hamlet was a scheme of personal aggrandizement. Atul and his kin lived at the west end of the hamlet, near to where the new club house and playing field were built, while Anil and Hrsikes and their kin lived at the east end of the hamlet, near to where the primary school was presently located. Atul's plan to transfer the primary school was thus interpreted by Anil and Hrsikes as a scheme to degrade their neighborhood in favor of his own. Haripado Bhunai, who also lives near the old primary school, shared the interpretation held by Anil and Hrsikes, and thus also opposed transferring the primary school.

Neither Anil nor Hrsikes nor Haripado took any immediate action, choosing to wait and see if the *anchal pradhan* affirmed the village council's right to effect a school transfer. If he did not, there would be no need for further action. Within a week, though, the *anchal pradhan* replied in writing that the school transfer could proceed as planned if approved by a majority of the village council members.

Atul quickly called another meeting of the village council, at which a majority of the council members present did vote to transfer the primary school. Notice of this decision was also forwarded to the *anchal pradhan*. Soon after, Anil sent his own letter to the *anchal pradhan* saying that the council decision should not be accepted as final because he and another member, Phani Babu, the village Brahman, had not been present and were strongly opposed to any transfer of the primary school. Moreover, Anil wrote, it was not the custom of Torkotala residents to reach decisions by a majority vote. In Torkotala decisions were customarily based on the unanimous agreement of all, which on this issue did not exist. As his final argument Anil also wrote that the primary school should not be transferred, or a new school built, because the old school could be repaired satisfactorily at far less expense.

On receiving the letters from Atul and Anil, the *anchal pradhan* soon withdrew his original ruling without suggesting further what the villagers might do. Four months passed in which the old school was not repaired and no plans for building a new school were made. It seemed that Anil had effectively opposed one of Atul's projects, thereby buttressing his own status as a man of power and influence and protecting certain interests in his neighborhood. Then, on March 19, 1964, the *anchal pradhan* made a surprise visit to Torkotala. A meeting of all villagers was called, at which the *anchal pradhan* conducted his own vote regarding the primary school transfer. Of 31 villagers present, 26 supported Atul and voted to transfer the primary school.

Even after the results of this vote Anil was not willing to see the primary school transferred. As advised by Anil, Hrsikes wrote a letter to the district magistrate stating his reasons, as secretary of the primary-school committee, for opposing the move. His hope was that the district magistrate, a higher-level government official, would overrule the *anchal pradhan*, which he did. Thus were Atul's plans to transfer the primary school again stymied, this time by Anil expanding the incident of the school to include a higher-level authority.

From 1964 until January 1968 Atul made no other attempts to have the primary school transferred to the west end of East Hamlet. Few villagers believed he had given up on the project, rationalizing Atul's long period of seeming inactivity by saying, 'Time flies, words last.' The memory of Anil's and Hrsikes's opposition, in other words, would not be forgotten; it was only a matter of time before the rivalry would be renewed, perhaps over the same issue, perhaps over another.

It was in January 1968 that Atul announced all arrangements were complete for a university-educated social worker from outside the village to staff and operate a junior high school in the area of the village club house if residents of Torkotala would finance and raise a building for the new school. A high school was raised within the year, labor and money for the new school coming in the main from Atul's supporters, and to a much lesser extent from Haripado Bhunai and his supporters. Haripado favored the new junior high school for the credit it would bring to the village. He was also promised that Rotinath, his wife's brother, would become a teacher in the new school, a position Rotinath did eventually receive. Anil opposed the new junior high school because its establishment would mean that Atul, at long last, had succeeded in adding a school to the club house and playing field area, thereby making his neighborhood the recreational and educational center of the village. To successfully establish a new junior high school would also mean that Atul had bested Anil – at least until the next confrontation.

By the end of 1968 Torkotala had two schools, a primary school at the east end of East Hamlet, and a junior high school at the west end of East Hamlet. Each school had become a symbol of factional loyalty and strength, with Atul and his factional supporters being identified with the junior high school and nearby club house and playing field, and Anil and Haripado and their factional supporters being identified with the primary school. Against this background Hrsikes called an *ad hoc* village meeting in November 1970 to discuss building a new primary school on the same site as the old primary school now stood. The old building had been repaired as needed over the years, but now the collapse of the rotted wood structure of the roof was imminent. Atul and his supporters were present in numbers at this meeting, and did not speak against a new primary school building. They, too, agreed that one was needed. But when Hrsikes called for pledges of labor and money for building the new primary school, Atul and his supporters were conspicuously silent. No explanation was offered for why they offered no pledges, and none was asked for. Yet all present understood that Atul was having his day: that he withheld support for the new primary school because in the past Anil and his faction made no contribution to building the junior high school.

The incidents of the club house and school do not end here, nor has the account given thus far included the many smaller incidents which fed into and fanned the specific competitions which were described. To do so would be to detail almost all of the factional competitions in Torkotala village during the last decade. An immediate competition between factional leaders may pass, but recollection of it rankles until an opportunity for continuing the rivalry presents itself. In this way each past competition becomes the source of future competitions, and factional politics is seen to have a dynamic and genetic history of its own.

Structure, process and meaning in factional politics

Like the politics of family life and the politics of caste, factional politics aims at the ultimate prize of rank. The units of rank are faction leaders, who are compared with respect to personal power, wealth, knowledge, honor and name or reputation. These are the qualities of a big man (*boro lok*), and it is among big men like Anil and Atul and Haripado that factional competitions are waged. More specifically, factional politics is identified by Torkotala villagers with competitions among big men, teamed with their supporters, to be recognized as the biggest of big men, as *the* leader.

Faction leaders are ranked via a series of competitions which have the cumulative effect of sorting out big men as more or less behaviorally dominant. Behavioral dominance confers rank by confirming those personal qualities by which big men as leaders are compared. Rank entails expectations of further behavioral dominance, which is realized through the control over persons and those material resources required to complete a project undertaken or successfully to oppose projects undertaken by a competitor. Material interests are thus not absent from factional competitions, be it the raising of a club house or relocating a school. But more than material interests are at issue. Factional competitions are also a realistic test of leadership and rank. The process of comparing leaders through the results of actual competition is here termed 'selection for rank.' It is a transformational process which highlights being the biggest of the big, *the* leader, as an achieved status resting on the personal qualities of individuals *qua* individuals, and not as members of a particular birth group. In that sense does factional politics further confirm the place and importance of individuals in Hindu society.

Victor Turner has formulated a processual model of local-level politics in which specific competitions typically pass through four distinct phases. (1) A public breach leads to (2) a crisis within a community. Then (3) redressive action is taken and, depending on its effectiveness, there results (4) a reconciliation of competitors or a social recognition of irreparable schism (Turner 1974: 37–42). In Torkotala, as in other Indian villages where there are reports of factional politics over time (see Beals and Siegel 1966; Lewis 1954; Nicholas 1965), it is more common for competition to take the form of extended rivalry in which selection for rank is an on-going process. Turner's phase 4 is never attained as each crisis becomes the source of future breaches, competition breeding competition in a continuing test of leadership. In this way does the process of selection for rank generate a continuing, if episodic, history of factional politics.

Beals and Siegel (1960b: 399) write that factional politics 'is essentially a phenomenon of socio-cultural change,' a product of external pressures on a political system that cannot be handled by applying routine or traditional devices. In Namhalli, the Mysore village studied by Beals, factionalism is dated from the famine of 1876–8, when the British management of this crisis presented villagers with an alternative political and legal system. Making an analogous historical argument for Torkotala factional politics is difficult because, as detailed in chapter 1, Torkotala has been subject to the external pressures of a series of superior rulers – Hindu, Moghul and British – from its very founding. If we know less about factional politics in Torkotala (or Namhalli) in the 1700s than the 1900s, it is more likely an artifact of the information retrievable than the absence of factional competition in a period of political isolation and social calm. The same point can be generalized. That is, a view of factional politics as a phenomenon of socio-cultural change implies a period of relative isolation and calm in which there were no, or significantly fewer, factional competitions. It is a view difficult to accept because villages of India probably never were – in that long-standing idealization – timeless, self-contained republics in which all lived in harmony and consensus. The external pressures cited by Beals and Siegel may provoke new material interests and thus provide new bones of contention for factional politics. But the process of selection for rank probably would generate factional politics during periods of relative stasis or change so long as Hindus remain concerned about differences in rank. The dynamic of factional politics in Torkotala is thus viewed as an endogenous process fueled by the Hindu concern with ranked inequalities. It is a process which seemingly generates factional competitions independently of external pressures associated with situations of change.

⌐ The importance of ranked inequalities among Hindus defines the cultural fuel, so to speak, which generates a history of episodic factional ∟competitions in Torkotala. But continuing factional competition is probably not peculiar to politics in rural India for, even if the culturally defined prize of competition were different, the structure of factions as political teams and the nature of factional leadership would both contribute to a history of self-perpetuating factional competition. Factional leadership is an achieved status. As an achieved status, it is also a status continually open to challenge. And even in the absence of open challenge, the achieved nature of factional leadership requires, periodically, the demonstration of those qualities by which leadership is realized, and leaders compared, Episodic factional competition is generated as well by the structure of factions as non-corporate political teams. Families and castes perdure in the absence of competition because they are not solely, or even primarily, political groups. Corporate political teams like political parties also perdure because they have institutionalized functions that continue apart from contested elections. But factions are non-corporate political teams that only exist for the purpose and at times of actual competition. For a faction leader to maintain the personal ties between himself and his following would thus seem to require periodic factional competitions.

In a comparative study of factionalism in thirty villages of a district in Mysore state, Alan Beals (1969) explored the hypothesis that factionalism – or in his terms, conflict between parties – will increase as village size increases, presumably because an increase in village size represents an increase in the number of potential competitors and thus provides greater opportunity for factional competition. The quantitative data for testing this hypothesis were drawn from census records and police reports which, Beals recognized, were limited as source materials. Police records, for example, probably under-reported actual factional competitions because 'whenever possible police officials and other outsiders were not told about existing conflicts' (Beals 1969: 36). The limitations of the data notwithstanding, Beals (1969: 42) concluded that his hypothesis was supported at a statistically significant level, even though he notes during the analysis of the data that 'there is no simple and direct relationship between the incidence of conflict and population size' (1969: 32). The evidence from Torkotala suggests both cultural and structural reasons for why no direct relationship should be expected. Simply, the value attached to individual rank within a transformational theory of human development, the nature of factional leadership as an achieved status, and the structure of factions as non-corporate political teams will each contribute to recurrent factional politics in villages large and small. But is there a minimal size required to support factional politics? On the basis of actual factional competitions reported in police records, Beals observes 'that in order to have party conflict at all, a village should have about one hundred households' (1969:39). Torkotala has but 65 Hindu households, plus another 73 tribal households. In total, then, there are more than one hundred Torkotala households. Yet it seems unlikely that factional competitions would not exist in Torkotala in the absence of any tribal households, particularly when the cleavage among Torkotala factions is internal to the Sadgop caste, and no faction leader relies exclusively on tribal Lodhas and Mundas for his following. It is more likely that the relationship Beals sought between village size and factional politics pertains not to the incidence of factional competition – which seems independent of village size or external pressures of social change – but to the manner in which competitions are managed. That is, smaller, more socially cohesive villages may be more successful in processing factional competitions locally and without the participation of police officials or other outsiders.

The structure of factional politics differs somewhat from that of other forms of village politics. Unlike families and castes as political teams, factions are voluntary, not ascriptive groupings. Members enter and remain in a faction for very personal and highly circumstantial reasons, which may vary over time. Also, unlike in a family or caste, the ties that bind faction members to a leader are not necessarily natural or moral ties. More often faction membership is based on transactional ties, bargains of a sort, in which each individual gives his support to a faction leader in expectation of some personal gains, direct or indirect, immediate or delayed. Continued membership in a faction then depends on a return for support given. It is because factions are voluntary teams based largely on transactional ties that their membership is so variable. Simply, individuals can switch their loyalties and support at will. As the incidents of the club house and school evidence, though, the voluntary nature of faction membership notwithstanding, the core and following of a faction leader may remain more or less stable over time. In Torkotala this is because faction members are attracted less by the issues at stake than the personal qualities of individual leaders. It is loyalty to a leader that lends stability to factions as political teams. Ties of factional loyalty, importantly, cross-cut divisions of caste and can divide persons of the same caste. In Torkotala the core supporters of Haripado, Anil and Atul come primarily from families of their own line, which divides Sadgops of the village into rough thirds. This limits Sadgop solidarity and encourages inter-caste alliances as each faction leader looks to recruit decisive support from outside the caste. Because factions are recruited across and largely irrespective of the caste divisions of society, they have a heterogeneous membership that is unique among teams in village politics.

The voluntary, transactional, heterogeneous nature of factions as political teams suggests why factional politics is often and sometimes openly guided by pragmatic rather than normative rules. Specifically, as factional competition is between teams that are not bound by natural and moral ties of birth, there is less constraint to pursue that competition according to normative rules. 'By all means, fair or foul,' could well be the slogan of factional politics. This translates behaviorally as winning through black arrows. In the incident of the school, to illustrate, Anil and Hrsikes effectively blocked Atul's effort to relocate the primary school by involving the district magistrate in a village affair. This was a successful tactic. It was also a suspect – Atul would say, an unfair – tactic because it expanded and transformed an instance of village politics in the direction of government politics. Village politics ideally involves only villagers, and should never involve outsiders, especially highly placed government officials, when this can be avoided. Notifying the *anchal pradhan* of the village council's decision to relocate the primary school, Atul says, was unavoidable, and merely to report a decision already taken is not really to involve the *anchal pradhan* in village politics. For Anil and Hrsikes to appeal the decision of the village council to an outsider, by contrast, is to follow the sneaky-clever, circuitous route of a black arrow.

Of all the forms of village politics, factional politics is most often and most openly guided by pragmatic evaluations of effectiveness. It is also the form of village politics which most often and most easily expands to include outsiders to the village. In that sense it represents a transitional form between village politics and government politics. Factions as a type of political team are common to both forms of rule. The prize factions compete for differs in each context, though, as will be detailed in chapter 5.

Whether pursued through normative rules or pragmatic rules, in the context of village politics factional competitions are generally accompanied by a moralistic language of claims. Each faction argues the righteousness of its own position and how it will advance social goals shared by the community, while exaggerating the very personal, even selfish ends of its opposition. In the incident of the club house, for example, activities of the Hitarthi Sangho were publicly promoted for the credit and benefit they would bring to the entire village, and not as a personal project for Atul Mahabarto and his supporters. Similarly, Anil's opposition to transferring the primary school was stated in terms of gain or loss for the village as a whole; it would be less expensive to repair the old primary school than to build a new one, so it was said. To provide another example, Atul's stated reason for helping found a junior high school emphasized the credit it would bring to the entire village. He did not state, as was also true, that his support of the high school represented another effort to best Anil Pal by establishing a school at the west end of East Hamlet. As these incidents evidence, whatever the actual goals of competing big men, in factional politics personal goals are usually masked publicly by a moralistic language of claims.

Summary and discussion

The first half of this study identified the basic units of the Bengali cosmos and society, how they are defined and differentiated locally, and how they are related one to the other in a Bengali construction of reality ordered on the premise of ranked inequalities. This chapter begins a discussion of how that system of ranked inequalities is variously maintained or altered, supported or challenged, through a variety of political acts. It also extends the discussion of Torkotala administration begun in chapter 1 in presenting local conceptions of politics and the relationship between polity, society and cosmos.

Torkotala Hindus refer to politics as *sason*, or rule, and then distinguish between two kinds of rule: government politics (the subject of chapter 5) and village politics. Village politics (*gramer kaj*) refers literally to the work (*kaj*) of the village (*gram*). Such work aims to uphold (*palana*) the customs of the *des* and of all the *jati* and *lok* within it. It is identified behaviorally with myriad family, caste and factional competitions over rank and the behavior appropriate to ranked social units. Informing this conception of village politics are four consciously held premises. (1) Politics is the administration of the divinely given natural and moral orders, *dharma* writ large, and the behavior appropriate to all individuals and birth groups, *dharma* writ small. (2) Politics is (ideally) moral activity in that the administration of dharma should itself be through means that are in accord with *dharma*. (3) Politics is the shared responsibility of all, for all are enjoined to act in accord with their own behavioral code and to ensure that others do the same. And (4) politics is subordinate to and inseparable from *dharma* in that it takes its definition of goals and moral means towards those goals from this concept.

These four premises constitute the theme of village politics. The politics of family life, the politics of caste and factional politics are the several forms of competition which Torkotala villagers identify as documenting that theme. Put differently, it is the Bengali concern with upholding a natural and moral order grounded on the premise of ranked inequalities which defines the context of meaning in which specific family, caste and factional competitions are engendered, fought and won. It is through competitions over rank and the behavior appropriate to ranked social units that the natural and moral orders of the universe are affirmed and maintained, sometimes with needed realignments in a given hierarchy. In that sense are theme and event, rank and rivalry, each intelligible in terms of the other.

This conjunction of rank and rivalry belies the usual Western distinction between religion and politics as clearly discrete, autonomous domains. In Torkotala, rivalries over rank have a social significance which transcends their nature as instrumental means towards an immediate material goal. Rivalries are also symbolic statements about the right and proper order of society, which in the context of village politics is defined by the religious framework of Hinduism. This highlights the nature of politics as two-dimensional: as a system of instrumental action and symbolic meaning. A two-dimensional understanding of Torkotala politics also reveals the limitations of universalistic definitions which posit politics as the ultimate domain of authority in society. In two of the definitions used most widely among anthropologists, for example, David Easton (1965: 21) defines the political as 'those interactions through which values are authoritatively allocated for a society,' while Swartz, Turner and Tuden (1966: 7) equate politics with those 'processes involved in determining and implementing public goals.' In the same vein Ronald Cohen (1973: 872) writes, 'We must operationally define the political system as the widest set of authority relations in society.' The example of Torkotala village politics, by contrast, reveals that while politics may always involve the administration of public goals and values, it does not always define those goals and values. In Torkotala, as elsewhere in rural West Bengal, village politics is inseparable from and subordinated to considerations of religion.

The theme of village politics provides a common significance to a number of ostensibly unrelated family, caste and factional competitions. All aim to uphold the natural and moral orders of society by upholding the behavior appropriate to ranked social units. Yet each form of village politics retains an event character of its own because the qualities deemed to merit the prize of rank and the structure and process of competition differ in each.

The politics of family life consists of interpersonal competitions between individual family members in which attributes of sex and age are the personal qualities deemed to merit the political prize. In this competition males rank over females, and seniors over juniors, because of the greater knowledge and skill presumed to come with life experience in a transformational theory of human development. Along with rank goes expectations of behavioral dominance. Persons of higher rank, that is, are expected to direct the activities of persons of lower rank. Persons of lower rank are expected to follow the directions and example of those who rank over them. Who directs whom is thus a demonstration of rank and behavioral dominance. Interpersonal competitions within a family occur most often when the expected association between rank and behavioral dominance is unsupported by the realities of daily life, so that one's senior, for example, is not more able or wordly-wise. The content of such competition (in the local idiom) involves exercising mastery and authority (*adhikara*) over others, lording it over others (*prabhutra kora*), being recognized as leader, head, chief, boss (*matabbor*).

In the politics of caste, competition is between corporate castes which aim actively to improve their rank in the local caste hierarchy, to caste-climb, or defensively to maintain their present position while also upholding those features by which a caste is uniquely defined and its rank established. High or low rank in this competition is defined within a transformational perspective as the natural and moral result of the defining features of a caste. Higher rank goes to the caste with the more *sattvik* features, lower rank to the caste with the more *rajasik* or *tamasik* features. The generalized life style or *jibika* of a caste is a reflection and realization of its defining features. Any change in life style, for better or worse, thus provides a basis for the politics of caste. Indeed, inter-caste competitions focus on claims to higher rank advanced on the basis of refinements in life style. Intra-caste competitions focus on rectifying or forestalling acts by individual caste members which threaten the defining features and rank of the corporate whole.

In factional politics competition is between leading individuals teamed with their supporters. As defined within a transformational theory of human development, individual Hindus can be compared and ranked on the basis of personal power, wealth, knowledge, honor and name or reputation. These are the qualities of a big man (*boro lok*), and it is among big men that factional competitions are waged for recognition as the biggest of the big, as *the* leader. Big men compete through a process of selection for rank, i.e. through a series of competitions which have the cumulative effect of sorting out big men as more or less behaviorally dominant. Dominance confers rank by confirming those personal qualities of power, wealth, etc. required to successfully complete a project once undertaken or to successfully oppose the completion of projects undertaken by competitors. Rank entails expectations of further behavioral dominance. Factional politics thus has an open-ended quality as competition breeds competition in a continuing selection for rank.

Selection for rank is an endogenous, self-perpetuating process that will generate factional politics in periods of relative stasis or change so long as individual Hindus strive for recognition as the biggest of the big. Though not explicitly stated during the course of this chapter, the politics of family life and the politics of caste also have an inherent dynamic. Interpersonal competition within the family will continue so long as individual Hindus strive to boss others while remaining sensitive to being bossed. Competitions within and between castes will continue so long as any change in the generalized life style of a caste is held a reflection and realization of its defining features, and thus its rank. Each form of village politics, in other words, is internally fueled by the Hindu concern with rank and the behavior appropriate to ranked social units. Or put differently, the myriad family, caste and factional competitions which constitute village politics are systematically related to a view of society and the cosmos as ordered on the premise of inequality. Village politics is a product, importantly, which reproduces itself in that rivalries over rank affirm and maintain the same premise of inequality by which they are generated in the first place.

The conjunction of rank and rivalry suggests why Torkotala is not now and probably never was a village in which all lived, stereotypically, in harmony and consensus. It also attests to the utility of political studies that are not narrowly focused on politics alone. This point was made indirectly in emphasizing the lack of native boundary between politics and religion, and thus the necessity of studying the relationship between politics and other social domains. It can also be made in emphasizing the nature of rivalries over rank as transformational acts. The prize of village politics and the qualities deemed to merit that prize in family, caste and factional competitions are defined for Torkotala villagers by the same transformational perspective which informs Bengali patterns of marriage, diet, food exchanges, work and ritual performances. And like marriage, diet, etc. village politics is itself a means by which the rank of an individual or caste can be transformed for better or worse. As noted in the Introduction, it is the nature of rivalries over rank as transformational acts which points to why political competitions, like life-cycle rites and other public ceremonies, are usefully studied as a social means to mark and facilitate status passage.

Torkotala residents distinguish between three forms of competition in village politics: argument (*jukti*), rivalry (*jhogra*) and open quarrel (*bibad*). Rivalry is the most frequent form, even the characteristic form, of family, caste and factional competitions. It is a form of competition, significantly, which may be pursued over prolonged periods of time, or recurrently at different times, without being too divisive. Rivalries are confrontations, not encounters. They are tests of rank which do not require a clear and immediate decision. In the context of village politics rivalries over rank function much like Gluckman's rituals of rebellion, or what Moore (Moore and Myerhoff 1975:234) terms 'processes of regularization.' They affirm and maintain the system of ranked inequalities which orders the Bengali cosmos and society, sometimes by redressing an actual or perceived inconsistency between rank and the behavior held appropriate to that rank. In doing so the proper rank of a given individual or caste may be questioned, but not the organizing premise of ranked inequalities.

Whatever the form of competition, families, castes and factions as political teams are each structured around the roles of leader and member or supporter. In families there is a single leader, the male head of household. Factions are led by a single big man. In castes there is in principle a collective leadership comprised of the male heads of its member households, but among these male heads may be big men who are recognized as the first among equals. Membership in both families and castes is by the circumstance of birth, and members of each team are bound to its leadership by natural and moral ties. For this reason the membership of families and castes as political teams is not easily subverted. Especially in castes, though, individual backsliders or even entire segments of a caste may seek transactional bargains of a sort in exchange for their continued support of the caste leadership. When this happens the personnel of a caste can be differentiated as morally committed core and transactionally committed followers. In families and castes core supporters generally outnumber followers.

Membership in a faction is voluntary, and the ties that bind a faction leader and his individual supporters are not necessarily natural or moral ties. More often they are transactional bargains of a sort in which support is given in expectation of some personal gain, if only to be associated with the ranking leader. In a faction transactionally committed followers often outnumber morally committed core supporters. The voluntary, transactional nature of factions as political teams suggests why the membership of a faction is more variable and more easily subverted than the membership of a family or caste. Yet factions as political teams can be more or less stable. In Torkotala this is because faction members are attracted less by the specific bones of contention at issue in a competition than by the personal qualities of a faction leader. It is loyalty to a leader, rather than commitment to an issue, which consistently divides Torkotala residents along the same lines of factional cleavage.

It is expected that intramural family or caste competitions will be guided entirely by normative rules which judge certain activities as morally right or wrong. The same is also expected of competitions between castes or factions. All politics is ideally moral activity. Yet it is recognized that when competitors are not bound by multiplex natural and moral ties competition is often guided additionally by amoral, pragmatic rules which advocate certain actions according to their relative effectiveness under a given set of circumstances. Whether actually guided by normative or pragmatic rules – white arrows or black arrows – the family, caste and factional competitions which constitute village politics are nevertheless accompanied by a moralistic language of claims.

The public statements which accompany instances of village politics provide what C. Wright Mills (1940) termed 'a vocabulary of motives.' As noted in the Introduction, a vocabulary of motives is not an indication of actual motives, and does not explain why individuals act the way they do. But it is an expression of socially accepted reasons for a particular act, of legitimate rationalizations for action whatever the actual motivation. Given its rhetorical nature, such a vocabulary has been described here as a language of claims. The importance of attending to the language of claims in political studies is that like other cultural statements a language of claims both directs and justifies action preferences.

Competition can be regarded as the inevitable product of social inequities. Or competition can be regarded as the avoidable result of individual misconduct in a just and moral society. The latter is the view of village politics held by Torkotala residents. In principle there would be no family, caste or factional competitions if all acted in accord with their own behavioral code. In fact rivalries over rank are a recurrent feature of Torkotala life. An ideology of order and harmony is opposed by the actuality of political competition. This seeming contradiction is rationalized by a language of claims which justifies political competition – however undesirable and potentially disruptive – as a moral means to rectify or forestall errant behavior. The only acceptable reason for engaging in village politics, in other words, is the moral claim to be acting to restore or maintain *dharma*, to ensure a lasting social order through the temporary disorder of politics. In this the rationale for village politics is analogous to reasons given for the appearance of kings and institutions of rule in Hindu society. Each is entirely avoidable if individuals and birth groups uphold *dharma* on their own. Yet each is entirely necessary in an age, the Kali Yuga, when *dharma* hobbles along on but one leg.

The language of claims which accompanies village politics is one means by which family, caste and factional competitions are pursued. Interwoven throughout the discussion of village politics is an indication of still others. News, rumor, gossip, stories, lies, criticism and invidious comparison, for example, are several types of political message common to each form of village politics. Vows and threats, verbal abuse and physical beatings, to ignore claims as not coming from a legitimate competitor or to recognize a competitor but actively oppose the claims made – these are still other indications of the manner and means of village politics. All add to an understanding of the 'how' of village politics. It has not been the purpose of this chapter to explore the pattern of political messages, or levels of abuse and violence associated with family, caste and factional politics. It also has not been its purpose to explore the full range of contentions which spark village politics, or the frequency with which specific bones of contention recur, or how they are differently managed. These are important questions, but for present purposes, this discussion of village politics has had a more synthetic and general goal: to clarify why family, caste and factional competitions are a regular, recurrent, even anticipated feature of Torkotala life by identifying those processes which generate them. In doing so this chapter also documents how a number of ostensibly unrelated, temporally discontinuous political events are related one to the other and all derive from a common concern with rank and the behavior appropriate to ranked social units. It is this underlying pattern of meaning which allows both participants and observers to see beyond the singularity of a given competition and speak more generally about paradigmatic examples of a broader theme – village politics.

But are there no competitions which contravene the theme of village politics? Are there no political events which challenge or alter a construction of reality grounded on the premise of ranked inequalities? There are! But with a logic that protects their own construction of reality Torkotala residents do not regard such competitions as negative examples of village politics. They are labeled instead as instances of government politics, to which the discussion now turns.

5. Sorkari kaj

The Bengali cosmos and society are informed by a common set of natural and moral laws. These laws and the resulting natural and moral orders are considered objective, divinely given ones inherent in the material nature of the universe. It is not for Hindus to change the orders of the cosmos and society, but to understand, guard and protect them. Also to act in accord with them. Following the approved pattern of marriage, the correct pattern of food and service exchanges, the occupation and life style appropriate to one's birth group, fulfilling the duties particular to one's life stage, performing the proper life-cycle rites – all of these activities reflect and realize the natural and moral orders of the Bengali cosmos and society, and thereby maintain and uphold them as well. The same activities also enable individuals to satisfy their material needs, to develop physically and morally, and, for some, even to achieve the ultimate quest of liberation from the round of rebirths on earth. Thus are individual actions and social order, social order and cosmological order all integrally, indeed inseparably, joined in this Bengali construction of reality.

Village politics is but another set of activities which reflects and realizes the natural and moral orders of the Bengali cosmos and society, and by which those orders are maintained and upheld. For whether in the context of family, caste or factional competitions, rivalries over rank affirm the fundamental premise by which the worlds of the universe, the several life forms which inhabit those worlds, and the various birth groups into which humans in society are divided are all defined and ordered: the premise of ranked inequalities.

The premise of ranked inequalities is fundamental for Bengalis. There exist nevertheless certain spheres of activity where the pervasive importance of this premise is honored more in its denial than in its affirmation, and still others where actual differences in rank are neutralized or left indeterminate. For example, Torkotala villagers evidence an open concern for equality in holding that all members of a birth group share the same defining features and thus the same rank with respect to outsiders. It is for this reason that the nature and code of an entire caste, as well as its rank, is

172

affected equally by the activities of any individual member. It is also for this reason that a caste council, like that of the Bagdis or Sadgops described earlier, will meet to judge its individual members as a body of peers in which all present, reflecting their common worth, in principle have equal rights to speak and be heard.

A concern for equality is also evident in ideas of friendship, support and partnership which describes the ideal relationship between siblings of either sex, as well as others who are likened to siblings. The rivalry between Khudi and Satya Dolai, which was resolved only after a reaffirmation and renewal of sibling solidarity, is an apt illustration of this concern for equality in the context of family politics. The same concern with sibling solidarity, and the equality which is implied thereby, is also evident in the relationship between members of the same caste, or supporters of the same factional leader, who literally address and refer to each other as 'brother' (*bhai*). So do members of the same village (*grambhai*), followers of the same teacher (*gurubhai*), and members of the same religious sect (*dharmabhai*).

A concern for equality is also evident at times in the relations between birth groups. Castes which exchange the same kinds of food are deemed equal, at least in that particular transaction, if not in others. So are *kul* or *bongso* which over time exchange women in marriage. In any single marriage Torkotala villagers, like Hindus elsewhere, hold that the groom's family ranks over and dominates the bride's, as they receive the unmatched gift of a virgin, as well as numerous other gifts both before and after the marriage. But even here the preferred marriage, *samanulom bibaha*, is between groups whose defining features are recognized as essentially similar, at par, equal. Kenneth David (1972) has described for Hindus of Ceylon (and the same would appear to be true in West Bengal) how mercantile castes also act with an eye towards equality in striving to make every business transaction a symmetrical, mutually satisfying and thereby equal exchange.

To claim an identity of defining features, or to recognize differences but emphasize the equality of exchange, are but two means to deny ranked inequalities by affirming their antithesis. There is another in that birth groups may avoid interacting with each other in a way that clearly attests to their relative rank. It was noted earlier that all known *kul* or *bongso*, even within a single caste, could not be ordered in an inclusive hierarchy of like units if they did not give or receive daughters in marriage. A similar kind of transactional standoff occurs when castes neither give nor receive food from the other. In such circumstances differences in rank may still be attributed to birth groups on the basis of their ascribed physical nature and behavioral code, but such attribution will find no confirmation in the transactions between birth groups.

Among individuals, this concern for equality is perhaps best represented

Table 12.   *Bengali personal pronouns*

Person	Singular	Plural	English translation
First	ami	amra	I
Second			
inferior form	tui	tora	you
common form	tumi	tomra	you
honorific form	apni	apnara	you
Third			
common form	se	tara	he/she (s.); they (pl.)
honorific form	uni	unara	he/she/(s.); they (pl.)
honorific form	tini		he/she

in the person of the *sannyasin*, who in renouncing active involvement in society renounces as well the ranked inequalities on which society is ordered (Dumont 1960). It is also evident in the everyday speech of individual Bengalis. As is common in Indo-European languages, all pronouns in Bengali are marked to indicate graded degrees of familiarity and honor, and each pronoun is used in agreement with only certain verb endings (cf. Brown and Gillman, 1960). Thus every sentence, whether in the second or third person, is marked for a ranked or non-ranked relationship. If two persons use the same pronoun form, the relationship is marked as non-ranked or equal. Two very close friends, to illustrate, can both use the *tui* form, as young children often do, or they may both use the *tumi* form. In either case the relationship is non-ranked, and the choice of *tui* or *tumi* indicates a measure of familiarity as well. For two persons both to use the *apni* form also marks a relationship as non-ranked or equal. But the choice of *apni* indicates a lack of familiarity or distanced formality.

Whenever two different pronoun forms are used, a ranked relationship exists, even if that relationship also be a familiar one. Thus an employer will address his employee as *tumi*, but be addressed in turn as *apni*. Or a husband will address his wife as *tui*, indicating great familiarity, but be addressed in turn as *tumi*. Mothers and fathers will address their children as *tui*, but be addressed, usually, as *tumi*. Because of the great familiarity between parents and their children, it is also sometimes heard that children address both parents as *tui*, or, more commonly, use the *tui* form when speaking to mother, while reserving the still familiar but more honorific *tumi* form for speaking to father. The use of third person pronoun forms, and the plural forms of both second and third persons follow the same pattern of usage and meaning as the singular forms.

There are circumstances when neither party to a conversation wants to use a pronoun form that will indicate either a ranked or non-ranked relationship. This occurs, for example, in conversation between persons completely unknown to each other, or when two persons are both being polite in not insisting that a known ranked relationship be openly marked by speech. More commonly, it occurs between persons known to each other when one party is not willing to admit of lower rank by using an honorific pronoun form. Party B, to illustrate, may be addressed as *tumi* by party A, who speaks first. Party B does not feel correct in using the familiar *tumi* form in return. But neither does he wish to accept an inferior rank by using the more honorific *apni* form. Alternately, persons of acknowledged higher rank may choose not to play on this fact, as is frequent among the politically-minded when seeking the support of others. In such circumstances the Bengali language permits a special construction where no pronoun is used, and all verbs are used in the undeclined verbal noun form. The sentence voice is passive, and no indication is given of relative rank. To illustrate, in active voice, using a pronoun and verb in agreement with that pronoun, a person may ask, '*Apni pujar janno taka deben?*' 'Will you (honorific) give money for the worship?' In passive voice, using no pronoun and a verb in the undeclined noun form, the same question is asked this way: '*Taka pujar janno daou habe?*' 'Will money be given for the worship?' Even for native speakers of Bengali this passive, circumspect speech is recognized as difficult when used in a prolonged conversation, and as a special kind of skill in itself – a skill, interestingly, which is described as political. For those able to use this mode of speech effectively, though, it does allow avoidance of the ranking of individuals implicit in the Bengali language.

In the circumspect speech of Torkotala villagers, in the belief that all members of a birth group share the same defining features and thus the same rank, in the symmetrical exchange of women or food or articles of trade, in the transactional standoff of symmetrical non-exchanges, in aspects of village politics, including the concern with sibling solidarity and the workings of caste councils – in all these spheres is the premise of ranked inequalities, pervasive and fundamental as it is to Bengali thought and action, nevertheless variously denied, neutralized or avoided. Put differently, and with a different emphasis, the concern for equality, or at least the idea of non-ranked individuals and birth groups, is neither foreign nor absent from Bengali thought and action. Nowhere is the concern for equality given greater importance, though, than in that set of activities which Torkotala villagers refer to as *sorkari kaj*, the work (*kaj*) of the government (*sorkar*), or government politics.

As noted at the outset of chapter 4, government politics refers ultimately to the activities of the central government in New Delhi, but includes as well the activities of government officers and agents at all levels of administration, plus the activities of political party workers and all other persons who share a certain goal orientation. Like village politics, government politics is identified behaviorally with rivalries over rank. Only in the context of government politics rivalries over rank aim to level, if not completely eliminate, the given system of inequalities and to substitute in its stead a polity, society and view of the cosmos ordered on the premise of equality. Government politics is in that sense innovative. It seeks to create a new and supposedly better order, one open to continual reshaping and improvement as members of the polity alter their own vision of the future.

An innovative, progressively oriented government politics which aims to redefine the social and political orders stands in marked contrast to a conservatively oriented village politics in which the social and political orders are viewed as divinely given and thus beyond the agency of human change. Yet village politics and government politics coexist in Torkotala, and while some villagers are partisan to but one form of rule, there are also residents who at times variously advance and act in accord with both. This will become evident in tracing the involvement in government politics of some of the same individuals introduced when presenting documentary cases of village politics. Doing so will also illustrate the limitation of assuming that exposure to the new necessarily leads to abandonment of the old, or that the old and new are incompatible alternatives. In Torkotala innovative change is sometimes rejected outright, even by those who generally favor a progressively oriented form of rule; sometimes added 'as is' to a flexible but enduring traditional order; sometimes added in a modified form that makes the new more compatible with the old.

To document these points three instances of government politics are presented involving, in turn, political equality through rural self-government, the reordering of social relations through legislation, and economic reforms through a labor dispute. Common to each of these documentary cases is the goal of progress and change towards a more equalitarian political, economic and social order. This goal and the involvement of outsiders in its furtherance is suspect among many Torkotala residents. Yet local suspicions can be allayed when efforts at innovative change are accompanied by an appropriate language of claims. An accompanying language of claims, even when appropriately chosen, does not guarantee the success of an innovative program, as will be evidenced by the negligible impact of Hindu Code legislation in Torkotala. But the publicly stated reasons used to justify an innovative program can be critical to the successful outcome of change efforts, as will be evidenced by the instances of Panchayati Raj and the Torkotala labor dispute.

All innovation involves change, but not all change involves innovation, since not everything that is adopted is perceived as new. Herein lies the basis for why a traditionalist and progressive form of rule each have a different language of claims. Village politics, it will be seen, is oriented to a Golden Age in the past, when people acted in greater accord with *dharma*, and life on the whole was deemed better. Change which recovers or restores what was is welcome. Innovation which further distances the present from the past is not. Government politics, by contrast, is oriented to a Golden Age in the future. Attaining that future Golden Age, when life will be different and better than it is presently or was in the past, requires innovation. Given this view of a future Golden Age, and the broader theme of which it is a part, government politics is for Torkotala residents more than a characteristic set of rivalries over rank. It is also a model of reality, and an orientation against which to interpret, judge and guide specific acts as they variously maintain or alter the ranked orders of the Bengali cosmos and society. For that reason government politics, like village politics, is two-dimensional: a set of instrumental acts and the embodiment of a pattern of meaning which informs a number of different, ostensibly unrelated acts. The ethnography supporting this statement was presented in half in chapter 4. The remainder is presented here, beginning with a discussion of those consciously held premises which constitute for Torkotala residents the theme of government politics.

Polity, society and cosmos

Politics aims at progress
Politics aims at progress (*unnoti*). Unlike village politics, government politics posits that every political and social order, as well as the world view which accompanies those orders and makes them seem uniquely fitted to the realities of life, is a human construction. Thus people can create the political and social order of their choice. Moreover, in creating a new political and social order, people are not bound by the reservoir of behaviors, values, symbols and meanings which collectively comprise local tradition. Within the context of government politics, change may be informed by the experience of all people, in all places, through all of history. Indeed, innovation is expected. So is a future better than the past – progress.

Many of the specific innovations Torkotala residents identify with government politics, including the concern for a more equalitarian and equitable society, were present in the slowly modernizing British colony of India, and the intrusion of government politics into Torkotala certainly predates Indian Independence. The critical period for Torkotala was probably in the 1880s when Prithvibillabh Pal lost his major land-holdings and villagers of the kingdom began to resort to the British courts or to British appointed revenue collectors to settle disputes over property. Prithvibillabh was the last Pal Raja, the first not to rule over the Narayanghar kingdom directly. Yet for present residents of Torkotala discussion of those innovations in village life identified with government politics are oriented to the more recent period of Indian Independence, and especially to the framing of an Indian-made constitution. The ['Dharmasastra of Delhi,] as the Constitution is sometimes called locally, has for Torkotala villagers much the same status as respected texts of the Indian Great Tradition. Villagers regard the Constitution as a normative text, and seek in it the goal and rationale of government politics.

The Indian Constitution became effective on January 26, 1950. It was drafted from December 1946 to December 1949 by a Constituent Assembly that included the principal leaders of the Indian National Congress; non-Congress leaders of diverse ideological persuasions, including communists, socialists and Hindu traditionalists; six out of nine provincial prime ministers; over one hundred members of the provincial legislatures; and members of certain minority communities not already represented by Congress or government leaders. Although indirectly elected, and there-fore not directly responsible to the mass of Indians, the Constituent Assembly was a truly national and highly representative body (Austin 1966:1–26). Torkotala residents thus seem justified in regarding the product of the Constituent Assembly as a statement of national purpose. Indeed, the Assembly was charged with drafting a constitution of purpose and practicality, with framing the basic goals of an independent India and providing an administrative blueprint to foster the achievement of those goals.

As a declaration of purpose, the major goals of an independent India are stated at the very outset of the Constitution in a Preamble which commits India

to secure for all of its citizens
JUSTICE, social, economic and political;
LIBERTY of thought, expression, belief, faith and worship;
EQUALITY of status and opportunity;
and to promote among them all
FRATERNITY assuring the dignity of the individual and the unity of the nation.

What is intended by such broad and evocative concepts as justice, liberty, equality and fraternity is explicated in Parts 3 and 4 of the Constitution, which detail Fundamental Rights and the Directive Principles of State Policy, respectively. Specifically, the Fundamental Rights guarantee that India will deny no one equality before the law, or discriminate on the grounds of religion, race, caste, sex or place of birth. All citizens are further guaranteed the freedoms of religion, assembly, association and movement. No one is to be deprived of life, liberty or property, except in accordance with the law. And various means are provided whereby citizens can move the judiciary to protect their rights when and if infringed upon. The Fundamental Rights, in sum, commit India to being a secular and equalitarian society structured around a universalistic legal system.

Expressed in the Directive Principles of State Policy is an additional commitment, that India shall be a welfare state. These Directive Principles are not justiciable, and cannot be enforced in court, but 'are nevertheless fundamental in the governance of the country and it shall be the duty of the State to apply these principles in making law' (Art. 37). They exhort the individual states of the nation to ensure that all citizens have humane conditions of work, adequate means of livelihood, a living standard that permits leisure, education and cultural opportunities, good health and proper nutrition. Undue concentration of wealth is to be prevented, and there is to be equal pay for equal work for both men and women. Other provisions of the Directive Principles aim to improve techniques of agriculture, animal husbandry and cottage industries, and to provide for a measure of self-government through the organization of village *panchayats*. As a body the Principles aim to promote the welfare of all Indians by ensuring the social, economic and political conditions necessary for each citizen to develop fully.

Only Atul Mahabarto, the head of the statutory village council, and the village school masters, including MGD, have certain knowledge of specific Articles included in the Fundamental Rights and the Directive Principles of State Policy. School children of the village have studied the Preamble. Adults of the village are aware of the broad commitments written into the Constitution through listening to their children (who typically study aloud), personal contact with government officials, and exposure to government-sponsored programs aimed to improve the social and economic conditions of villages in the Narayanghar area. Food distributions, free primary schools, adult education classes, rural libraries, economic cooperatives, medical dispensaries, irrigation projects, demonstration fields for new agricultural methods, new varieties of seed and fertilizer and insecticides, legislation affecting customary practices of marriage, divorce, adoption, inheritance and succession to property, landholding ceilings, land redistribution programs, elections and Panchayati Raj are all examples of such programs which affect Torkotala villagers. From them villagers have formed their own understanding of the Constitution as a declaration of purpose.

The ideal of fraternity, for example, is interpreted locally as a commitment to nationalism. 'Not the king (*raja*), but the state (*rastra*)' is the way Torkotala residents voice this ideal that all citizens, whatever their local loyalties as personified in their loyalty to the king, will recognize an encompassing loyalty and fraternity that is Indian. From their own participation in elections, both state and federal, and the workings of Panchayati Raj, Torkotala villagers are also aware, and convinced, that India is committed to the ideal of democracy. Far less convincing is the ideal of a democratic state governed by a rule of law which applies equally to all citizens and in which all citizens are equal before the law. In district courts, as in local jails, with registry officers, as with tax collectors, Torkotala villagers have learned that the law is applied differently to the high born, the influential and the wealthy, just as one would expect by the premises of village politics.

Progress in the context of government politics also includes the ideas of a secular state and a welfare state. India is not a Hindu state, as neighboring Pakistan is an Islamic state, and Torkotala villagers are aware that the government guarantees all citizens the right to follow their own faith. They are also aware that government officials and agents at all levels of administration have assumed responsibility for improving the social, economic and political conditions of life in Torkotala as elsewhere in India. The ideas of a secular state and a welfare state are sometimes at odds with each other, as will be discussed below. But like nationalism, democracy and the rule of impartial law, secularism and the welfare state are all identified by Torkotala villagers with progress in accord with the ideals of a modernizing nation.

Politics is (ideally) moral activity

As with village politics, it is expected that government politics will be pursued through moral means. Yet it is also recognized that competitions between natural and moral communities – the villagers versus outsiders to the village – will often proceed outside of a single, agreed upon, moral code. This is not to say that government politics proceeds without regard to evaluations of right and wrong common to village politics, or others established by government-backed statutory law; it does not. But Torkotala villagers fully expect government officials and political party workers to pursue their aim of progress by all available means. And what makes their actions particularly suspect is that with few exceptions Torkotala villagers do not know or cannot use effectively the political rules and resources manipulated by these outsiders to the village.

Politics is open to all

Government politics is not held the shared responsibility of all Torkotala villagers; nor is it expected that all villagers will actively further the work of effecting progress and change in village life; or even that all villagers will be unopposed to such work by others. But it is expected that government politics will be open to all who wish to participate and that all who wish to participate will do so as political equals.

Politics is superordinate to and (supposedly) separate from dharma

Village politics is subordinate to and inseparable from *dharma* in that it takes its definition of goals, as well as its definition of moral means towards those goals, from this generalized concept of behavioral codes.

Government politics does not. It looks instead to the Indian Constitution and legal system as its ultimate ground of authority, and uses the institutional system and statutes contained therein to establish politics as superordinate to *dharma* – which is interpreted by government officials as synonymous with religion – and to establish politics and religion as discrete domains. Government politics aims not to maintain the distinctions and behaviors of rank which are supported by *dharma*, but to level, if not completely eliminate, them. Further, both the Indian Constitution and specific statutes make it criminal to discriminate against individuals, denominations or institutions on the basis of religion.

Contained within the Indian Constitution is the basis for a clear separation of politics from religion, a separation symbolized in the ideal of a secular state. Article 25 guarantees all individuals the right to profess, practice and propagate religion. Article 26 extends the same guarantees to every religious denomination and minority. Still other provisions guarantee the state will not discriminate against individuals on the basis of religion in matters of employment (Art. 16) or education (Art. 29), and that there will be no separate electorates on the basis of religion (Art. 325). In other ways, too, the Constitution provides for the ideal of a secular state. Article 27 guarantees there will be no special taxes for the promotion of religion. And Article 28 guarantees there will be no religious instruction in state educational institutions.

The separation of politics from religion, clear as it is in the Constitution, nevertheless remains suspect for Torkotala villagers. For along with the ideal of a secular state, Indian national planners and local government officials also advance the ideal of a welfare state in which the model of social, economic and political justice is based on a premise of equality. This concern for equality is contrary to that which informs polity, society and cosmos under the premises of village politics, and has meant that government politics is very much involved with matters of religion. The state, to illustrate, has expanded its jurisdiction at the expense of *dharma* by assuming jurisdiction over matters of marriage, divorce, adoption, inheritance and succession to property, all of which are now covered by the Hindu Code legislation to be discussed later. Other customary practices deemed anti-social, including the immolation of widows, infanticide, animal sacrifice, and temple prostitution, are also regulated by law, as is the involvement of religious figures in political affairs. Additionally, the state has undertaken to reform temple administration, to abolish untouchability, and to eliminate communalism, all in the name of a welfare state.

The effect of these and other provisions has been to establish government officials and agents at all levels of administration in the role of active social reformers. Thus do Torkotala villagers regard the clear separation of politics from religion implied in the ideal of a secular state to be contravened by the actual activities of government, to be more supposed than real.

To premise that individuals are fundamentally equal or unequal is a political and moral judgement, a way of viewing people in the world. Both premises are voiced and acted upon in Torkotala today. The former informs those competitions identified with village politics. The latter is not foreign or absent from village politics, but is identified most closely with government politics. Put differently, village politics and government politics exist side by side in Torkotala, providing villagers with alternate sets of premises about individual worth and the relationship between polity, society and cosmos. This is in itself a change resulting from the increased presence of government officers and agents in Torkotala. Still other changes will be evident in the pattern of support and participation given by villagers to three documentary cases of government politics. Each of these cases can be read as a record of the efforts of outsiders and partisan villagers to extend a modern political and legal system into a local administrative unit recognized as having an alternative system of political meaning and action.

Panchayati Raj

Article 40 of the Indian Constitution directs the several Indian states to establish village councils (*panchayats*) and to endow them with such resources and authority as may be necessary to enable them to function as units of self-government. The Constitution does not also set forth the organization and function of these *panchayats*, but guidelines for state legislation on these matters were provided in 1959 by a government-sponsored study team (popularly called the Mehta Committee) set up for that purpose. The Mehta Committee proposed a tiered system of rural self-government consisting of village (*gram*), area (*anchal*) and district-level (*zilla*) councils, each having delegated responsibility, powers and resources for planning and executing development programs in their respective jurisdictions. Through these development programs it was intended that rural India would come to share the economic and social advances already evident in urban centers, thereby reducing a major barrier to national unity and a major problem concern for national planners – rural poverty and social backwardness.

Panchayati Raj was intended as something more than a new approach to community development, though. On the one hand it was intended to actualize the constitutional commitment expressed in Article 40 to a decentralized economic and political democracy. And on the other hand it was intended to incorporate local administrative units – village

India – into the broader national polity, principally by extending those features of a modern parliamentary democracy which already characterized central government activity into rural areas. In their day-to-day operation, for example, *panchayats* are to rely on bureaucratic procedures, participation in their activities is to be open to all persons as a right of Indian citizenship, and leadership positions are to be achieved and circulated through open and regularly recurrent elections in which *panchayat* officers are answerable to their constituencies. Also, associated with Panchayati Raj are judicial courts (*nyaya panchayats*) which rely on a predominately secular and impersonal system of coded law and which operate on the premise that all persons have equal rights before the law. In all of these respects does Panchayati Raj aim at extending into rural India those features associated with modern political and legal systems.

Directed by the Constitution to establish a system of village councils, it remained for each Indian state to pass its own legislation providing for the formal organization and operation of Panchayati Raj locally. In West Bengal this legislation is contained in the West Bengal Panchayat Act of 1957, the Panchayat Rules Act of 1958, and the West Bengal Zilla Parishad Act of 1963. The provisions of these Acts can be summarized as follows. Panchayati Raj is organized in three tiers. At the village level it consists of a village assembly (*gram sabha*) of all adults, male and female. The assembly is a corporate body which may sue, be sued, acquire and dispose of property, etc. It is led by an executive body, the village council (*gram panchayat*), elected by villagers from amongst their own numbers. Intermediate between the district and village levels is the area council (*anchal panchayat*) which has jurisdiction over several village councils, who then elect an area council head from amongst themselves. Also included on the area council are a few other persons, Muslims or persons from scheduled castes or tribes, for example, who would not be represented otherwise. Having the same jurisdiction as an area council are judicial councils (*nyaya panchayats*) consisting of five members selected by the area council. Like village and area council members, judicial council members serve for four years before having to stand for re-election. The district council (*zilla parisad*) provides the third tier in this system of rural self-government. It includes the heads of the several area councils under its jurisdiction, some members of the state legislative assembly, and a few other persons to provide for minority representation. The district council is linked to the state government, which exercises powers of suspension and control over all three tiers of the Panchayati Raj system.

The formal organization and stated goals of Panchayati Raj are known to Torkotala villagers, not from their own reading of the relevant legislation, but from explanations given them by outsiders: the BDO and his staff of officers, which include the *panchayat* extension officer. It was also the BDO, in 1962, who organized the first *gram panchayat* election in Torkotala. At his direction Torkotala was divided into three voting wards, a northern ward which includes the Munda hamlets, a southern ward which includes the Lodha hamlets, and a central ward which includes the Hindu hamlets. From each ward were to be elected three *panchayat* members, thereby guaranteeing equal representation to each of the three major social divisions of the village. As part of his efforts to organize the *gram panchayat* election, the BDO made it clear that all adults of the village, male and female, could stand for election and could vote for the election of others. The BDO also explained to villagers why the right to vote was a privilege, how it gave all persons, regardless of birth group and rank, an equal voice, and why persons elected as *panchayat* members were responsible to the electors who gave them their position.

The *gram panchayat* selection took place several months after the BDO's initial organizing efforts, in August 1962, under his supervision. The village assembly met as provided for by law to nominate council members, three from each voting ward. But no nominations were ever asked for or received from the villagers. Prior to the meeting, and contrary to the provisions of law, Atul Mahabarto and Anil Pal, with the apparent consent of the BDO, met privately to compose a list of *panchayat* nominations of their own. Their list included just nine nominees, one for each available *panchayat* seat, thereby eliminating the need for an actual election. Indeed, none was held. The assembled villagers merely approved by voice the list of nominees Atul and Anil placed before them.

Members of the Torkotala village *panchayat* were not chosen in a contested election; nor did nominations for *panchayat* membership come from the village assembly as provided for by law. Why the BDO allowed this to happen was never clarified to Torkotala villagers, and none pressed terribly hard for an explanation, it being an accepted, even expected, practice of local leaders to make their decisions in private, behind-the-scenes meetings, and then later to face the public or the opposition with a united front. A consensus had developed as to why Atul and Anil sought to avoid an actual election. The practice of elections, and the rule of the majority, are held alien to Torkotala, where decisions are customarily taken by unanimity. An election was avoided, according to this logic, in order to avoid its potentially divisive effect. Perhaps of even greater concern was a problem which arose shortly before the *panchayat* election date. The Lodhas of the village decided not to nominate any of their number to sit on the *panchayat*, saying that the Hindus, their landholding employers, would never listen to them anyway. Rather than publicly discuss how the three seats originally allotted to the Lodhas could be fairly redistributed, Atul and Anil sought to resolve this problem privately. They decided to retain three *panchayat* seats for Munda representation, and divide the remaining

Table 13. *The Torkotal village panchayat, 1962*

Member	Caste or tribe
Atul Krishna Mahabarto, *Adhyaksa*	Sadgop
Satya Chandra Dolai, *Upo-adhyaksa*	Bagra-Khatriya
Phani Bhusan Chakraborti	Brahman
Anil Baren Pal	Sadgop
Sridam Rana	Kamar
Iswar Sit	Rajok
Fakir Singh	Munda
Suklal Singh	Munda
Gurkha Singh	Munda

six seats equally between higher-caste Hindus and lower-caste Hindus. Table 13 lists the members of the Torkotala *gram panchayat*, formed on August 27, 1962.

Once the *panchayat* was formed it remained for its members to elect one of their number as council head, or *Adhyaksa*. As noted earlier, both Atul and Anil wanted the position and began campaigning for it long before the BDO ever entered Torkotala to organize an election. Both men, for example, attended the marriage of Khudi Dolai's daughter, and eventually recognized Bagdi claims to being Bagra-Khatriyas in order to win the backing of the Bagdis and their clients in the forthcoming *panchayat* election. Both men also backed certain projects of the recently formed Munda society for the same reason. Atul and Anil were aware that in an election where all villagers had the right to vote, and each vote would count equally, it was necessary to expand their social contacts and political following as widely as possible. They were also aware that the factional rivalry between them meant neither man could rely on the full backing of his caste fellows, the Sadgops, which made winning the support of non-Sadgops in the village still more important.

Much of the campaigning for the position of *Adhyaksa* occurred long before the Torkotala *gram panchayat* was ever formed. After the *panchayat* was formed Atul and Anil campaigned further, now concentrating their efforts on fellow council members, their electors. Atul promised to appoint Satya Dolai as assistant council head, *Upo-adhyaksa*, if he delivered his own vote and that of Iswar Sit and Fakir Singh, who did agricultural labor for Bagra-Khatriyas and were thus counted as their economic clients and political followers. Atul made a similar promise to Gurkha Singh, hoping thereby to win the support of three Munda *panchayat* members. Of the remaining *panchayat* members, it was expected that Sridam Rana, the village Kamar, would vote for Atul Mahabarto because his home was located on land owned by Mahabartos, while Phani Bhusan Chakraborti,

Table 14.   *Panchayati Raj meetings in Torkotala village, 1963–1971*

Year	Village assembly (*gram sabha*)	Village council (*gram panchayat*)	Inspection visits by government officials
1963	3	15	1
1964		6	1
1965	1	5	1
1966	2	2	
1967		5	1
1968	2	5	1
1969		7	
1970			
1971			1
Total	8	45	6

the village Brahman, would vote for Anil Pal because persons of the Pal line financed his initiation (*upanoyana*) ceremony.

Atul Mahabarto won the election for *Adhyaksa*, receiving the votes of Satya Dolai, Iswar Sit, Sridam Rana and Fakir Singh. Soon after, ignoring legislation which provides for the assistant council head to be chosen through a separate election, Atul appointed Satya Dolai as *Upo-adhyaksa*. Atul and Satya have led the Torkotala village council in the absence of a second election ever since 1962. And with one exception the membership of the village council has remained unchanged as well. Sridam Rana left Torkotala in 1968; his seat on the *panchayat* remains unfilled.

Another provision of Panchayati Raj legislation instructs the *Adhyaksa* to keep records of every meeting of the village assembly and village council, including minutes, a listing of all persons present, and an account of all finances with itemized expenditures. Separate registries also record all lands included in the *panchayat* jurisdiction, a listing of all villagers who qualify for government food handouts, a listing of tax assessments for each villager, and a listing of official *panchayat* correspondence. All of this documentation is held available for inspection by authorized government officials who visit Torkotala, and is summarized yearly in reports forwarded to the head of the area council. Together the record books and registries provide a complete and continuing history of the Torkotala village assembly and council from January 1963, the date of the first recorded *panchayat* meeting.

Table 14 indicates the number of times the Torkotala village assembly and council have met since 1963, the distribution of meetings over those years, and the number of times government officials have visited Torkotala to inspect the workings of this system of rural self-government. The Torkotala village assembly has met eight times in nine years, but not since

1968. The village council has met 45 times in nine years, but not since 1969. There have been six inspection visits since 1963. Even the relative inactivity of the assembly and council does not give an adequate picture of the ineffectiveness of Panchayati Raj in Torkotala, though. For as suggested in the earlier discussion of factional politics, the successful completion of any project in Torkotala requires that Atul Mahabarto, Anil Pal and Haripado Bhunai, as leaders of the three principal village factions, work in cooperation with each other, or at least not in active opposition. Yet throughout the history of Panchayati Raj in Torkotala this has not been the case.

Haripado Bhunai, the village *Mukhya*, never sought membership in the village council, arguing from the time when Panchayati Raj legislation was first explained to villagers by the BDO that the concept of elected authority, and the rule of the majority, were alien to Torkotala and inherently divisive. Villagers, in his opinion, should continue to follow the established customs of the village, which include being led by their *Mukhya* and making all decisions through consensus and unanimity. Haripado in effect advanced the theme of village politics and countered whatever importance the BDO and others attributed to this new system of rural self-government by labeling it, pejoratively, as an instance of government politics, i.e. a scheme by government officials and other outsiders to alter life within Torkotala. By first refusing to seek *panchayat* membership and later refusing to involve himself in *panchayat* affairs, Haripado also undermined the effectiveness of the village council by not lending it the legitimation that would accrue from his personal support and that of his factional following. This said, it must be added that Haripado never actively opposed development projects undertaken by the *panchayat* which, in his opinion, promised to benefit the village as a whole. The sinking of new tube wells, the laying of new roads, drainage projects, the dissemination of information about medicines, new seeds and fertilizers, and the sponsorship of cultural events like fairs and plays and poetry readings are all examples of such projects which Haripado, while never actively supporting, has also never actively opposed.

Anil Pal, for his part, originally sought involvement in this new system of rural self-government through council membership and election as *Adhyaksa*. Like his one-time school friend Atul, Anil was in sympathy with many of the stated goals of Panchayati Raj. And like Atul, he recognized that the powers invested in the office of *Adhyaksa*, as well as the money distributed through that office, could be manipulated and used to personal advantage, even while advancing certain village causes. Anil's involvement in the village *panchayat* was short-lived, though, for within a year after losing the election for council head, he withdrew from active participation in council affairs and like Haripado began to speak of the *panchayat* pejoratively as an instance of government politics. Rather than participate under the leadership of Atul, Anil now sought to belittle that leadership by undermining the effectiveness of the village council. After 1963, the first full year of *panchayat* activities, in which he attended 5 out of 15 meetings, for example, Anil never again attended another meeting of the village council. Further, in addition to avoiding *panchayat* activities as Haripado did, Anil actively opposed every project which Atul was known to support. The incident of the primary school transfer described earlier is an example of such active opposition.

The Torkotala village council continues to exist and to be active even without the support of Haripado and Anil and their respective factional followings. But lacking this support, the *panchayat* has become over the years less a village council than a factional council, a legally constituted and government funded body through which Atul Mahabarto and other progressively minded villagers can advance factional goals. In that sense has the council been co-opted to the personal advantage of Atul and his supporters. Yet the *panchayat* does advance projects that benefit Torkotala villagers as a whole, and in spite of its becoming a factional council, has effected many of the social, economic and political changes envisioned by the national planners of Panchayati Raj. In addition to specific development projects, for example, the extension of voting rights to all adults and the introduction of popular elections have, in combination, allowed previously subordinated but numerically significant groups like the Bagra-Khatriyas and Mundas to gain a say in village affairs. Their votes must be bargained for in any *panchayat* election. And even in the absence of a second election the Bagra-Khatriyas and Mundas have secured an increased say in village affairs because Atul Mahabarto is aware that he must use the office of *Adhyaksa* to advance the well-being and political participation of as many villagers as possible against the day when there is another election. Then, too, because the formal existence, if not the actual effectiveness, of any village council is independent of particular men, the mere existence of Panchayati Raj in Torkotala has opened the way for the advance of a new leadership. By their very lack of involvement with *panchayat* affairs established village leaders like Haripado and Anil have allowed others, like Satya Dolai, to seek and gain positions endowed with legal power.

In many ways the activities of the Torkotala village assembly and council do not conform to the provisions of Panchayati Raj legislation. *Panchayat* members were not chosen in a contested election. Nor was the *Upoadhyaksa*. The assembly and council do not meet regularly. And new council members, or even a new leadership, are not chosen every four years. On all of these counts is Atul Mahabarto sometimes criticized for acting outside the law, for acting immorally, in order to maintain the personal advantages of his present position. Government politics is ideally moral activity, but in this instance the ideal, Anil and Haripado would say, is far from realized. In the behavior of Anil and Haripado and their factional supporters is reflected another premise of government politics. Namely, that participation in government politics is open to all, though not all may wish to participate or even welcome the aim of government politics in effecting progress and change. Anil, for one, seems to have no interest in the development projects undertaken by the village council. Haripado does, welcoming those projects deemed to benefit the village as a whole. But his opinion of government politics is not unmixed, for to the extent that *panchayat* activities are successful the given social and political orders of the village are likely to change. It is to protect and maintain those same orders for which Haripado, as the traditional headman of Torkotala, is responsible.

Prior to 1962, there was no Torkotala village council in the sense of a formally organized and constituted body. When matters of public importance arose they were discussed in *ad hoc* village meetings called for that specific purpose. Such meetings were, and still are, held irregularly in Torkotala. They are referred to, significantly, as *des jama*, a gathering (*jama*) of the *des*, and not as *panchayats*, a term which villagers recognize as a recent addition to their vocabulary. Participation in such *ad hoc* village meetings is in principle open to all within the village. In practice, only adult males are likely to attend such meetings, and actual attendance is usually predicated on receiving a direct call to the meeting. Active, effective participation is limited still further to those males who head their own households, and especially to those who head households having substantial landholdings. Both presently and in the past this has meant that effective participation in *ad hoc* village meetings is limited primarily to persons of the Sadgop caste. Indeed, such a meeting is often indistinguishable from a meeting of Torkotala Sadgops.

It is not unusual for the village *Mukhya* to preside over an *ad hoc* meeting of the village. But neither is it necessary. Any villager can call such a meeting, and preside over it as well. In that sense these meetings, unlike meetings of the statutory village assembly or council, lack a formal leadership. Also unlike the statutory assembly or council, *ad hoc* village meetings have no specified powers or functions apart from those which villagers in attendance are willing and able to give them. All power and authority rests entirely in the personal qualities and resources of the villagers in attendance. Decisions can only be enforced by the common agreement of all present to abide by them – expressed as unanimity – and not by the sanction of any outside government agency or set of codified laws. Another feature of *ad hoc* village meetings is the differential judgements passed according to the defining features and rank of individuals. In every adjudication of a dispute, or judgement of errant behavior, villagers adjust their decisions and penalties according to what is considered just, given the birth group and life stage of the individuals involved. Justice is meted out in accordance with the premise of inequality. There is not, as there is meant to be in the judicial councils associated with Panchayati Raj, or in the judicial courts of West Bengal state, an emphasis on the impersonal assessment of evidence and the application of impartial law according to specific events and transactions.

In many ways, then, the village assembly and village council introduced into Torkotala under the auspices of Panchayati Raj represent significant departures from the system of *ad hoc* village meetings which existed prior to them, and now co-exist with them. Panchayati Raj is intended as and is in fact both an instance and an invocation of social and economic, but especially political equality. For that reason does the extension of Panchayati Raj into Torkotala represent a process, not of regularization but of adjustment and innovation. This is evident behaviorally in the leveling, however gradual and minimal, of inequalities between castes and tribes in the context of local self-government. It is evident also in the language of claims which accompanies Panchayati Raj. Specifically, unlike village politics, which is regarded as the avoidable result of individual misconduct in a just society, the competitions occasioned by instances of government politics are regarded differently as the inevitable product of social inequities. The goal of government politics is not to maintain the given order, which is deemed unjust, but to fashion a new and more equitable order grounded on the fundamental equality of all. The language of claims which accompanies instances of government politics like Panchayati Raj thus rationalizes competition as a conduit of progress and change. From the temporary disorder of politics is to come a new and better order.

Panchayati Raj in Torkotala does serve as a vehicle of community development, and has served to extend into this local administrative unit some of those features of a political democracy which already characterize higher administrative units of the state. But Panchayati Raj in Torkotala is not an unqualified success and does not operate fully as planned by its national architects. The village council is today only sporadically active, has only limited support among Hindus and no support among Lodhas, and since its formation in 1962 has become progressively less a village council than a factional council. It is avoided by many and has been co-opted by others.

This pattern of avoidance and co-option probably recurs elsewhere in rural India where their coexist two sets of understandings about the right and proper order of village life. Beteille (1965). Bailey (1963) and Epstein (1962), for example, each describe how the avoidance pattern of Haripado

Bhunai is repeated where the extension of Panchayati Raj meets resistance from men who already occupy established positions of village leadership on the basis of those personal qualities discussed in chapter 4 as criterial for big man status, and with the same result as in Torkotala. Namely, the avoidance of established leaders tempers the effectiveness of the local *panchayat* while opening the way for a new set of leaders advanced by popular vote and willing to capitalize on the concept of elected authority. These new leaders, like Satya Dolai, may not have the personal qualities of a big man, but they come to have the legally defined powers of office in a statutory council. In villages where established local leaders like Atul Mahabarto do not avoid the new *panchayat*, they may nevertheless co-opt the powers of office to buttress the personal basis of their position as a faction, caste or village leader. A likely result, as in Torkotala and the Uttar Pradesh village described by Retzlaff (1962), is that the distinction between *ad hoc* councils and the local statutory council, though never entirely lost, becomes increasingly blurred as the leadership of both is in the same person, who does not often or clearly distinguish when he is acting on the personal powers of his big man status and when he is acting on his legal powers as a *panchayat* officer.

The Hindu Code

For framers of the Indian Constitution, a democratic state in which political participation is open to all citizens was deemed desirable in its own right. It was additionally desirable because a politicized citizenry was valued as a catalyst for a range of other social and economic changes identified with a modernizing nation. Through citizen involvement in politics it was expected that other goals of a secular, welfare state would also be furthered as villagers, townsmen and urban dwellers took it upon themselves to define a future better than the past, and actively worked towards that future.

The activities of the Torkotala village council document the catalytic importance of political participation, for through them an increased measure of political activity did result in an increased measure of social and economic equality. Yet whatever their faith in the importance of a politicized citizenry, the framers of the Indian Constitution left little to the vagueries of mass political participation. The Constitution is a declaration of social purpose, a vision of the common weal. It is also, importantly, an administrative blueprint for realizing that vision within the institutional structure of a federal republic with powerful legislatures at the federal and state levels, and an all-India judiciary united through appeal to a supreme court as the court of final jurisdiction. Like the Constitution, these legislatures and courts are a forum for defining national direction, and also instruments for encouraging or precipitating social and economic change.

The Indian parliament since Independence has sought to effect changes in a great many spheres. Of particular interest here is legislation in response to the Directive Principle contained in Article 44 of the Constitution: '... to secure for the citizens a uniform civil code throughout the territory of India.' India at Independence had virtually a complete codification of all fields of commercial, penal and procedural law, both criminal and civil. But the codification begun by the British, and based more or less on English law, did not extend to the Hindu personal law that governed family affairs. In this area, as with matters of caste and religious endowments, the British courts acted in accord with a principle established by Warren Hastings when the British first took effective control of the judicial system in Bengal, namely

> In all suits regarding inheritance, marriage, caste and other religious usages
> and institutions, the law of the Koran with respect to Mohammodans and those
> of the Shaster with respect to the Gentoos shall invariably be adhered to
> (Art. 23 of Regulation II, 1772, cited in Hooker 1975:61).

This principle was consistent with the British practice of ruling with minimal interference in Indian religious affairs. Its application proved difficult, though, because the British erred in assuming that the Hindus, like themselves, had an authoritative body of textual law which, once discovered and learned, could be applied in the courts. In fact, there is no single *sastra* or normative text authoritative throughout India; the multiple *sastras* are at points inconsistent and even contradictory; and *sastra* is not the only, or always even the foremost source of Hindu law. Even respected texts can be superseded by customary practice, which itself is not uniform throughout India and by its nature undergoes gradual flux (Galanter 1968).

Hastings' Regulation II of 1772 also established a second principle. In difficult cases the British judge was to act according to 'justice, equity and good conscience.' Whatever was originally intended by this principle, it allowed British judges to apply English law where, for example, the textual sources of Hindu law were silent, vague, inconsistent or contravened by customary practice; or where indigenous law simply offended British sensibilities (Derrett 1963; Galanter 1968). The application of Hindu personal law in the British courts thus included an admixture of English law.

The British were reluctant to undertake any reform of Hindu personal law. Yet in their interpretation of Hindu texts and their attempt to act with 'justice, equity and good conscience,' some changes in the personal law of

Hindus resulted nevertheless. The British sense of humanitarianism, for example, led to the legal abolition of female infanticide and the immolation of widows, the practice of *sati*. It also resulted in occasional legislation regarding wills, the remarriage of widows, and civil marriage – reforms designed not to alter the laws for all Hindus, but to provide an alternative for those individuals who wished to avoid the strictures of Hindu law. During the last decades of their rule, seemingly contrary to earlier principles of ruling with minimal interference in Indian religious affairs, the British also undertook to alter Hindu law as it applied to everyone. There were restraints placed on child marriage, rules of inheritance were made more favorable to women, and protection was given to widows, among other legislative reforms. These pre-Independence reforms, as Galanter (1978:494) notes, did not constitute a thorough reworking of Hindu personal law, but did, importantly, mark the successful attempt by a government power to modify normative religious texts and customary practice as the principle sources of Hindu law.

A unified body of civil law that applies throughout a territory is a salient feature of modern legal systems. By the time the Indian Constitution was drafted the goal of a unified civil code was already accepted by a large section of the national leadership and found expression in Article 44. Since Independence there has not been any serious effort to implement Article 44 literally, and it is unlikely that there will be such an effort in the near future, because enacting a uniform code for all Indians would require abolishing the personal law of Muslims and other non-Hindus. The parliament has acted, though, to introduce wholesale changes in the personal law of Hindus, and in doing so has abandoned status-oriented religious texts as an orienting normative frame in favor of the more equalitarian standards of a modern legal system.

To reform and unify Hindu personal law, the Indian parliament in 1955–6 passed a series of Acts known collectively as the Hindu Code. The Code consists of four Acts, which extend to the whole of India except the state of Jammu and Kashmir, and applies to all Hindus, Buddhists, Jains and Sikhs. It does not apply to Muslims, Christians, Parsis or Jews, who are recognized as having their own personal laws. Each of the Acts, and their impact on social relations in Torkotala, will be discussed in turn. In doing so, the discussion ignores consideration of earlier legislation passed during British rule or immediately after Independence which has been incorporated into the Hindu Code. The focus of discussion, in other words, is not the history of Hindu Code legislation, but the behavioral impact among Torkotala residents of the broad reforms included in the legislation. At issue is the effect of progressive legislation on those relations of social inequality based on differences of caste and sex.

The Hindu Marriage Act 25/1955

The Hindu Marriage Act (HMA) omits as a condition of marriage that a bride and groom must be of the same caste, but stipulates that a bride must have completed the age of 15 and a groom the age of 18 at the time of marriage (s. 5). It also recognizes that Hindu marriages can be solemnized without civil ceremony where the established custom is for the bride and groom to take together seven steps before the sacred fire (s. 7). This is, in fact, how all marriages in Torkotala have been solemnized.

In Torkotala in 1971 one daughter and two sons of the village were married. All were under the age set by the HMA as a condition for marriage, as were their spouses. Indeed, among Hindus of the village there are but two females who passed the age of 15 without being married. Both were high school students when they turned 16. There are but five males of the village who passed the age of 18 without being married. Four were in high school or college when they turned 19. The fifth is exceptional in having decided never to marry. In general, then, Torkotala Hindus pay no heed to the legally stipulated ages for marriage. The relevant provision of the HMA is known to them, but consistent with a transformational perspective on human development, age *per se* is not held a criterion for adult status or indicative of the physical-cum-moral growth considered requisite for entering the adult life stage marked by marriage.

Regarding inter-caste marriage, in Torkotala only 3 out of 127 unions (2%) did not conform to the *samanulom* pattern of males and females marrying persons of the same caste. Two of these unions involved a higher-caste widower remarrying with a lower-caste female. This is sanctioned by the HMA, but in both instances the males involved say they were not influenced by the removal of a judicial bar to inter-caste marriage. They describe their remarriage with a woman of lower caste as a form of *anulom* marriage common among relatively poor widowers. In the third union a male born of the Sadgop caste lives with a Lodha woman and their children. This too is sanctioned by the HMA, though proscribed by a customary bar against Hindu–tribal marriages. Jogi Pal was outcasted for violating Sadgop and Hindu *dharma*.

The HMA also provides for either party to a marriage to petition the local district court for judicial separation, annulment or divorce (ss. 9–18), though no petition for divorce is to be presented within three years of marriage (s. 14), and a divorced person is not permitted to remarry within one year (s. 15). These provisions thus allow for the dissolution of unions, but also pose conditions intended to protect the viability of marriages. In Torkotala no one has ever petitioned the court for a judicial separation, annulment or divorce, though there has been at least one clear opportunity to do so. That involved Nirod Janna, a Tantoby by caste, and his wife Basanti.

Nirod and his elder brother, Sarat, married two sisters of Torkotala, and took up residence in the village. By all accounts Sarat and his wife, Veena, lived in relative harmony. Nirod and Basanti did not. Basanti behaved indecorously in speaking openly to unrelated males in the market and along village roads. It is rumored that she was involved sexually with some of these men. Nirod, in response to such rumors, separated from Basanti and took up residence in a small hut in the compound of his brother's wife. As this compound was adjacent to Basanti's, Nirod and his wife still saw and spoke to each other on occasion, but Nirod never again worked the fields of his wife, ate from her fire, or slept in her hut. The separation occurred about ten years ago. Though Nirod could have petitioned the district court for a divorce on grounds of adultery, he did not.

Nirod had lived apart from Basanti for about three years when Sarat died. After Sarat's death, Nirod continued to dwell in Veena's compound and gradually assumed those work tasks once done by his elder brother. Eventually he also slept in Veena's hut. Basanti is aware that she can now formally divorce Nirod. She has not done so during the last five years, and expresses no plans ever to do so. Why not? Why did Nirod also not seek a divorce through the courts?

It has been argued that Indian villagers like Nirod and Bansanti avoid using the judicial system when they know about and have the opportunity to do so because of the expense involved, the time required for court action, the uncertainty of how a judge will decide, or the lack of understanding or acceptance of the procedural and substantive rules applied in the courts (Cohn 1959, 1965; Kidder 1973). There may also be simply no necessity to use the courts. In this instance both Nirod and Basanti were aware of the relevant provisions of the HMA, and both assert they would engage lawyers, go to court, and bear the needed expense if that was the only way to effectively separate from each other. But it isn't. In their case petitioning the court, or even other villagers, is simply unnecessary. Both wish to live apart from one another, and need no one's sanction to do so. Moreover, neither Nirod nor Basanti require the legal rights entailed with a judicial divorce. The HMA prohibits plural marriages (s. 17), but in Torkotala there is no customary bar to prevent either Nirod or Basanti from remarrying without first undergoing divorce proceedings.

The Hindu Succession Act 30/1956

It was noted when discussing the politics of family life that inheritance and succession to property among Bengali Hindus is governed by a customary pattern of law known locally as Dayabhaga. Under Dayabhaga law the father has sole and complete rights over ancestral and personal property during his lifetime. This is true of immovable property such as land, and movable property such as livestock and household effects. The father can divide this property while still alive, allotting it according to his pleasure. If left undivided, upon his death the estate is inherited in equal shares by surviving sons. Widows and daughters have no similar claim to inheritance as right of survival; only the right of maintenance, which in practice usually depends on their continued residence in the family household.

The HSA affirms local practice in providing that property can be disposed of by will or other testamentary form (s. 30). It breaks with Dayabhaga practice in providing that in intestate succession a man's widow and surviving children, male and female, shall inherit in equal shares (s. 10). The same holds true for female property. It can be allotted by will or other testamentary form, but in the absence of the same, devolves in equal shares upon the widower and surviving sons and daughters.

In none of the 65 Hindu households in Torkotala has the present male head of household or his father before him distributed ancestral property during his own lifetime. Over these two generations – which span the passage of the HSA – landed property has passed to surviving sons in accord with Dayabhaga practice in every instance but one. The exception involved Krishna Prasad Dolai, a Bagra-Khatriya, who used his knowledge of the HSA to avert the customary exclusion of widows and daughters from an inheritance that would have obtained if he died intestate.

Krishna Prasad died in 1966. He had two wives at the time, both married prior to the ban on plural marriages contained in the HMA. Guna Bala, the first wife, was barren. Shandai, the second wife, bore a son and a daughter. Neither wife got on well with the other. As neighbors now tell it, though Shandai pleased Krishna Prasad by bearing his children, she could not displace Guna Bala as his favorite or as female head of household. In anger and jealously Shandai made frequent long visits to her father's home, usually leaving her children behind. Guna Bala, in Shandai's absence, cared for the children and maintained Krishna Prasad's household.

On one visit Shandai stayed at her father's home for an entire year. This prompted Krishna Prasad, who was in failing health, to meet with other Bagra-Khatriyas of the village. He left with his caste fellows verbal directions governing the inheritance of his property. The same directions were later given to a Midnapore lawyer who drafted a will accordingly.

Under Dayabhaga law Krishna Prasad's only son would inherit all of his property, including fifteen acres of rice land. If the son was still a minor when Krishna Prasad died, the land probably would be managed by his mother, Shandai, as Krishna Prasad had no living adult male relatives. In his lawyer-executed will, by contrast, Krishna Prasad provided that upon his death Guna Bala would inherit in her name two acres of rice land, as would his daughter. The remaining acres of rice land and all other property would be inherited by his son. The will also provided that if Krishna Prasad's son and daughter were minors at the time of his death, their inheritances would be managed by Guna Bala until the son was 18 and the daughter was married.

This was the first and only instance that Krishna Prasad ever contacted a lawyer. Doing so involved much initiative and some expense in seeking in Midnapore Town an unknown person who could be entrusted to draft a will in accord with statutory law. Krishna Prasad made that effort because customary practice would not provide Guna Bala or his daughter an inheritance, and could not insure that Shandai upon his death would not benefit by managing the inheritance of her son. This is not to say that Krishna Prasad was committed in principle to the reforms contained in the HSA. Only that unlike Nirod and Basanti Janna, he could not find a satisfactory remedy to his particular plaint apart from legislation contained in the Hindu Code. Yet Krishna Prasad seemingly was not entirely certain about the force of law either, for in confiding his will to caste fellows of the village he, in effect, enjoined them to see that it was enforced. A lawyer-executed will is an instrument of government politics. Making the enforcement of that will a shared public responsibility of many caste fellows is an instrument of village politics. Krishna Prasad used both to his own purpose.

The Hindu Minority and Guardianship Act 32/1956

Among Bengali Hindus it is customary for children sired in marriage to be under the ultimate guardianship of their father. In the absence of their father because of his death or permanent departure, minor children come under the effective care of their mother, provided that she continues to live in the home of her husband or his lineal relatives. A woman cannot usually take her children to live elsewhere over the objections of males of her husband's line. In that sense are males of the line the ultimate guardians of a man's children in his absence. The HMGA, by contrast, gives the mother first right to be the effective and ultimate guardian of her children in the absence of their father (s. 6).

No one in Torkotala has ever sought to take advantage of this provision of the HMGA. When Shandai left the home of Krishna Prasad Dolai, for example, she also left her children behind, and after Krishna Prasad's death she did not try to establish rights of guardianship. She also did not claim a right to maintenance from his estate, though she could have under provisions of the Hindu Adoption and Maintenance Act (1956, ss. 18–19). In local practice the right to maintenance usually depends on living in one's husband's household. A widow who leaves her husband's village for her natal village, as Shandai did, in effect renounces the right to benefit from her husband's property.

The Hindu Adoption and Maintenance Act 78/1956

The practice of adoption is associated for Torkotala residents with men who have no sons of their own, but seek a son to fulfill a debt by ensuring the perpetuation of the line and the continued performance of ancestor worships after one's own death. In a family without any natural sons, adopted sons are generally of the same caste, though there is no bar against adopting a son of another caste. There is also no proscription against adopting a daughter, though this occurs infrequently because for Hindus there is no cultural importance attached to being without female children. Adoption is customarily a right of men only. This was reformed by the HAMA, which entitles any qualified adult, male or female, to adopt a son or daughter of any caste (ss. 7–8).

No one in Torkotala has formally adopted a son or daughter. It is not uncommon, though, for children to be integrated into a family and raised as if they were natural children without legal adoption. This occurs among relatives under two sets of circumstances. A relatively poor family with many children may send one of its sons or daughters to live and assist around the house of a wealthier relative with fewer children than needed to handle chores in the house or field. Or if both parents of a child die while he or she is still a minor, the child may be integrated into a family of relatives. Without formal adoption, children integrated into a family do not share rights of inheritance with natural children.

A child may also be integrated into a family of non-relatives without being adopted. Most often this involves a widow living alone who requires the practical assistance of a male. Consider, for example, the documentary case involving Amodini Mahabarto, a Sadgop widow without children of her own, and Banksi Das, a Bagra-Khatriya Boisnab.

Amodini was childless and still a teenager when her husband, Manibrata Mahabarto, died. After the death, Amodini's husband's father's brother, Guru Prasad Mahabarto, provided her with a hut in a far corner of his own compound, and approximately ten acres of rice land. Their oral agreement was that Amodini could use the land during her lifetime, but could not sell or otherwise alienate the land. When Amodini died the land would pass to Guru Prasad's own sons, Atul and Pulin Mahabarto. Guru Prasad did not expect to outlive Amodini.

During the same year that Amodini was widowed, Banksi Das was orphaned. Guru Prasad arranged for Banksi to work for Amodini, and to live in a shelter near her hut. In exchange for food and some wages Banksi would do those tasks outside the household not allowed decorous women or widows, and give some measure of protection by his presence around the household. This arrangement, minus the formal payment of wages, lasted for nearly 25 years. Over that period Amodini and Banksi came to address each other as mother and son, and to share much as a family would. In 1951 the census taker, an outsider to the village, even listed Banksi as the head of Amodini's household, and entered their names as a single family unit. In 1954 Amodini sponsored Banksi's marriage, just as his natural parents would have if still alive. In 1971 Banksi's 14-year-old son lived near and assisted Amodini in the same manner as his father had once done. Amodini refers to the boy as her grandson.

Amodini never adopted Banksi. Banksi expresses no regret over not having been adopted. For both the practical and emotional benefits of their relationship existed independently of any ties established through a legal adoption. A legal adoption was in that sense unnecessary, just as a legal divorce was unnecessary for Nirod and Basanti Janna. Local practice sufficed. Amodini also recognizes two other considerations that mitigated against adoption. The land loaned her by Guru Prasad, after various land reform legislation of the mid-1960s, is now registered in her name and considered her property. Adoption would give Banksi a justiciable claim on this land, which Amodini intends Atul and Pulin to receive out of respect for her oral agreement with their now deceased father, Guru Prasad. She admits to avoiding adoption in order to avoid the inheritance rights which accrue to an adopted son. Unlike Krishna Prasad Dolai, Amodini does not wish to avert a customary pattern of inheritance by taking advantage of a provision of the Hindu Code. In this she has the support of Atul and Pulin Mahabarto, who were responsible for explaining to Amodini the full implications of a legal adoption. Formal adoption would also require Amodini, who lives the model life of a Hindu, to merge her identity and defining features with a son of lower caste. To Amodini this represents an adverse mixture of qualities in a way, and to an extent, that her present relationship with Banksi does not. To adopt Banksi would thus involve a clash of perspectives. The HAMA does not recognize caste, or all that is entailed by a transformational perspective. Amodini does, and for her the considerations of *dharma* central to a transformational perspective take precedence over the considerations of progress and change central to Hindu Code legislation.

The legislation contained in the several Acts of the Hindu code represents an effort to use lawyer's-law to reorder relations of caste and sexual inequality for Hindu society as a whole. In Torkotala such legislation exists alongside of and in competition with local ways that support the already established order of social relations identified with a transformational theory of rank and human development. These local ways do not have the sanction of federal and state courts, but they do have the authority of *dharma* and the force of longstanding usage. They define Torkotala as a semi-autonomous social field (Moore 1973) which is subject to the Hindu Code, but within which that legislation only has limited effectiveness. The time, money and knowledge required to take advantage of provisions of the Hindu Code contribute in part to that limited effectiveness. Also, and importantly, Torkotala Hindus sometimes simply prefer to order their family life in accord with local ways and contrary to provisions of the Hindu Code. This is true even of persons like Atul Mahabarto who in the main favor the changes identified with a progressive government politics. Atul, as head of the Torkotala *panchayat*, actively works to improve the lot of tribals and lower-caste Hindus of the village, and to involve them politically in council affairs. He also encourages females of the village to attend day school or adult education classes at night, and has educated his daughter through high school. Yet in matters of family life, Atul avers he will not leave land to his wife or daughter, or countenance an inter-caste marriage for any of his children. Atul also strongly advised Amodini not to adopt a lower-caste son.

It is the pardox of legislation as an instrument of directed change that while law is self-defining it is not self-executing. Drafters of the Hindu Code can limit the contexts in which caste is recognized judicially and can level the inequalities between sexes by extending to females rights already held by males. But they cannot control the acceptance of that legislation. Torkotala residents simply use or ignore the provisions of the Hindu Code according to their own purposes. Put differently, in Torkotala today the impact of civil legislation like the Hindu Code is contingent on citizen acceptance and voluntary use because the courts, police and other agents of the state do not take the initiative in enforcing that legislation. No one in Torkotala, for example, has ever been served process for allowing underage children to marry, or for excluding females of the family from their legally defined inheritance rights. Nor is it likely that such action will be initiated because in matters of personal law the Indian legal system acts – or more correctly, reacts – almost wholly in response to citizen-initiated complaints. The Hindu Code exists. But in the absence of citizens voluntarily accepting its provisions or initiating complaints against others who do not, the legislation contained in the Hindu Code has not had the impact envisioned by its drafters.

The negligible impact of Hindu Code legislation in Torkotala is due ultimately to a lack of voluntary acceptance by villagers who continue to order their social relations in accord with an alternative set of local law ways. That Torkotala villagers have not been induced or compelled to accept the Hindu Code depends as well on the reactive stance of the state in advancing this innovative social legislation. To clarify with a comparison, both the Hindu Code and Panchayati Raj have the same authoritative source in a Directive Principle of the Indian Constitution, and both represent instances of directed change aimed at modernization. The extension of rural self-government into Torkotala, for example, can be regarded as a program of political modernization. How does one extend into local administrative units, villages, those features of a participatory democracy which already exist in other administrative units of the nation? Government officials and their agents can await local initiative and then respond to requests by villagers to establish the system of *panchayats* provided for in Article 40 of the Constitution. Or the state can initiate efforts to establish a system of rural self-government, as it did, by deputing agents charged to explain Panchayati Raj legislation to rural citizens, to oversee the first *panchayat* election, and then to provide incentives for the actual operation of these councils by funneling money and other government aid through them. Whereas the first approach would be reactive in relying on local initiative, the second is proactive in that officials and agents of the government – outsiders to the community – took the first steps required to innovate locally. To the extent that Panchayati Raj succeeded in advancing a measure of political and economic equality, that success depended in large part on the proactive stance of change agents from outside the village community.

By contrast, in Torkotala the several Acts of the Hindu Code have had less than the impact desired by legislators, in part because of the reactive nature of the Indian legal system with respect to civil law. As the courts, police and other administrative agents of the state do not take the initiative in enforcing provisions of the Hindu Code, this innovative social legislation is both easily ignored and ignored without fear of negative sanctions by the state. Unlike the clear material rewards associated with participating in Panchayati Raj, the positive incentives for embracing the Hindu Code also remain unclear to Torkotala villagers. And villagers wonder why their own acceptance and voluntary use of the Hindu Code should be forthcoming when district-level officials are observed ordering their family life and patterns of inheritance in the same manner as they do. Local government officials, in other words, do not themselves appear committed to the new behaviors required by law, which was not true of the BDO and others who advanced the program of Panchayati Raj.

The negligible impact of Hindu Code legislation in Torkotala notwithstanding, the very existence of the Hindu Code does represent an instance and invocation of progressive change in several respects. The Indian parliament has successfully asserted itself as a central authority which can reorder social relations, in law if not in action, for Hindus throughout India, thereby subjecting Hindus of every caste and region to a degree of uniformity unprecedented in Indian history. In doing so the parliament has brought Hindu family life entirely into the ambit of legislative rule. Appeals to religious texts, like appeals to customs of locality, caste and family, are in the main no longer acceptable in the eyes of the state. The personal law of Hindus is now man-made law, and the inequalities of caste, indissoluble marriage, the favored position of males, and other practices supported by *sastra* and custom have been replaced by emphases on individual rights and the equality of all persons. In that sense does the Hindu Code mark a step towards legal modernization, even as residents of Torkotala remain out of step with it.

The Torkotala labor dispute

In 1969, when the Torkotala labor dispute occurred, West Bengal was governed by the second United Front (UF), a loose coalition of leftist political parties united primarily by their opposition to the Congress party which had governed the state from 1952 to 1967, when the first UF government was returned. Leading the UF coalition, both in popular support and the active formulation of its party platform, were the Communist party of India (CPI) and the Communist party of India (Marxist) (CPM), who differed with each other on pragmatics, but nevertheless advocated many of the same reform programs, including efforts to improve wages and working conditions for agricultural laborers in villages throughout West Bengal.

Efforts to raise the dignity and rewards of labor are common to communist-party platforms throughout India. That reforms of this kind should have particular saliency and suport in Torkotala in 1969 is related to the local pattern of wage and labor relationships. Specifically, in Torkotala, as in other villages of the area, agricultural laborers are divided into two categories: *munis* are employed by a single landholding family on a yearly basis, and usually from year to year; *mojur* work on a short-term, temporary basis for one or several landholders.

Both males and females are included in the *munis* category. A *munis* receives for work done a daily measure of food, which includes enough for himself and some extra for his family, a specified number of clothes yearly, and a minimal, but fixed, amount of cash, most often paid monthly. In addition, a *munis* is the occasional recipient of largess from his or her employer, and can usually count on receiving loans and other kinds of aid in times of personal or family crisis. In return, *munis* are expected to do whatever work is required of them, whether in the fields, the compound, or the house, and to provide the patron–employer wide-ranging political support as well.

UF party workers voiced no major complaint against the wages paid to agricultural laborers employed as *munis*. *Munis* wages were not generous, but they were sufficient for a family to subsist on, and, most importantly, they provided a source of income year round even when there was not much agricultural work to be done. UF party workers did complain about the wages and working conditions of those agricultural laborers employed as *mojur*.

Both male and female laborers are referred to as *mojur* if they are employed on a short-term, temporary basis, say to complete a specified job like plowing the fields, or from day to day. In 1969 the going wage for short-term male labor was 1.50 rupees daily (slightly less for females), and food, which consisted of parched rice in the early morning before work began and boiled rice at midday. *Mojur* could eat their fill during the working day, but received no additional food for when not working or for their family, and neither the *mojur* nor the family received any clothes. In return for these wages, a *mojur* worked from sunrise to sunset, with some rest at midday when the heat was greatest.

In Torkotala it is a mark of a middle-class household to employ one or two *munis* and then supplement this standing source of labor with *mojur* on a job or daily basis as needed. This practice works to the advantage of landholders because continuing labor expenses are kept at a minimum, and there is never a shortage of unemployed laborers to hire on a short-term basis as needed, even during peak work periods. *Munis* also fare reasonably well. They have year round employment, and can depend on the patronly support of their employers to supplement basic income. Also, a *munis* is often allowed to sharecrop part of his employer's lands, and in this way can accumulate some wealth and, occasionally, even lands of his own. In particular, Mundas of the village have accumulated moderate landholdings in this way. *Mojur* do not fare as well. Their wages are insufficient to permit savings against those days when there is no work to be had, which is most of the year. And even when work is available, *mojur* wages are insufficient to support a family, thereby requiring that spouses and children all seek temporary work. Because employment is on a short-term basis, a *mojur* also does not benefit often from largess from his employer. Some landholders will advance pay against future work when unemployed laborers are most in need. But when paid in advance *mojur* wages are calculated at one rupee daily, which makes such labor worth even less than usual, and only perpetuates the poverty and daily struggle for subsistence that characterizes life for short-term agricultural laborers.

It was to reform this pattern of wage and labor relationships that UF party workers in the Narayanghar area advocated a minimum wage of two rupees (slightly lower for women), and a fixed daily allocation of 250 grams of parched rice and 1 kilogram of uncooked rice for all agricultural laborers who worked as *mojur*. Associated with these reforms were still others. The UF sought to prohibit the hiring of migrant workers from western Midnapore – the same area from which the Lodhas and Mundas of Torkotala originally migrated – as a cheap source of labor. And they wished to establish an eight-hour working day for all agricultural laborers, *munis* and *mojur*.

Both laborers and landholders of Torkotala were aware of the reforms advocated by the UF even before party workers entered the village. They had attended political rallies held in nearby Narayanghar Town, timed to coincide with market days, and from radio broadcasts and word of mouth were aware of similar reform efforts in villages elsewhere in West Bengal. The landholders in particular were aware that physical violence was not uncommon in villages where party workers organized agricultural laborers in defiance of their employers. Indeed, it was this fear of violence, coupled with a feeling that there was no effective way to oppose the advocated reforms, which prompted Torkotala landholders to let it be known that in the future they would pay 1.75 rupees daily to all temporary laborers. This was less than the amount the UF was calling for, but Torkotala *mojur* did not object. Regarding the other reforms advocated, Torkotala landholders had long ago stopped hiring migrant laborers from the west, and both landholders and laborers thought the UF demand for an eight-hour working day a somewhat misguided product of communist ideology. As one Munda laborer expressed it, 'Rice must be harvested when ripe, and threshed when needed, no matter how much work is required.'

Because of earlier statements by landholders of the village, in late October, when rice was fast ripening in the field, Torkotala was calm and without expectation of a labor dispute. When harvesting actually began in November, the village was torn by an explosive quarrel (*bibad*). What happened? Rather than pay temporary laborers the increased daily wage of 1.75 rupees, Torkotala landholders hired some laborers as if they were *munis*, offering them the same wages as *munis*, but with the understanding that they would work through the harvest season only. The landholders created, in other words, a new category of *kal munis* or seasonal laborer in order to avoid paying higher wages to all *mojur*.

This action incensed the unemployed *mojur* of the village and local UF party workers, who accused the village landholders of acting immorally, of employing a black arrow. Spurred on by party workers, the laborers thus decided to prevent the so-called seasonal *munis* from working. Village roads were patrolled and all seasonal *munis* were physically prevented from proceeding to work, while regular *munis* were allowed to proceed unmolested. In addition, the *mojur* of the village, who previously had been willing to work for 1.75 rupees daily, now announced a demand of two rupees daily. If two rupees were not paid, they warned, then the landholders would find no labor available at all.

Nearly a week passed in which the laborers continued to prevent all but regular *munis* from proceeding to work, and the landholders refused to employ any *mojur* at two rupees a day. Rice continued to ripen in the field, with an ever-increasing threat of spoilage if it was not cut soon. Unemployed laborers, in need of food and vengeful for not being given the expected opportunity to work, took to harvesting needed amounts of rice at night by stealth, thereby pressuring landholders with a loss of another kind. If their crop did not rot in the field, it would be stolen from the field. Towards the end of the week, laborers of the village exacerbated the quarrel further by physically preventing some regular *munis* from going to work.

With but a few exceptions, in 1969 all *mojur* in Torkotala and all persons hired as seasonal *munis* were Lodhas or Mundas. Positions as regular *munis*, by contrast, were typically held by landless Hindus, though some of the earliest Lodha and Munda settlers in Torkotala still retained their original positions of employment as *munis*. Given this distribution of jobs, it was not difficult for the unemployed laborers to effect a near-total work stoppage by calling on the loyalties of their fellow tribesmen, and then physically intimidating some of the Hindu *munis*. For the same reason, it was not difficult for the middle-class landholders of the village, all Hindus, to depict the labor dispute as an attempt by outsiders to instigate a communal quarrel – tribals versus Hindus – where none had existed in Torkotala previously. Such communalism, it was argued, would benefit no one within the village; only political party workers from outside. In this way did landholders of the village appeal to the loyalty of all villagers, tribal and Hindu, to their *des* in order to end the labor dispute. Coupled with this appeal to loyalty to the *des*, landholders also cast suspicion on the true motives of UF party workers, and especially the CPI and CPM members, who were suspect locally because of their communist ideology. (Torkotala residents had voted in the main for another party within the UF coalition, the non-communist Bangla Congress.)

When an appeal to loyalty to the *des* failed to end the labor dispute, the landholders sought to break the work stoppage against them by undermining its leadership. Tribal laborers of the village were being led by a Hindu, Byomokes Maiti, one of the larger landholders of the village. Other landholders sought to exploit this seeming paradox. Why should Byomokes be leading tribals in a labor dispute if not for selfish, suspect ends? And why should tribals of the village follow a Hindu, especially a Hindu landholder? Confronted with these questions, spokesmen for the Lodhas and Mundas replied, in effect, that they continued to work for Byomokes, and to follow his lead, because he paid them two rupees daily. If other landholders paid the same wage, they would find willing laborers as well.

Again the landholders had failed to break the work stoppage against them. They could not rally the Lodhas and Mundas in an appeal to common loyalty to the *des*, and they could not undermine the leadership provided by Byomokes. Meanwhile their crops were either rotting in the field or being stolen. Given these circumstances, the landholders next decided to patrol their fields at night (one or two owned guns) and to begin harvesting the rice crop themselves. This was a radical decision, for any physical labor involves one with the *rajasik* and *tamasik* aspects of life, and is thus to be avoided. Moreover, it is the mark and privilege of a middle-class landholder to avoid the demanding work of laboring in the fields by hiring others to work in his stead. The decision to harvest their own crops was made nevertheless, and the landholders drew up a schedule by which they would work each person's land in turn.

Work started the very next day. And for three days the landholders of the village proceeded to harvest their own crops, without the aid of tribal laborers, but with the assistance of a new-found camaraderie and a unique sense of fun and adventure. In recounting the events of those days, some landholders are still amused by how certain wealthy villagers, who had never been known to work in the fields, awkwardly gave their hand. On the fourth day fun and adventure gave way to fear, for the unemployed laborers, carrying bamboo staves in their hands, marched to the fields in mass, opposed the landholders, and demanded that they stop harvesting the rice crop, or else. A quarrel (*bibad*) threatened to become a war (*juddho*); words and verbal abuse (*gala gali*) threatened to give way to blows and beatings (*mara mari*). The landholders responded that they had every right to harvest their own fields. In fear of violence, and knowing they were no physical match for the stave-bearing laborers, the landholders nevertheless stopped their work and left the fields, proceeding directly to the police station in Narayanghar Town.

The police, themselves fearful of the UF, and especially the CPI and CPM party workers, who were alleged to beat or even assassinate political opponents, did nothing in response to the complaint lodged by Torkotala landholders. So the landholders next approached the BDO and the head of the area *panchayat*, the *anchal pradhan*, who agreed to arbitrate the labor dispute. Several more days passed, making the labor dispute almost two weeks old, before the BDO and *anchal pradhan*, accompanied by several UF party workers, unexpectedly arrived in Torkotala and called for a village meeting. Laborers and landholders assembled. Spokesmen for each were allowed publicly to present their side of the dispute. Then the BDO, *anchal pradhan* and UF party workers met privately before presenting their resolution of the labor dispute. Specifically, they instructed the landholders to stop harvesting their own crops, as this eliminated the only source of income agricultural laborers of the village had. Also, it was held unseemly for men of their class to do physical labor. The laborers, for their part, were instructed to return to work for 1.88 rupees daily. This was less than the demanded wage of two rupees but more than the wage originally offered by landholders.

The open quarrel between agricultural laborers and landholders of Torkotala ended after this arbitration, but not the competition between them. For while the Torkotala labor dispute resulted, finally, in an increased measure of economic equality for short-term laborers – higher wages – and for all laborers a heightened sense of political effectiveness when organized for a common purpose, the dispute also left a legacy of mutual distrust and rivalry. *Mojur* complain that the system of advanced wages for future work, which allowed them some income even when there was no work to be done, has been discontinued entirely, and that the 250 grams of parched rice and one kilogram of uncooked rice which they demanded and won has turned out to be less than they received previously when allowed to eat their fill. Now landholders fastidiously provide the measured allotment only. *Munis* complain that they no longer receive the same amount of largess from their employers, and that loans are much harder to come by.

The importance of the Torkotala labor dispute can be narrowly summarized as documenting efforts at economic equality by agricultural laborers acting in accord with the premises of government politics. Its broader significance goes beyond the specifics of wage and labor relationships, for the dispute divided the village in a way that family or caste or factional competitions never did. Economic interests here combined with social differences, so that tribals and Hindus of the village found themselves in a competition mitigated by few cross-cutting interests and no mutually acceptable third party to act as a peace maker, at least not within the village. Laborers appealed to government officials and UF party workers to support their efforts at economic equality. With the exception of Byomokes Maiti, landholders pejoratively labeled all such interference in village affairs by outsiders as an instance of government politics.

As noted in chapter 3, distinctions of class have probably existed in Torkotala since its founding by Sadgop landholders and their landless laborers, the Bagdi. Yet as categories of individuals who share only a certain level of personal accomplishment, classes in Torkotala have not had the social importance of face-to-face interactive groups like families and castes, or even more ephemeral, loosely tied associations of individuals, like disciples of the same guru. The broader significance of the Torkotala labor dispute thus includes its rarity as an instance in which inclusion in a class became the locus of conscious identification and class interests provided an orientation for individuals who do not usually act together out of a common economic interest. For the Lodhas and Mundas, the labor dispute was the first occasion on which individuals of these different tribes acted jointly out of class interest. Class-based action was not similarly novel to the middle-class landholders of Torkotala. They had arranged, for example, first to settle Lodhas and Mundas in the village, and before that to hire tribals as migrant laborers during the peak labor season of harvest. But it was novel for landholders of Torkotala to be opposed by their laboring employees.

Those minimal landholding Hindus counted among the village poor did not participate actively in the labor dispute. Households of this class do not employ agricultural laborers year round as *munis*, and of necessity use family labor instead of *mojur* to harvest their rice crop. The landless Hindus of Torkotala, from whom the middle-class landholders draw most of their *munis* labor, also were not active competitors in the labor dispute, but were involved indirectly. Some were physically prevented from reaching work by Lodhas and Mundas who patrolled the village roads. Others did not try to reach work in fear of bodily harm. And a few, perhaps more familiar with the village back roads, successfully reached the compound of their employer and did their work as usual. The labor dispute nevertheless had a similar consequence for all Hindu *munis*, for it resulted in the reordering of relations between middle-class landholders and agricultural laborers, whether tribal or Hindu.

To explain more fully, after the arbitration by government officials and UF party workers, Lodha and Munda *munis* let it be known that they were well satisfied with their wages and working conditions and wished to be treated just as before the dispute. They were not. Neither were the Hindu *munis*, whom their landholding employers lumped together with the tribals as part of the same laboring class. Specifically, the element of patronage which personalized the tie between a landholder and his long-term agricultural laborer was shorn from the relationship. No longer were landholders responsive to requests for loans or intercession in times of family or personal crisis. *Munis*, both tribal and Hindu, were now treated as *mojur*, as laborers to whom a landholder owed only wages for work done. *Munis* labor, in effect, was commercialized, and from the vantage point of Torkotala landholders their relationship with all *munis* was redefined as part of the market economy UF party workers spoke about so often. It was no longer part of the moral economy of the village.

In characterizing the relationship between agricultural laborers and their landholding employees, one could emphasize the complementary nature of occupational tasks and the more or less mutually beneficial aspects of the relationship for both the givers and receivers of service. Or one could emphasize the inequality between landholders and their landless or minimal landholding laborers who must of necessity work in their employ. Here the relationship would be characterized by exploitation rather than reciprocity.

In Torkotala prior to the labor dispute in 1969 neither of the above characterizations would have been entirely accurate, nor would they have been entirely misleading. Through their *munis*, landholders secured a dependent source of labor, which also constituted a political following. *Munis*, for their part, secured a continuing source of employment in a village with surplus labor. Inequalities existed between landholders and their landless or minimal landholding employees, but *munis* were compensated for those inequalities by a sense of economic security and an umbrella of political protection. Whatever exploitation existed was additionally compensated for by the patronage a *munis* received from his landholding employer. A *munis* was not simply a laborer, but also a family friend of long standing, sometimes a fictive 'little brother' or 'little sister,' and a reliable ally. Further, like the subject of a king, or the offspring of a father, a *munis* was the *praja* or dependent of his employer. As a dependent he owed full loyalty to his landholding employer; but he was also due the affection, generosity and protection expected from a king to his subjects or a father to his offspring. Such patronage mitigated exploitation and provided an integrative bond which cross-cut the divisive inequalities which separated landholders and laborers.

Since the labor dispute, *munis* have been hired on a wage basis only, meaning without obligations of patronage. In that sense did this instance of progress and change in the name of government politics have the double-edged consequence of gaining higher wages for short-term laborers at the expense of long-term laborers. For landholders, too, the labor dispute had a double-edged consequence. The commercialization of labor reduced the total expense of working their fields and compounds, and made those expenses more predictable by reducing the diffuse obligations they had towards laborers. But there now exists in Torkotala consciousness of two new political teams – agricultural laborers versus landholders – that add to the divisions of family, caste and factions the division of class.

Structure, process and meaning in government politics

Other instances of government politics could be presented. But like those already considered they would evidence that government politics aims to alter the system of ranked inequalities supported by village politics, and to substitute in its stead a social and political order grounded on the fundamental equality of all persons. Efforts towards this goal may emphasize differently the immediate political gains of extending a democratic system of rule into local administrative units like Torkotala, the social gains of removing judicial recognition of certain religiously based inequalities, or the economic gains of a more equitable reward for labor. But whatever the immediate goal of specific instances of government politics, all aim at the ultimate goal of a more equalitarian society. Progress towards this goal defines the context of meaning in which government politics is pursued.

Not all Torkotala residents favor the progressive goal of government politics, and even partisan villagers may not favor the full range of changes associated with government politics. Not surprisingly, therefore, in Torkotala efforts at directed change are marked by recurrent, even anticipated competition. As in village politics, such competitions take the form of argument (*jukti*), rivalry (*jhogra*) and open quarrel (*bibad*). And as in village politics, rivalries are the characteristic form of competition in government politics, if only because of the difficulties inherent in maintaining a continuous state of open quarrel among co-residents of a village. But in contrast to village politics, open quarrels are more frequent and carry far less opprobrium in government politics. Why? Torkotala residents recognize that not all villagers accept the goal of progress and change, or welcome the alterations of day-to-day village life attendant on India becoming a modernized nation-state. They recognize also that competitors from different natural and moral communities (villagers versus outsiders) will not always act within a single, agreed upon, moral code, as is also true of villagers who accept different premises about the relationship between polity, society and cosmos. Further, it is recognized that some of the innovations identified with government politics are themselves conducive to the direct and open encounters which define quarrels. The election process favored by advocates of Panchayati Raj, for example, is held by Haripado Bhunai and others to generate open quarrels in requiring a clear choice between candidates for council membership and leadership. The black-letter law of the Hindu Code, if accepted, entails a clear rejection of certain customary practices. And United Front party workers, through their accounts of peasant movements, convinced some Torkotala laborers that direct and even violent encounter was the only sure and immediate means of labor reforms.

The reduced negative sanction which attaches to open quarrel in the context of government politics reveals an affinity with factional politics. In other respects, too, government politics and factional politics are alike structurally. The prize of each differs. But in the organization of teams both are founded on voluntary ties of association in which individuals *qua* individuals pursue interests that cross-cut their membership in birth groups like family and caste. Government politics is identified with outsiders to the village, and with the rules and resources of the state. These same persons, rules and resources are considered alien to village politics, but if used at all it is faction leaders who are most likely to draw upon them. In the incident of the school, for example, faction leaders variously involved government persons like the BDO and the head of the area council, political party workers and another outsider, a university-educated social worker. Common to all political competitions in Torkotala are still other specifics, including the use of rumors, lies and gossip, verbal abuse and physical beatings, or the threat of physical beatings, which describe in part the manner and means of both village politics and government politics.

The contrasting themes and events of Torkotala politics reflect very different understandings of order, each with its own validation. Village politics premises a social and political order which is objective, divinely given and inherent in the material nature of the universe. It is not for men to change that order, but to understand, guard and maintain it. Village politics is thus essentially protective of the traditional. Validating this image of a traditionalist politics is a cyclical vision of time, which holds that the creator of the universe generates the phenomenal world out of his cosmic body, sustains it for a time, then causes it to degenerate and be reabsorbed in him, only later to begin the cycle anew. Like the universe at large, human society also passes through an interminable series of long cycles, each consisting of four ages. The Golden Age, when *dharma* was upheld in its entirely, is quite literally in the past. So are the Silver and Bronze Ages when *dharma* walked on three and then two feet respectively. What confronts men in their own lifetime is the Iron Age or Kali Yuga, when *dharma* hobbles along on but one foot. To forestall an even further degeneration of behavioral codes and ultimately the destruction of the known world, it is for men to protect what remains of the rule of *dharma*. Village politics is but one set of activities towards that end.

Government politics, by contrast, premises that social and political order is a human construction, and thus subject to continual reshaping and improvement in accord with human efforts. Moreover, in creating a new order, men are not bound by local tradition. Innovation is expected. So is progress, a future better than the past. Validating this image of a progressive politics is a vision of time as a forward trajectory, having a single beginning and a single, purposeful end, which in contemporary India is seen as progress in accord with the ideals of a modernizing nation-state. The Golden Age of government politics is in the future, not in the past, and is accessible to men through their own efforts at reform.

The premises, images and validations which inform village politics and government politics bear importantly on the process of political change in Torkotala today. For while change is not unique to either form of politics, each form of rule does have its own manner of rationalizing change, and thus its own language of claims. To illustrate, traditionalism – as distinct from tradition – is a language of claims which justifies present practice in terms of the presumed practice of a past Golden Age. Traditionalism in the context of village politics does not entail an unchanging set of acts, premises and institutions which have persisted from time immemorial. It refers to no set conditions or time, but to a positive evaluation of the past order. As such, traditionalism is not antithetical to change, but requires that innovations be accommodated so that they are regarded not simply as new, but also, paradoxically, as old, as reviving or restoring an original and better state that for some reason has been lost in the Kali Yuga. In practical terms this means that events like the Bagdi claim to a new and higher rank are justified publicly as a corrective to the right order of castes – temporarily disrupted – and not as a challenge to that order. It means also that truly innovative aspects of government politics are often characterized, falsely, as restorationist. During the extension of Panchayati Raj into Torkotala, for example, the theme and language of claims associated with a traditionalist village politics were manipulated for the purposes of a progressive politics.

Government officials regularly depict Panchayati Raj as an elaboration of a historic pattern of rural self-government that is documented in the Vedas and the great epics, Ramayana and Mahabarata, as well as in Kautilya's Arthasastra. As the BDO explained it to Torkotala residents, during the Golden Age of ancient India villages were the basic unit of republican government and councils were the basic instrument of village rule. Rural self-government through councils was lost during the centuries of Muslim and British rule. To restore it became the goal of the pre-independent Indian National Congress, prodded by Mahatma Gandhi, who saw self-ruling villages as a necessary first step in preparing for a viable, independent democratic state. After Independence, it was this same system of rural self-government through councils which was formalized as national policy with the incorporation of Article 40 into the Indian Constitution, and which later became known as Panchayati Raj.

Village councils did exist in ancient India, and in parts of northern India (though not in Bengal) they were known as *panchayats*. But the councils of ancient India, like the informal meetings (*des jama*) of Torkotala today, were very different from their supposed statutory counterparts. They were *ad hoc* bodies for dealing with the broadest range of village affairs, not formally organized and constituted bodies with specified functions, power, revenue sources, etc., which is characteristic of councils instituted under Panchayati Raj legislation. Also, unlike the *panchayats*, councils of ancient India were not popularly elected bodies. Their leadership did not circulate regularly and was not in any real sense open to persons without hereditary rights and/or dominant economic status. Their source of support derived from local custom and the personal influence of their active membership, and not from the political and legal systems of a superordinate power.

Panchayati Raj legislation, in sum, did not restore the historic councils of some past system of rural self-government. It created a new kind of council intended to actualize the premises of government politics and to effect progress and change through the devolution of power, both economic and political. Yet in extending Panchayati Raj into villages like Torkotala, government agents manipulated the premises, images and validations of village politics to ease the accomodation of this political innovation. By associating the modern *panchayats* with a supposed ancient counterpart, these new councils were given a history and genealogy within the Indian Great Tradition which in effect then served to validate their (re)-introduction. The same process of validating the new through association with the old also explains why these councils were termed *panchayats*; they would be better understood by this traditional sounding name than by any other technically more accurate neologism.

The use of traditionalism as an instrument of political innovation is best directed towards those who view the Golden Age as being in the past. It is far less effective, even counter-productive, when addressed to those who view the Golden Age as in the future. This suggests why efforts by United Front party workers to improve wages and working conditions for agricultural laborers in rural West Bengal were accompanied by a different and more progressive language of claims, that of modernism. Specifically, at rallies timed to coincide with market days in the Narayanghar area, and when visiting within Torkotala, UF party workers depicted a new and better order that could be realized if agricultural laborers organized and acted in their own interests. UF party workers acknowledged that local history was characterized by the dependence of many agricultural laborers on a relatively few large landholders. But they marshalled the evidence of world history to argue that this was not a necessary dependence, and also not an irreversible dependence. Party workers spoke, for example, of Russian and Chinese peasants overcoming conditions of bonded labor and improving their lot through political action. They spoke also of laborers in other West Bengal villages who had effectively pressed for higher wages or even caused village land to be redistributed and now worked that land for their own benefit. The accuracy of these statements could not be contested by Torkotala residents, who know little of Russian or Chinese history, or even the details of labor disputes in other areas of West Bengal. But this was in an important sense unimportant because for Torkotala laborers the comparative experience of Russian or Chinese peasants or other Bengalis sounded plausible. The Lodha and Munda laborers of Torkotala share little of what UF party workers understand by a communist orientation. But like the party workers, they are not committed to historic forms of work and service and welcome the immediate, material benefits promised as a result of labor reforms. For them a progressive language of claims that conjures a future different and better than the present or past is a convincing language of claims.

The meaning of any political event is not determined by the particulars of the event itself. Meaning is socially authored, and the meanings attributed by actors may be manipulated for their own purpose. This suggests why an appropriate language of claims can ease the reception of an innovative change. It also points to why the success of an innovation depends on more than the immediate material benefits to be gained. Namely, any effort to change the present order is perceived and judged by Torkotala villagers within the broader context of views about polity, society and cosmos. It is to those views, as defined by the themes of village politics and government politics, that a traditionalist and progressive language of claims are addressed.

This observation suggests two general propositions. First, when politics is held subordinate to a broader normative framework like *dharma* – as in village politics – changes which challenge the basic premises, images and validations of order will be accommodated more readily when innovated in the name of traditionalism. Innovation can then be rationalized not simply as new, but also as old, as restorationist, as recapturing a past Golden Age. The threat of increased disorder and the further degeneration of *dharma* associated with advancing time is in this way mollified, and change, paradoxically, is interpreted as serving the broader goals of the past and present order.

Innovating the new in the guise of the old suggests how traditionalist understandings can be manipulated in the support of innovative programs like Panchayati Raj. For those already committed to a progressive politics an appropriate language of claims stresses advancing time as the conduit for a new and better order. Specifically, when politics is held superordinate to alternative normative frameworks, including *dharma* – as in government politics – changes which challenge the basic premises, images and validations of order will be accommodated more readily when innovated in the name of progress. Innovation can then be rationalized as hastening the Golden Age of the future. This confidence in what the future will bring, plus a disaffection with the present and past order, suggests why tribal laborers in Torkotala organized in response to reforms advocated by UF party workers. Simply, where politics provides the orienting normative framework, efforts at directed change will be evaluated in their own terms, no matter how radical the break with historic forms, for politics is then considered the ultimate arbiter of public goals and values. For Torkotala Hindus politics does not provide the orienting framework for those aspects of family life addressed by the Hindu Code legislation, which suggests why this instance of government politics was ill served by a progressive language of claims which hailed the removal of judicial recognition of inequalities of caste and sex ? ¡ a step towards modernity. As with Panchayati Raj, the extension of Hindu Code legislation into Torkotala would have been better served by a traditionalist language of claims.

Summary and discussion

The theme and events of village politics were discussed in chapter 4. In this chapter was presented an analogous discussion of *sorkari kaj*, the work (*kaj*) of the government (*sorkar*), or government politics. Both forms of rule, importantly, are identified behaviorally with competitions over rank, and are pursued through much the same manner and means. But whereas village politics supports and maintains a social and political order grounded on the premise of inequality, government politics aims to level, if not completely eliminate, that system of inequalities and to substitute in its stead a social and political order grounded on the premise of equality. Informing local conceptions of government politics are four premises. (1) Politics aims at progress, a future better than the past. (2) Politics is (ideally) moral activity in that efforts toward progress should proceed in accordance with law and those uncodified evaluations of right and wrong common among Hindus. (3) Politics is open to all who wish to participate and all who do participate will do so as political equals. And (4) politics is (supposedly) separate from *dharma* – which government officials equate with religion – in that its ultimate ground of authority is the Indian Constitution and legal system, which also establish politics as super-ordinate to religion.

These four premises constitute the theme of government politics. The extension of Panchayati Raj into the Narayanghar area, the effort to reorder social relations through Hindu Code legislation, and the Torkotala labor dispute are three instances of the kinds of events which Torkotala residents identify as documenting that theme. Each in its own way both challenges and alters the given order in rural West Bengal by allowing for an increased measure of social, economic and political equality. It is this concern to establish a more equalitarian order that defines the context of meaning in which the competitions identified as instances of government politics are situated. It is through such competitions that a more equalitarian order is both affirmed and realized, if only in part. In that sense are theme and event, rank and rivalry, each intelligible in terms of the other.

This conjunction of rank and rivalry again underscores the utility of political studies that consider the relationship between politics and other social domains. It also evidences the differing importance that can be given to politics as a normative framework whose authority extends – or does not extend – to other social domains. In village politics the conjunction of rank and rivalry was seen to belie the primacy of politics as the domain of ultimate authority, or even as a domain discrete from religion. The goal of village politics, the moral means towards that goal and individual political responsibility are all inseparable from and subordinate to considerations of *dharma*. In government politics, by contrast, the Indian Constitution and legal system supplant *dharma* as the broadest normative framework for politics, and also establish politics and religion as formally separate domains in a secular India. Politics, not religion, becomes the arbiter of public goals. For that reason is government politics, unlike village politics, consistent with universalistic definitions of politics as the ultimate domain of authority in society (Easton 1965; Swartz, Turner and Tuden 1966; Cohen 1973).

Louis Dumont (1971) has argued that politics is a primary normative framework only in individualistic societies of the West. In India, as in other group-oriented societies, Dumont holds, it is religion which provides the normative framework that 'encompasses' all social life. The limitation of Dumont's argument is that while individuals and groups may be differently valued, any actual society, including Hindu India, is neither entirely individualistic nor entirely group-oriented. This point was made in chapter 3. This chapter and chapter 4, when taken together, evidence that actual societies may also include more than one set of relations between politics and religion.

The conjunction of rank and rivalry also points again to the nature of political competitions as two-dimensional. As in village politics, the competitions identified as instances of government politics have a social significance as instrumental means towards an immediate material goal. But more is at stake than winning a *panchayat* election, or ensuring a desired succession of property, or improving the wages of labor. Political competitions are also symbolic statements about the right and proper order of things, which in the context of government politics includes a greater measure of social, economic and political equality. The many and varied instances of government politics reflect this goal of an equalitarian order symbolically. They also realize it socially. For that reason do instances of government politics function not as rituals of rebellion or processes of regularization, but as processes of adjustment and innovative change.

Village politics is protective of the present and past order of things. Validating this traditionalist politics is a negative evaluation of advancing time, for the Golden Age, when life was best, is seen in the past. Government politics, by contrast, posits that social and political order, as well as the world view which accompanies those orders and makes them seem uniquely fitted to the realities of life, are human constructions, and thus open to continual reshaping as individuals seek to establish the kind of social and political order in which they wish to live. Government politics is thus essentially progressive in being open to innovation. The Golden Age, when life will be better, is seen in the future.

For some Torkotala residents there is no conceivable alternative to the ranked orders of their polity, society and cosmos that does not threaten horrific chaos. As a result they are closed to the future as hastening the further dissolution of order symbolized in the cycle of ages. Other Torkotala residents can envisage an alternative to the present order of things, and are open to advancing time as a vehicle of positive change. Among them, significantly, are the leading big men of the village, who at times variously act in accord with the premises of village politics and government politics, being wholly committed to neither, and evaluating the competitions identified with each in situational terms. It is the fluid support of these leading big men – with the result that some innovative changes identified with government politics are favored, but not others – which highlights the limitation of opposing village politics and government politics as mutually incompatible forms of rule. Village politics and government politics have contradictory themes and posit starkly contrasting models of reality, but just as Torkotala Hindus are neither entirely individualistic, nor entirely group-oriented, so too they are neither entirely traditionalist nor entirely progressive in their politics.

In Torkotala today a traditionalist and progressive politics coexist. In practical terms this means that the new does not necessarily displace the old, and the old does not necessarily reject the new; also that when innovative changes do occur they are often additive to a flexible but enduring traditional order. Panchayati Raj, for example, is a fixture in Torkotala today. Yet this innovation has not displaced those *ad hoc* councils which existed prior to statutory councils, and now coexist with them. Nor has the village *panchayat* escaped being modified and co-opted by some Torkotala residents for the purposes of factional competitions that are part of village politics. Other government-sponsored innovations, like the reordering of social relations through legislation contained in the Hindu Code, have been almost totally ignored by Torkotala residents, who clearly favor customary patterns of handling matters of personal law. The labor strike as an instrument of economic reform, by contrast, is now well accepted by at least some Torkotala residents and represents a genuine addition to the manner and means of local politics, as does the organization of political teams by class.

Government politics is always identified by Torkotala residents with outsiders who seek to alter village life. Yet local response to specific instances of government politics is not uniform or easily predicted because each effort at directed change has an event character of its own and impacts a different aspect of village life. Far more predictable is that efforts at directed change will be rationalized in terms of local conceptions of a past or future Golden Age. This highlights the role of an accompanying language of claims as part of the manner and means of Torkotala politics. It also underscores the importance of going beyond an attention to the substantive content of political themes to consider also their function in justifying the interested participation of individuals in specific competitions. It is worth recalling again C. Wright Mills' observation that varieties of situated action – such as village politics and government [politics – will each have their characteristic vocabulary of motives.

Mills' point is also relevant when considering the reasons given by Torkotala residents for engaging in government politics. In the context of village politics competition is regarded as the avoidable result of individual misconduct in a just society. In principle there would be no family, caste or factional competitions if all acted in accord with their behavioral code. Yet such competitions are a recurrent feature of village life. Why? In its language of claims village politics occurs and is justified as a moral means to maintain or restore *dharma*. That is, village politics ensures a lasting social order through the temporary disorder of competition. Competition in the context of government politics is viewed differently as the inevitable product of social inequities. The prize of government politics, as a result, is not to maintain the given order, which is deemed unjust, but to fashion a new and more equitable order premised on the fundamental equality of all. The language of claims which accompanies government politics thus rationalizes competition as a conduit of progress and change. From the temporary disorder of government politics is to come a new and better order.

Government politics premises the fundamental equality of all. This is not an entirely novel idea in rural West Bengal. It was present in the slowly modernizing colony of British India and as noted at the outset of this chapter is also not absent or alien to village politics. It is today an idea of increasing importance, though. Torkotala never was, in Charles Metcalfe's stereotype of village India, a self-contained, self-reliant little republic complete unto itself. But during the period of rule by the Pal Rajas and the later period of British rule, the broadest *des* in which Torkotala residents interacted regularly was the now former Narayanghar kingdom, and neither the Pal Rajas nor the British interfered much with the given order of life within the village or kingdon that did not touch upon their revenue collections. This altered with Independence. Torkotala residents now recognize themselves as part of the larger *des* of West Bengal and India. Agents, policies and programs of West Bengal and the nation now impinge on village life in a way and to an extent that the Pal Rajas and the British never did. The innovative changes in village life that have resulted from this combination of Torkotala residents looking outwards and outsiders entering into the village have been multiple and varied. But as the cases presented in this chapter are intended to document, it is their common goal of a new and more equalitarian order which allows one to see beyond the singularity of such diverse events as a *panchayat* election, the enactment of Hindu Code legislation, and a labor dispute and speak more generally about paradigmatic examples of a broader theme – government politics.

Conclusion

The opening paragraph of the Introduction to this study identified the twin goals that run throughout and link the separate chapters: namely, to provide a descriptive analysis of rank and rivalry in a village of West Bengal, and to advance a holistic style of analysis that attends to systems of both meaning and action.

This Conclusion will not review the descriptive portions of the study, nor how they extend the ethnography of stratification and politics in rural India. The separate chapters are themselves organized as a progressive summary and synthesis of the ethnography presented. And for a further review, the Introduction can be reread. Attention will be focused here on the style of analysis undertaken, for now that the ethnographic portions of the study are complete, it is possible to examine the overall argument presented. There is a conjunction of rank and rivalry in rural West Bengal, and this is probably true throughout Hindu India. But in documenting this conjunction ethnographically, how has the argument been structured? What explanation has been offered? To address these questions is to clarify why the study is organized as it is, and, at bottom, what claims of understanding are being made.

Dharma refers to the natural and moral behavior appropriate to an individual or group of individuals and to society as a whole. The *dharma* of a Hindu is defined in part by the *des* or physical-cum-social community in which he lives, for each *des* has a customary way of life that is in some ways different from all other places. The *dharma* of a Hindu is also defined in part by the *kal* or time in which he lives, for every *des* has a history which is unique and dissimilar, and even in the same *des* what is deemed right and proper behavior has not been unvarying through time. And the *dharma* of a Hindu is defined in part by his own *gun* or qualities and *asrama* or life stage, for the behavior appropriate to individuals differs according to their own nature and physical-cum-moral maturity. Place, time, qualities and life stage – these are the four coordinates of Hindu action.

The four coordinates of Hindu action are a constant against which the

219

dharma of any individual or group of individuals is defined. The specific behaviors which constitute *dharma* are not similarly constant, for they differ across time and place, they differ among individuals living at the same time and in the same place, and they differ during the course of an individual's own life. This insight is part of the view of their own society held by Torkotala villagers, and points to why the first questions asked of a newcomer seek to situate a person spatially and socially. Simply, Torkotala villagers are aware of the need to contextualize human action.

The order of chapters in this study, and the order in which topics are raised in each chapter, reflects a similar effort to contextualize the discussion of rank and then rivalry. Chapter 1 opens with a discussion of the land, people and local history of Torkotala. The aim is to define the spatial and temporal settings of this study, and to provide a first introduction to its principal subjects, be they named individuals, kin groups, castes or factions. In doing so, chapter 1 uses the historical experience of Torkotala also to present a self-contained argument that the Indian village probably never was, as idealized, a closed and static political entity, a so-called village republic. But in the perspective of the whole, the contribution of chapter 1 is to define the socio-historical context in which a more problem oriented discussion of rank can be pursued. Without it any discussion of rank would float free of social moorings.

Chapters 2 and 3 also include self-contained arguments. Most notably they advance a transformational theory of rank and human development, and in doing so extend past discussions of rank that focus too narrowly on caste or misrepresent either physical attributes or patterns of interaction and behavioral dominance as distinct and separate criteria of rank in Hindu society. Yet, as in chapter 1, in the perspective of the whole chapters 2 and 3 are also prefatory. They preface the later discussions of village politics and government politics by exploring the broad cultural context in which political competitions are generated in a regular and recurrent fashion. It is this early attention to cultural context, when combined with the prior discussion of land, people and local history, which enables the discussions in chapters 4 and 5 to move beyond the orthodox political questions of who, what, when and how to pursue the more elusive question of why: why are political competitions a chronic feature of village life in India?

In developing a transformational theory of rank and human development, chapters 2 and 3 focus on those understandings of rank shared by all Torkotala Hindus in favor of noting the intra-cultural variability that segments the population. That cultures include core understandings, and that the premise of inequality represents a core understanding of Hindu culture, perhaps needs no more justification than already provided ethnographically for a people aptly dubbed *Homo hierarchicus*. But as any discussion of shared understandings that neglects the social distribution of knowledge may be regarded as incomplete for some purposes, it is perhaps worth recalling that this study was planned and carried out in the field as an exercise in political anthropology. Segments of the Torkotala population differently value an inequalitarian social order and differently act to maintain or alter the ordered ranks of society. But whether a partisan of village politics or government politics, it is the common concern, even preoccupation, with rank that defines the context of meaning in which all Torkotala residents compete politically. The contribution of chapters 2 and 3, in the perspective of the whole, is to document this common concern with rank.

It is only in chapters 4 and 5 – after each of the four coordinates of Hindu action have been drawn and used broadly to define the sociocultural context of Torkotala politics – that the conjunction of rank and rivalry is first discussed. And while an attention to systems of meaning and action runs throughout the earlier discussions of a transformational theory of rank and human development, it is only here that the goal of advancing a holistic style of analysis that attends equally to cultural and social structural material is most fully realized in studying politics as two-dimensional.

Political competitions in Torkotala are instrumental acts aimed at material prizes. But whatever the specific bone of contention which sparks a competition, and whatever the immediate material prize at stake, political competitions in Torkotala are also statements about the right and proper order of society. They reflect the themes of village politics and government politics symbolically. And they realize those themes socially. The contribution of chapters 4 and 5 is to explore how the effort of Torkotala residents to advance and act in accord with the themes of village politics and government politics generates rivalries over rank, and how those rivalries, in turn, support or challenge the given system of inequalities. This is to document the conjunction of rank and rivalry. It is also to use each in explaining the other.

To explain can be to state why some concepts and ideas follow from other concepts and ideas, and thus identify relationships of logic and meaning as is characteristic of a cultural analysis. To explain also can be to state why some acts follow from other acts with greater or lesser probability given certain conditions, and thus identify relationships of cause and function as is characteristic of analyses of social structure and process. Both types of explanation are pursued at points in this study, but the product that results is not exactly like the one or the other. It differs from both in recognizing the limitation of each.

A strictly cultural explanation is limited in not examining how formal relationships of logic and meaning apply to actual behavior. And even when the fit between systems of meaning and action is examined, explanations that treat culture as primary are still limited by the paradox of culture. That is, while no course of human behavior is intelligible apart from culture, no actual course of behavior is determined or can be predicted on the basis of concepts and ideas alone, for actual behavior is also contingent on other factors. Culture, as Geertz has remarked (1973:14), is not a causal power, but a context for interpretation. As applied to this study, it is the paradox of culture which points to the inappropriateness of expecting or claiming that a common concern with rank at a cultural level will itself lead to a uniformity of political action. It does not. Torkotala residents divide as partisans of village politics and government politics, and over time the same individuals may vary in their support for each of these two forms of rule. Nonetheless, it is the common concern with rank and inequality that defines the context of meaning in which all political competitions in Torkotala are generated, perceived, typed, pursued and justified. Culture may not be causal, but as context it cannot be ignored.

A strictly social explanation is in an important sense impossible because behavior is unintelligible apart from cultural context. But even when the fit between systems of action and meaning is examined, the explanation of human events is complicated by the paradox of causality. Specifically, while it is possible to generalize from a number of occurrences to isolate the cultural and social structural reasons for why acts of a certain type (say rivalries between brothers) recur, causal statements about types of acts are of a different sort than statements about individual cases, and prediction from one to the other is always uncertain. Brothers may not compete with each other at all, or may do so for ideocentric reasons. The same point applies to rivalries among other family members, among caste fellows, between castes, between big men as factional leaders, and between partisans of village politics and government politics. In each case an understanding of the generic type does not in itself explain specific instances of the type. The limited aim of this study has been to clarify why certain types of political competition are not an infrequent, unanticipated or aberrant feature of village life in West Bengal, as is probably true throughout Hindu India.

The paradox of causality also has a second dimension. That is, a causal explanation requires the possibility of discrete causal judgements. But the more complete and accurate an account of human events is, the more do all past events seem responsible, at least in part, for any given occurrence in the present. The possibility of discrete causal judgements, in other words, conflicts with the need for completeness required for a causal understanding of social behavior. As applied to this study, it is the completeness required for a causal explanation which underscores why politics is best studied as two-dimensional. Specifically, a narrow focus on the bones of contention which spark a political competition, and the immediate material prize at stake, would provide an incomplete explanation of why family, caste or factional competitions, or instances of government politics, recur. Politics in Torkotala is not solely about material interests. It is also about morality and ideas of a just society. And both the ideas and interests which move political events may not be unique to politics at all, which is why this two-dimensional study also examined the relations between politics and other social domains.

A cultural analysis and the analysis of social structure and process are both concerned with necessary or determinative relationships. In this study, too, necessary connections are identified whenever possible. Scattered throughout chapters 2 and 3 are propositional statements about rank – relative highness and lowness – and the behavior appropriate to ranked individuals and birth groups. Scattered throughout chapters 4 and 5 are propositional statements about rivalries over rank; why they occur, among whom, when, and the manner and means by which they are pursued, including the language of claims which typically accompanies instances of village politics and government politics. But even in advancing propositional statements, it is recognized that the explanation of human events in terms of necessary or determinative relationships can only be approximated, not fully realized, at least not without falsifying or ignoring the open-endedness and complexity of social life. For that reason this study claims, at bottom, not to fully explain the conjunction of rank and rivalry in a causal sense, but to offer a well-documented interpretation of why it exists.

If a name be needed, this study offers a holistic interpretation of rank and rivalry in rural West Bengal. Like a cultural analysis and analyses of social structure and process, a holistic interpretation aims to account for something in the sense of establishing what it is, which is description, and in the sense of establishing – to the extent possible – why it follows from something else, which is explanation in the strict sense. Descriptively a holistic interpretation takes as its smallest unit of study the correspondence between systems of meaning and action rather than focusing on either alone. It aims to lay bare the embeddedness of action in systems of meaning and the fit between what people do and what people say or otherwise indicate as reason for why they do what they do. Neither systems of meaning nor action are ever perfectly consistent or ever perfectly integrated with each other given the piecemeal manner in which both are constituted and undergo change over time. Yet both do tend towards a certain consistency and integration, if only because the members of a society act to lend significance and order to their day-to-day lives. The focus of a holistic interpretation is on both the product and the process of this effort. Or put differently, the focus of a holistic interpretation is on how actors in a given society maintain or alter a certain fit between systems of meaning and action, and the social and cultural forms that result from this on-going process.

In this study a holistic interpretation is pursued through a documentary method that attends both to cultural and social structural material without treating either as in some sense secondary, derived or epiphenomenal. As applied in chapters 2 and 3 , of particular interest is how the Hindu concern with rank at a cultural level is evidenced behaviorally in a number of different and seemingly unrelated acts, including marriage, diet, the exchange of food and services, occupation and those ritual performances that both mark and facilitate passage through a series of life stages. Of particular interest in chapters 4 and 5 is how the Hindu concern with rank generates political competitions at all levels of social organization in Torkotala, and how those competitions variously support or challenge the given system of inequalities. The separate halves of this study, in combination, thus document the pervasive and fundamental importance of concepts, ideas and understandings of rank for both the Bengali construction of reality and Bengali patterns of acting within that reality. The separate halves of this study, in combination, also document why the ranked orders and ordered ranks of the Bengali cosmos and society, though apparantly static, are not static at all, but constantly renewed, or transformed, through the widest variety of social acts, including rivalries over rank.

Appendix: Caste ranking by opinion

The opinion ranking technique used in Torkotala village was patterned after that used by McKim Marriott (1968). The 14 castes and tribes resident in Torkotala and the four non-resident castes which visit the village regularly were selected for comparison. To determine the rank order of these 18 birth groups in a local hierarchy, 28 villagers were interviewed to collect opinion data. These informants were chosen to include, where possible, one male head of household from each of the castes and tribes in Torkotala. For some castes there was only one adult male head of household, as among the Rajok, Hari, Mahisya Boisnab and Brahmans, and thus there was no real selection to be made. Where the population of a caste or tribe was larger, the names of all adult male heads of household were written on a piece of paper and placed in a box from which they were drawn at random. For these larger birth groups at least two informants were selected. The assumption guiding this selection process was that persons of different castes or tribes might view local rankings differently according to their own position in them. Thus it was deemed important to sample opinion from all castes and tribes represented in the village. It was also assumed that persons who were not male heads of households might view the local rankings differently. Thus interviews were also conducted with an aged widower, three unmarried male youths, and three adult females. Table 15 lists the persons interviewed, their caste or tribe, and their status as male head of household, youth, wife, widower or widow.

To elicit the opinion data the names of the 18 birth groups chosen for comparison were written in Bengali on separate cards, one name for each card, and the informant was asked to order the castes and tribes in order of their rank in Torkotala village. The first two cards were handed to the informant with this question: 'In this village which *jati* is higher and which *jati* is lower? Or are they equal?' ('*E grame ki jati uccu, ki jati nicu? Ba e duto soman?*') Thereafter one card at a time was handed to the informant with exactly the same question. For those informants who could not read, or only barely, every card was read aloud and paired with every other card until its place in the ranked order was determined. Where castes and tribes were determined to be of the same rank, to be equal, the cards were placed side by side in one line. Otherwise higher-ranking castes and tribes were placed above lower-ranking ones. This seemed like a perfectly reasonable way of doing things to Torkotala villagers. Everyone asked to rank the castes and tribes in this manner was able to do so (though in two instances informants (8.1, 11.1) could not rank a particular caste). And others in the village not originally selected for interviewing even volunteered to place the cards in order once it became known what was being done.

An analysis of the opinion data gathered in this way indicates that castes and

225

Table 15.   *Respondents for the opinion ranking operation*

Caste Code Numbers

Resident castes

1 Bagal	8 Lodha
2 Bagra-Khatriya	9 Mahisya Boisnab
3 Bagra-Khatriya Boisnab	10 Munda
4 Brahman	11 Rajok
5 Hari	12 Sadgop
6 Jogi	13 Tantoby
7 Kayastha	

Non-resident castes

14 Kamar	16 Malakar
15 Kumar	17 Napit

Informants

Caste and informant number	Life stage	Caste and informant number	Life stage
1.1	Male householder	10.1	Male householder
1.2	Male householder	11.1	Male householder
1.3	Male householder	12.1	Male youth
2.1	Male householder	12.2	Male householder
2.2	Male householder	12.3	Male householder
2.3	Widow	12.4	Male householder
3.1	Male householder	12.5	Widow
3.2	Male householder	12.6	Widower
4.1	Male householder	12.7	Male householder
4.2	Male youth	12.8	Male householder
6.1	Wife	13.1	Male householder
7.1	Male householder	13.2	Male youth
8.1	Male householder	17.1	Male householder
9.1	Male householder		

tribes can indeed be placed in a series of ordinal ranks. Table 16 provides the responses of 28 informants. Where a bracket is drawn grouping several responses together, the bracket includes castes or tribes which were assigned equal ranks. Out of 28 informants, 16 viewed at least two castes as having equal rank; the remaining 12 informants distinguished 17 discrete ranks.[1] The number of discrete ranks distinguished by all informants ranged from 10 to 17, with the average number of ranks distinguished being 15.4.

Table 17 presents the opinion data after it has been counted and sorted and arranged in matrix form. To arrive at these figures every caste and tribe was compared with every other and the number of instances in which each was ranked higher or lower. The totals are then presented for each caste with the number indicating instances of higher rank being placed first and separated by the number indicating instances of lower rank by a slash (/). A figure such as 25/3, then, indicates that 25 out of 28 informants ranked the caste or tribe higher than the one it was being compared to; 3 informants did not. Significant breaks in the matrix were

Table 16. Opinions on caste rank held by 28 respondents in Torkotala village

Caste code[a] and individual serial number of respondents

Rank of caste	1.1	1.2	1.3	2.1	2.2	2.3	2.4	3.1	3.2	4.1	4.2	6.1	7.1	8.1	9.1	10.1	11.1	12.1	12.2	12.3	12.4	12.5	12.6	12.7	12.8	13.1	13.2	17.1
Higher	4	4	4	4	4	4	4	9	4	4	4	4	4	8	4	4	4	4	4	4	4	4	4	4	4	4	4	4
	12	7	12	7	12	12	9	3	12	7	12	12	9	4	7	3	9	12	12	12	12	12	9	12	12	12	12	12
	7	9	9	12	9	7	3	4	7	12	9	16	7	7	12	9	3	7	7	7	7	9	3	9	7	7	7	7
	9	12	7	17	17	9	12	12	17	9	7	7	12	12	9	7	7	9	9	9	3	16	12	7	3	17	17	16
	14	3	17	9	7	2	16	16	9	16	16	17	16	16	14	12	12	16	16	3	3	17	7	6	6	3	3	3
	16	2	16	14	3	3	17	17	16	14	13	14	17	17	15	2	16	14	14	2	2	14	16	16	14	2	13	2
	17	1	7	16	14	16	14	7	14	3	14	15	13	2	16	16	17	17	17	14	16	15	17	17	2	13	6	14
	3	14	14	3	2	17	2	14	3	2	2	9	6	1	16	10	14	1	3	17	8	3	3	3	16	6	1	13
	2	16	3	2	16	14	15	2	15	6	15	2	2	13	17	14	6	3	2	13	17	2	2	2	13	1	16	8
	1	13	2	6	1	6	8	1	6	15	17	3	1	14	13	13	2	2	1	1	14	6	15	15	15	16	15	11
	6	15	1	1	8	13	13	15	13	17	3	1	15	6	6	17	1	6	6	6	1	1	14	13	11	15	14	10
	11	17	6	13	6	8	1	8	11	1	11	13	14	11	2	6	13	13	15	15	13	13	13	1	8	8	11	5
	13	6	15	13	13	11	6	6	8	13	6	11	8	10	11	1	11	15	13	8	8	8	1	8	10	10	10	
	15	11	13	11	11	15	11	10	10	8	8	8	11	5	8	15	8	11	11	11	10	11	8	11	5			
	8	8	8	15	1	10	10	11	10	5	5	10	10		10	8	10	8	8	10		10	11	10				
	10	5	10	10	5	5	5	5	5		10	5	5		5	11	5	10	10	5		5	10	5				
Lower	5	10	5	5	10											5		5	5				5					
Number of ranks	15	17	16	13	16	17	17	17	17	11	16	10	17	14[b]	11	17	16[c]	17	17	15	16	16	17	16	14	16	16	16

[a] Caste code numbers are given in Table 12.
[b] Respondent 8.1 could not rank caste no. 9.
[c] Respondent 11.1 could not rank caste no. 15.

227

Table 17. *Matrix of opinions on caste rank in Torkotala village*

	Brahman	Sadgop	Kayastha	Mahisya Boisnab	Bagra-Khatriya Boisnab	Bagra-Khatriya	Malakar	Napit	Kamar	Jogi	Bagal	Kumar	Tantoby	Rajok	Lodha	Munda	Hari
Brahman		28/0	28/0	28/0	28/0	28/0	28/0	28/0	28/0	28/0	28/0	28/0	28/0	27/1	28/0	28/0	28/0
Sadgop			20½/6½	24½/2½	27/1	28/0	28/0	28/0	28/0	27/1	28/0	28/0	28/0	28/0	27/1	28/0	28/0
Kayastha				20½/5½	17/10	25½/2½	23½/4½	27½/2½	27½/2½	27/1	28/0	28/0	28/0	28/0	27/1	28/0	28/0
Mahisya Boisnab					21½/6½	23/4	23/4	23/4	27/0	26/1	27/0	27/0	27/0	27/0	26/1	28/0	27/0
Bagra-Khatriya Boisnab						16/12	14/14	18½/8½	26/2	25/3	27/1	22½/5½	26/2	27/1	27/1	28/0	28/0
Bagra-Khatriya							16½/11½	18½/9½	26/2	25/3	28/0	23½/4½	26/2	28/0	27/1	28/0	28/0
Malakar								18½/9½	25/3	23/5	25/3	21/7	25/3	28/0	27/1	28/0	28/0
Napit									24/4	22/6	27/1	23/5	24/4	28/0	26/2	27/1	28/0
Kamar										19/9	20/8	20½/7½	20/8	26/2	24/4	27/1	28/0
Jogi											15/3	17/11	17/11	24/4	22/6	27/1	28/0
Bagal												14/14	18/10	26/2	25/3	27/1	28/0
Kumar													17/11	26/2	23/5	27/1	28/0
Tantoby														25/3	21/7	27/1	28/0
Rajok															25/3	25/3	28/0
Lodha																25/3	28/0
Munda																	25/3
Hari																	

Note: row caste is ranked higher by majority in cell, column caste by minority.

Table 18.   *Collective   ranking   of   castes   in
Torkotala village*

Rank	Birth group
1	Brahman
2	Sadgop
3	Kayastha, Mahisya Boisnab
4	Bagra-Khatriya Boisnab
5	Bagra-Khatriya, Malakar, Napit, Kamar
6	Jogi, Bagal, Kumar, Tantoby
7	Rajok
8	Lodha
9	Munda
10	Hari

Note: based on opinions given in tables 16 and 17.

marked where one or a number of castes or tribes was held to rank higher than others by a 2 to 1 margin, at the least. This margin of 2 to 1 was selected arbitrarily but seems justified as a clear and unambiguous marker of discrete ranks. A total of 10 out of a possible 17 discrete ranks are distinguished, using this criterion of a 2 to 1 margin.

Table 18 summarizes the opinion data presented in matrix form in a collective ranking – a ranking which expresses the collective opinion of the 28 informants interviewed – having 10 discrete ranks. From this collective ranking it is apparent that while Torkotala villagers are agreed that all castes and tribes can be ranked, every birth group does not occupy a distinct rank. Rather, several castes are seen as occupying an equal rank, as forming a block in which constituent castes are not distinguished as high or low, big or small, or the like. Further, while the opinion data collected shows a remarkably high degree of agreement regarding rank order, that agreement is not perfect.

Notes

Introduction

1   For a critique of attributional theories, see Marriott (1959); of interactional theories, Dumont (1970) and Tyler (1973); of the purity-plus-power argument, see the review symposium of Louis Dumont's *Homo Hierarchicus* organized by T.N. Madan (1971), as well as Yalman (1969), Marriott (1969), Khare (1971), Leach (1971) and Lynch (1977).

2   The language of this comparison is less precise than it could be because words are deeds of a verbal sort. The contrast being drawn is between verbal deeds or acts and deeds or acts other than speech.

1. Des

1   The designation Navasakhya, meaning 'nine branches or subdivisions,' was originally applied to nine artisan and trading castes. Now it is applied to as many as 14 castes, including Tili, Mali, Tambuli, Gopa, Napit, Madhunapit, Gochali, Kamar, Kumar, Gadhanik, Tanti, Sankhabanik, Kamysyabanik and Kuri-Moira (Dutt 1969: 108–9).

2   A description of Torkotala castes and tribes is presented in chapter 2. See table 3 for a listing of traditional and present-day occupations.

3   An account of Bagdi efforts to be recognized as Bagra-Khatriyas is presented in chapter 4.

4   Partial genealogies of the Bhunai, Mahabarto and Maiti–Pal lineages are illustrated in figure 8.

2. Jati

1   In reading the paradigm, it may be asked how *rajagun* can activate *sattvagun* and *tamagun* when it is itself suppressed. Two different conceptions of 'activity' are not involved here. Rather, all life forms, like Brahma, are ever animate – only more or less so. Thus to say that *rajagun* is suppressed is to describe a relative, not an absolute, disposition. Even when relatively suppressed, *rajagun* is still active and can still activate the other *gun*.

2   Bengali scholars generally argue that the Kshatriya and Vaisya *varnas* in Bengal have not been eliminated forever; only that in this age of Kali Yuga they remain unnoticed or degraded to the rank of Sudra for failure to observe their appropriate behavioral codes (see Dutt 1969: 78–90).

230

3 In fact, there is in Torkotala village an exception to this general rule, which is discussed separately in chapter 3.
4 The appendix describes the opinion-ranking operation and presents the opinion data by which the castes and tribes of Torkotala were ranked.
5 For a more developed statement about the changing membership of Bengali *kul*, and of the changing features of the women who pass between them, see Inden and Nicholas (1977). Kenneth David (1973) makes a similar argument for the changing features and membership of women among Jaffna Tamils.
6 The same is also reported for Jaffna Tamils (David 1973:522).
7 For somewhat different listings of hot and cold foods in Tamil Nadu and Madhya Pradesh, see Brenda Beck (1969) and Lawrence A. Babb (1973). A general discussion of post-digestive effects of foods is found in Jack M. Planalp (1977).

3. Lok

1 See Manu Dharmasastra, chapters 2, 3 and 6.
2 Widows are also referred to as *buri*, even when not physically decrepit, perhaps because they are no longer able to act as adult women in certain important ways, including sexually and ritually.
3 For a description of the ritual content of the *samskaras* in Bengal, see Inden and Nicholas (1977). For a discussion of *samskaras* elsewhere in India, see Pandey (1969) and Babb (1975).

Appendix

1 The eighteenth birth group, the Mahisya, had to be deleted from the ranking part way through the operation because its sole representative was jailed on suspicion of theft. All opinions collected about Mahisyas after the jailing were strongly influenced by this incident.

Bibliography

Austin, Granville. *The Indian Constitution: Cornerstone of a Nation*. Oxford University Press, 1966.

Babb, Lawrence A. Heat and control in Chhattisgarhi ritual. *Eastern Anthropologist* XXVI, 1 (1973): 11–28.

– *The Divine Hierarchy*. New York: Columbia University Press, 1975.

Bailey, F.G. *Tribe, Caste and Nation*. Manchester University Press, 1960.

– Closed social stratification in India. *European Journal of Sociology* 4(1963):107–24.

– *Politics and Social Change*. Berkeley: University of California Press, 1963.

– Parapolitical systems. In *Local-level Politics*, edited by Marc Swartz. Chicago: Aldine, 1968, pp. 281–94.

– *Stratagems and Spoils*. New York: Schocken, 1969.

Beals, Alan. Social structure and the prediction of conflict: a test of two hypotheses. *Contributions to Indian Sociology* n.s. 3 (1969): 32–44.

Beals, Alan and Siegel, Bernard J. Conflict and factionalist dispute. *Journal of the Royal Anthropological Institute* 90 (1960a):107–17.

– Pervasive factionalism. *American Anthropologist* 62 (1960b): 394–418.

– *Divisiveness and Social Conflict*. Stanford University Press, 1966.

Beck, Brenda E.F. Color and heat in South Indian ritual. *Man* n.s. IV, 4 (1969):553–73.

Benoit-Smullyan, Emile. Status, status types and status relationships. *American Sociological Review* 9 (1944):151–61.

✓ Beteille, André. *Caste, Class and Power*. Berkeley: University of California Press, 1965.

– The politics of 'non-antagonistic' strata. *Contributions to Indian Sociology* n.s. 3 (1969):17–31.

Bhagavad Gita. Trans. R.C. Zaehner. Oxford University Press, 1969.

Bhattacharya, J.N. *Hindu Castes and Sects*. Calcutta: Editions Indian, 1968.

Brown, R. and Gillman A. The pronouns of power and solidarity, In *Style in Language*, edited by T.A. Sebock. Cambridge, Mass.: MIT Press, 1960, pp. 253–76.

Bujra, Janet. The dynamics of political action: a new look at factionalism. *American Anthropologist* 75, 1 (1973): 132–52.

Cohen, Abner. *Two-Dimensional Man*. Berkeley: University of California Press, 1976.

Cohen, Ronald. Political anthropology. In *Handbook of Social and Cultural Anthropology*, edited by John J. Honigmann. Chicago: Rand McNally, 1973, pp. 861–82.

Cohn, Bernard S. Some notes on law and change in North India. *Economic Development and Cultural Change* 8 (1959): 79–93.

Anthropological notes on dispute and law in India. *American Anthropologist* 67, 6 (1965): 82–122.

Notes on the history of the study of Indian society and culture. In *Structure and Change in Indian Society*, edited by Milton Singer and Bernard S. Cohn. Chicago: Aldine, 1968, pp. 3–28.

David, Kenneth. The bound and the unbound variations in social and cultural structure in Jaffna, North Ceylon. PhD dissertation, University of Chicago, 1972.

Until marriage do us part: a cultural account of Jaffna Tamil categories of kinsmen. *Man* n.s. VIII, 4 (1973): 521–35.

Derrett, J.D.M. Justice, equity and good conscience. In *Changing Law in Developing Countries*, edited by J.N.D. Anderson. London: George Allen, 1963. pp. 114–53.

Dhillon, Harvant Singh. *Leadership and Groups in a South Indian Village.* New Delhi: Government of India Press, Planning Commission, Program Evaluation Organization, 1955.

Dube, S.C. *Indian Village.* London: Humanities Press, 1955.

Dumont, Louis. World renunciation in Indian religion. *Contributions to Indian Sociology* 4 (1960): 33–62.

The functional equivalents of the individual in caste society. *Contributions to Indian Sociology* 8 (1965a):85–99.

The modern conception of the individual in caste society. *Contributions to Indian Sociology* 8 (1965b):13–61.

The individual as an impediment to sociological comparison and Indian history. In *Social and Economic Change*, edited by V.B. Singh and Baljit Singh. Bombay: Allied Publishers, 1967.

Homo Hierarchicus: The Caste System and its Implications. University of Chicago Press, 1970.

Religion, politics and society in the individualistic society. *Proceedings of the Royal Anthropological Institute* 1971:31–41.

Dutt, Nripendra Kumar. *Origin and Growth of Caste in India.* 2 vols. Calcutta: Firma K.L. Mukhopadhyay, 1969.

Easton, David. *A Framework for Political Analysis.* Englewood Cliffs, New Jersey: Prentice Hall, 1965.

Epstein, Scarlett T. *Economic Development and Social Change in South India.* Manchester University Press, 1962.

Firth, Raymond. Factions in Indian and overseas Indian communities. *British Journal of Sociology* 8 (1957): 291–342.

Fox, Richard G. *Varna* schemes and ideological integration in Indian society. *Comparative Studies in Society and History* II, 1 (1969):27–45.

Galanter, Marc. The displacement of traditional law in modern India. *Journal of Social Issues* XXIV, 4 (1968):65–91.

Remarks on family law and social change in India. In *Chinese Family Law and Social Change*, edited by David C. Buxbaum. Seattle: University of Washington Press, 1978, pp. 492–7.

Garfinkel, Harold. *Studies in Ethnomethodology.* New Jersey: Prentice Hall, 1967.

Geertz, Clifford. *The Interpretation of Culture.* New York: Basic Books, 1973.

Goodenough, Ward Hunt. *Description and Comparison in Cultural Anthropology.* Chicago: Aldine, 1970.

234   *Rank and rivalry*

Gough, Kathleen. The social structure of a Tanjore village. In *India's Villages*, edited by M.N. Srinivas. Bombay: Asia Publishing House, 1952.

Brahman kinship in a Tamil village. *American Anthropologist* 58 (1956):826–53.

Criteria of caste ranking in South India. *Man in India* XXXIX (1959):115–26.

Gusfield, Joseph R. Tradition and modernity: misplaced polarities in the study of social change. *American Journal of Sociology* 72 (1966):351–62.

Hooker, M.B. *Legal Pluralism*. Oxford: Clarendon Press, 1975.

Inden, Ronald B. *Marriage and Rank in Bengali Culture*. Berkeley: University of California Press, 1976.

Inden, Ronald B. and Nicholas Ralph W. *Kinship in Bengali Culture*. University of Chicago Press, 1977.

Kessinger, Tom G. *Vilyatpur 1848–1868*. Berkeley: University of California, 1974.

Khare, R.S. Encompassing and encompassed: a deductive theory of caste system (review article on *Homo Hierarchicus*). *Journal of Asian Studies* 30 (1971):859–68.

Hindu social inequality and some ideological entailments. In *Culture and Society*, edited by Balakrishna N. Nair. Delhi: Thomson Press, 1975, pp. 97–114.

Kidder, Robert. Courts and conflict in an Indian city: a study of legal impact. *Journal of Commonwealth Political studies* XI, 2 (1973): 121–39.

Kroeber, A.L. and Kluckhohn, C. *Culture: A Critical Review of the Concepts and Definitions*. Papers of the Peabody Museum 47, no. 1. Cambridge, Mass.: Harvard University, 1952.

Kroeber, A.L. and Parsons, T. The concepts of cultural and social system. *American Sociological Review* 23 (1958):582–3.

Langer, Suzanne. *Philosophy in a New Key*. Cambridge, Mass., 1960.

Leach, Edmund R. What should we mean by caste. In *Aspects of Caste in South India, Ceylon and North-West Pakistan*. Cambridge University Press, 1960.

Hierarchical man: Louis Dumont and his critics. *South Asian Review* 4, 3 (1971):233–7.

Lewis, Oscar. Group dynamics in a North Indian village. *Economic Weekly* 6 (1954):501–6.

Lynch, Owen M. Method and theory in the sociology of Louis Dumont: a reply. In *The New Wind*, edited by Kenneth David. The Hague: Mouton, 1977.

Madan, T. N. *Family and Kinship: A Study of the Pandits of Rural Kashmir*. Bombay: Asia Publishing House, 1965.

On the nature of caste in India: a review symposium on Louis Dumont's *Homo Hierarchicus*. *Contributions to Indian Sociology* n.s. 5 (1971):1–81.

Mandelbaum, David G. *Society in India*. Berkeley: University of California Press, 1970.

Mannheim, Karl. On the interpretation of Weltanschauung. In *Essays on the Sociology of Knowledge*. London: Routledge and Kegan Paul, 1952, pp. 33–83.

Manu Dharmasastra, edited by F. Max Muller. Delhi: Motilal Banarsidass, 1964.

Marriott, McKim. Little communities in an indigenous civilization. In *Village India*. University of Chicago Press, 1955, pp. 171–222.

Interactional and attributional theories of caste rank. *Man in India* XXXIX (1959):92–107.

Caste ranking and food transactions: a matrix analysis. In *Structure and Change in Indian Society*, edited by Milton Singer and Bernard S. Cohn. Chicago: Aldine 1968, pp. 133–71.

Review: Homo Hierarchicus: essai sur le systeme. des Castes. *American Anthropologist* 71 (1969): 1166–75.

Marriott, McKim and Inden, Ronald B. Caste systems. In *Encyclopaedia Britannica* (3rd ed.), 1974. *Macropaedia* 3:982–91.

Toward an ethnosociology of South Asian caste systems. In *The New Wind: Changing Identities in South Asia*, edited by Kenneth David. The Hague: Mouton, 1977, pp. 227–38.

√Mayer, Adrian. *Caste and Kinship in Central India*. Berkeley: University of California Press, 1960.

Mead, George Herbert. *The Philosophy of the Present*. Chicago: Open Court, 1932.

Mills, C. Wright. Situated actions and vocabularies of motive. *American Sociological Review* 5 (1940): 904–13.

Moore, Sally Falk. Law and social change: the semi-autonomous social field as an appropriate subject of study. *Law and Society Review* 7 (1973): 719–46.

Moore, Sally Falk and Myerhoff, Barbara G., editors. *Symbol and Politics in Communal Ideology*. Ithaca, New York: Cornell University Press, 1975.

Nadel, S.F. *Foundations of Social Anthropology*. London: Cohen and West, 1953.

Neale, Walter C. *Economic Change in Rural India*. New Haven: Yale University Press, 1962.

Nicholas, Ralph W. Villages of the Bengal delta: a study of ecology and peasant society. PhD dissertation, University of Chicago, 1962.

Factions: a comparative analysis. In *Political Systems and the Distribution of Power*, edited by Michael Banton. ASA Monograph 2. London: Tavistock, 1965, pp. 21–62.

Structure of politics in villages of South Asia. In *Structure and Change in Indian Society*, edited by Milton Singer and Bernard S. Cohn. Chicago: Aldine, 1968, pp. 243–84.

Social and political movements. In *Annual Review of Anthropology*, edited by Bernard J. Siegel and Alan Beals. Palo Alto, California: Annual Reviews Inc., 1973, pp. 63–84.

Pandey, Raj Bali. *Hindu Samskaras*. Delhi: Motilal Banarsidass, 1969.

Parsons, Talcott and Shills, E. *Toward a General Theory of Action*. Cambridge, Mass: Harvard University Press, 1961.

Planalp, Jack M. Thermal environmental relationships of diet in North India. *Papers in Anthropology*, University of Oklahoma 18, 2 (1977): 147–52.

Pocock, David. *Kanbi and Patidar: A Study of the Patidar Community of Gujarat*. Oxford: Clarendon Press, 1972.

Retzlaff, Ralph. *Village Government in India: A Case Study*. New York: Asia Publishing, 1962.

Ricoeur, Paul. The model of the text: meaningful action considered as text. *Social Research* 38, 3 (1971): 529–62.

Robinson, Marguerite S. *Political Structure in a Changing Sinhalese Village*. Cambridge University Press, 1975.

Ross, A.D. *The Hindu Family in its Urban Setting*. University of Toronto Press, 1961.

Rudolph, Lloyd I and Rudolph, Suzanne. *The Modernity of Tradition: Political Development in India*. University of Chicago Press, 1967.

Sarma, J. Formal and informal relations in the Hindu joint household of Bengal. *Man in India* XXXI (1951): 51–71.

Schneider, David. *American Kinship: A Cultural Account*. Englewood Cliffs, New Jersey: Prentice Hall, 1968.

Silverberg, James. Caste-ascribed 'status' versus caste-irrelevant roles, *Man in India* XXXIX (1959): 148–62.

Silverman, M. and Salisbury, R.F. A house divided? Anthropological studies of factionalism. *Social and Economic Papers* No. 9, Institute of Social and Economic Research, Memorial University of Newfoundland, 1977.

Simmel, Georg. *Conflict and the Web of Group Affiliations*, Trans. Kurt Wolff and R. Bendix. New York: The Free Press. 1955.

Singer, Milton. *When a Great Tradition Modernizes*. New York: Praeger, 1972.

Sinha, Surajit and Bhattacharya, Ranjit. *Bhadralok* and *chotolok* in a rural area of West Bengal. *Sociological Bulletin* 18, 1 (1969): 50–66.

Srimad Bhagavata Mahapurana. Trans. C.L. Goswami. Gorakhpur, India: Motilal Jahan, 1971.

Srinivas, M.N. *Religion and Society Among the Coorgs of South India*. Oxford University Press, 1952.

∫ *Social Change in Modern India*. Berkeley: University of California Press, 1966.

Srinivas, M.N. and Shah, A.M. The myth of the self-sufficiency of the Indian village. *Economic Weekly* XII (1960): 1375–8.

Stevenson, H.N.C. Status evaluation in the Hindu caste system. *Journal of the Royal Anthropological Institute* 34 (1954): 45–65.

Swartz, Marc J., Turner, Victor W., Tuden, Arthur, editors. *Political Anthropology*. Chicago: Aldine, 1966.

Turner, Victor W. *Dramas, Fields and Metaphors: Symbolic Action in Human Society*. Ithaca, New York: Cornell University Press, 1974.

⌐ Tyler, Stephen. *India: An Anthropological Perspective*. Pacific Palisades, California: Goodyear publishing Co., 1973.

van Gannep, Arnold. *The Rites of Passage*. Trans. M.B. Vizedom and G.L. Caffee. University of Chicago Press, 1960.

van Velsen, J. The extended-case method and situational analysis. In *The Craft of Social Anthropology*, edited by A.L. Epstein. London: Social Science Paperbacks, 1967.

Winckler, E.A. Political anthropology. In *Biennial Review of Anthropology*, edited by Bernard J. Siegel. Stanford University Press, 1970.

Yalman, Nur. De Tocqueville in India: an essay on the caste system. Review article on 'Homo Hierarchicus: Essai Sur le System des Castes. *Man* n.s. 4, 1 (1969): 123–31.

Index

action systems 7–8, 222, 223
adoption 198–9
artha 86, 87, 89, 113, 114
asat Sudra 24, 53–4, 58

Bagal 60
Bagdi 24, 25, 26–8, 34, 58, 80, 117, 135–42
Bagra-Khatriya 24, 41–2, 58–60, 102, 135–42
Bagra-Khatriya Boisnab 58–60
bhadralok 102–4
'big man' 149, 160–1, 191
birth groups 3, 50–69 *passim*
Brahma 47, 48, 49, 69, 70, 74, 82, 83, 84
Brahman 24, 25, 58, 61, 102

castes, of Midnapore district 24; of Torkotala village 24–5
causality, paradox of 222–3
chotolok 103–4
clan 65, 68, 80
classes 100–5, 202–9
cold foods 74
Communist Party (Marxist) 202–9 *passim*
Communist Party of India 202–9 *passim*
Constitution of India 178–9, 181, 182, 191, 192, 193
cosmology, Hindu 3, 47–50
crier 34, 35, 44
crops 23
cultural analysis 5–9, 14, 17–18, 80, 221–2
culture, as a system of meaning 6, 15, 222; paradox of 222

Dayabhaga law 122, 195–6
des, as compound and household 29–30; as district 40–2; as hamlet and neighborhood 26–9; as kingdom 20, 30–40; as village 20–6
dharma 3, 50, 54, 69, 70, 71, 86, 87, 89, 110–11, 112, 113, 114, 170, 180, 181, 194, 211, 219–20
diet 74–8
documentary method 10–11, 19, 110, 224

equality, economic 202–9 *passim*; political 182–91 *passim*; premise of 172–5, 176, 177–82 *passim*, 218; social 191–202 *passim*

factional politics 13, 147–65, 167–8
family 65, 68–9, 80, 114–33 *passim*
fieldwork 16–19
food exchanges 74–8
fraternal rivalries 116–24

goals of Hindu life 86, 87, 113–14
government politics 9, 12, 14–15, 109, 122, 138, 172–218
guardianship 197–8
gun 3, 48–50, 53, 69–84 *passim*

Hari 62–3, 76
headman, *Adhyaksa* 41, 42, 44, 137, 153, 185, 186, 188; *anchal pradhan* 158, 159, 164; *Mukhya* 33, 34, 35, 39–40, 42, 44, 67, 112, 138, 150, 153, 154, 187, 189; *Raj Mukhya* 33–4, 35, 42, 44, 67
Hindu Adoption and Maintenance Act 198–9

237

Hindu Code Acts 191–202, 214, 217
Hindu Marriage Act 194–5
Hindu Minority and Guardianship
   Act 197–8
Hindu Succession Act 195–7
holistic analysis 8, 19, 108–9, 223–4
holism 4–5
hot foods 74

inequality, among castes 54–64,
   133–47 *passim*; among
   classes 100–5; among descent
   lines 64–8; among factional
   leaders 147–65 *passim*; among
   families 68–69, 114–33 *passim*;
   among family members 114–33
   passim; among individuals 4–5,
   81–2, 98–105; among life
   forms 47–50; among worlds 47
impurity 70
individual, as microcosm 5, 81, 82–4,
   105; as social unit 4–5, 7, 81, 106;
   as unit of rank 4–5, 81–2, 98–105,
   107, 161; development and
   transformation 5, 81–2, 84–98,
   105–7
individualism 4–5
inheritance 122

jati, as categories of castes 51–4; as
   caste or tribe 54–64; as clan, line
   or family 64–9; as non-
   Hindus 50–1
Jogi 60

kama 86, 87, 89, 113, 114
Kamar 63
Kayastha 61
king, role of 110–11, 112, 113, 115
kulinism 66–7
Kumar 63

labor, agricultural 202, 203–9 *passim*
labor dispute 202–9, 213, 217
landholdings 101, 102
language of claims, defined 15; of
   government politics 176–7, 190,
   213–14, 217–18; of village
   politics 119, 128–9, 133, 147,
   164–5, 170–1, 211–13, 214, 217–18
'law of the fish' 110

life-cycle rites 91–8
life forms 3, 47–50
life stages, popular 87–91;
   textual 85–7, 89, 90
lineage 65–8, 80, 173
Lodha 26–8, 42, 50–1, 55–7
lok, see individual; also see worlds of
   the universe

Mahisya 62
Mahisya Boisnab 62
Malakar 63
marriage 71–4, 173, 194–5
meaning systems 6–8, 222, 223
Mitaksara law 122
modernism 213
mukti 86, 87, 114
Munda 26–8, 42, 50–1, 55, 57

Napit 63

occupation 59, 78
opinion ranking 225–9

Pal Rajas 31–2, 37–40, 43, 177
Panchayati Raj 41–2, 57, 137, 138,
   182–91, 201, 211–13, 217
partition 121–4
political analysis 9–10, 110, 166, 177,
   216
political competitions, between
   castes 8–9, 12, 133–47; between
   classes 202–9, 217; between
   factions 8–9, 13, 147–65; between
   family members 9, 12, 114–33;
   between villagers and non-
   villagers 9, 180, 210; forms of 133,
   146, 168–9
political culture 10, 109
politics, as transformational 13–14,
   132, 134, 140–1, 144, 145, 161, 167,
   168; as two-dimensional 10, 110,
   166, 177, 216; in relation to
   religion 113–14, 166, 180–2, 214,
   215–16
politics of caste 12, 133–47, 167, 168
politics of family life 12, 114–33,
   166–7, 168
prakriti 48, 69, 82, 83
pronouns, Bengali 174–5
purity 70